Xenophanes of Colophon: *Fragments*
A Text and Translation with a Commentary
Edited by J.H. Lesher

Xenophanes of Colophon was a philosophical poet who lived in various cities of the ancient Greek world during the late sixth and early fifth centuries BC. In this book, James Lesher presents the Greek texts of all the surviving fragments of Xenophanes' teachings, with an original English translation on facing pages, along with detailed notes and commentaries and a series of essays on the philosophical questions generated by Xenophanes' remarks. Also included are English translations of all the ancient *testimonia* relating to Xenophanes' life and teachings, and a discussion of how many of the *testimonia* pose impediments to achieving a consistent interpretation of his philosophy.

The Xenophanes who emerges in this account fully warrants classification as a philosophical thinker: moral critic and reflective student of nature, critic of popular religious belief and practice, and perhaps the first to challenge claims to knowledge about divine matters and the basic forces at work in nature. As with earlier works in the Pheonix series, this volume aims to make an important portion of Presocratic writing accessible to all those interested in ancient philosophy and the first phase of European natural science.

(Phoenix Supplementary Volumes XXX; Presocratics IV)

J.H. LESHER is professor of philosophy at the University of Maryland.

D1158628

PHOENIX

Journal of the Classical Association of Canada
Revue de la Société canadienne des études classiques
Supplementary Volume xxx / *Phoenix* Presocratics Volume IV
Tome supplémentaire xxx / Les Présocratiques *Phoenix* tome IV

Phoenix Presocratics / Les Présocratiques *Phoenix*
General Editors / Rédacteurs en chef
David Gallop *Trent University*
T.M. Robinson *University of Toronto*

Xenophanes of Colophon

FRAGMENTS

A TEXT AND TRANSLATION

WITH A COMMENTARY BY

J.H. LESHER

UNIVERSITY OF TORONTO PRESS

Toronto Buffalo London

© University of Toronto Press Incorporated 1992
Toronto Buffalo London
Printed in Canada
Reprinted in paperback 2001
ISBN 0-8020-5990-2 (cloth)
ISBN 0-8020-8508-3 (paper)

Printed on acid-free paper

National Library of Canada Cataloguing in Publication Data

Xenophanes, ca. 570-ca. 478 B.C.
Xenophanes of Colophon : fragments :
a text and translation with a commentary

(Phoenix. Supplementary volume ; 30 = Phoenix.
Tome supplémentaire, ISSN 0079-1784 ; 30)
Greek text with English translation and commentary.
Includes indexes.
Reprint. Originally published: Toronto : University of Toronto, 1992.
Includes bibliographical references.
ISBN 0-8020-8508-3

1. Xenophanes, ca. 570-ca. 478 B.C. 2. Philosophy, Ancient.
I. Lesher, J. H. (James H.) II. Title. III. Series: Phoenix.
Supplementary volume (Toronto, Ont.) ; 30.

B258.X32E5 2001   182   C2001-902936-5

This book has been published with the help of a grant from the Canadian Federation for the Humanities, using money provided by the Social Sciences and Humanities Research Council of Canada, and a grant awarded by the General Research Board of the Office of Graduate Studies and Research, University of Maryland at College Park.

For my mother

and in memory

of my father

CONTENTS

ACKNOWLEDGMENTS

I am indebted to the editors of this series for inviting me to undertake this volume and for providing both criticism and encouragement along the way to its completion.

I am also grateful to my colleague John Duffy for many discussions of questions of translation, to Lawrence Jost, John Kazazis, and Hugh Lee for helpful suggestions, and to Ellen Roth, librarian of the Center for Hellenic Studies, for assistance in obtaining research materials. A portion of part 2, chapter 4 was presented to a seminar on Presocratic philosophy at the University of Pennsylvania. I am grateful to Charles Kahn and the members of his seminar for their helpful comments. Aryeh Finkelberg, Andrei Lebedev, and Alexander Mourelatos were kind enough to supply prepublication copies of their recent papers on Xenophanes. Darlene King has done her usual excellent job of transforming masses of manuscript into an orderly text. Many improvements resulted from the careful attention given to the text by Joan Bulger and John St James of the University of Toronto Press, and by the typesetter, Philippa Matheson.

This book was written during an extended period of sabbatical leave from the University of Maryland arranged through the good offices of (then) Provosts W.E. Kirwan and I.L. Goldstein.

J. H. LESHER
University of Maryland
1992

ABBREVIATIONS

D-K   Diels-Kranz
GG   Goodwin and Gulick
KRS   Kirk, Raven, and Schofield
LSJ   Liddell, Scott, and Jones

PREFACE

This study, like the other volumes in this series, focuses on the views of one member of a group of philosophers who lived in ancient Greece before and during the time of Socrates. But whether its subject, Xenophanes of Colophon, was really a philosopher has long been a matter of debate. For Harold Cherniss, Xenophanes was 'a poet and rhapsode, who has become a figure in the history of philosophy by mistake.'[1] A popular anthology of Greek philosophy (one which I assign to my own students)[2] omits Xenophanes altogether from its selection of readings and discussions. The view of Xenophanes as, at best, a marginal philosopher goes back to Aristotle who regarded him as a religious thinker rather than a serious student of philosophy.[3] There are also enough dubious elements in the portrait of Xenophanes as Eleatic monist to warrant real scepticism about his claim to being the founder of Eleatic philosophy.

Yet Xenophanes has impressed some scholars as 'a paradigm of the Presocratic genius'[4] in virtue of the wide range of his interests and his ability to provide rational explanations for matters commonly supposed to lie beyond human understanding. One can always debate claims to genius, but the study that follows will fully warrant a positive assessment of Xenophanes as philosopher: outspoken critic of common opinion and the leading poets of Greece, advocate for inquiry into natural causes, proto-epistemologist, and innovator in both religion and morality.

We should concede that, at least on the basis of what we know of them, his teachings did not possess the degree of rigour and profundity attained by Parmenides (few have!), nor were they expressed with the artistry of Heraclitus. Yet Xenophanes did make a series of insightful observations across a range of topics that was unusually broad, even for an Ionian thinker: on the nature of the divine, superstitious practices, and misconceptions about the gods; on the proper measures of moral excellence and social utility; on eclipses, rainbows, fossil finds, and the origins of the cosmos; and on the tenuousness of our conceptions of the gods and of how 'all things' are. These teachings, I shall argue, left a philosophical legacy to Parmenides, even if Xenophanes was not 'the founder' of Eleatic philosophy. There is in any case ample reason to study his ideas as well as his verses, and to include him in our histories of early Greek philosophy along with his Milesian, Samian, and Ephesian counterparts.

But there are obstacles in the path of adequately understanding and assessing his ideas. The world he probably knew best was that of aristocratic households 'throughout the Greek land'; the interests of his actual and intended audiences must have been vastly different from our own. This distance in time and culture compounds the difficulties already created by the meagreness of the information that has come down to us from antiquity. It is a commonplace that we possess only a fraction of the teachings of the Presocratics and that we must rely for our sources on persons who often quoted from the Presocratics with an ulterior motive in mind. A recent study has challenged the legitimacy and credibility of the whole reconstructive enterprise,[5] and even if the study fails to prove that universal claim,[6] it nevertheless reminds us of the barriers that lie between us and the *ipsissima verba* of the philosophers. Whether our natural responses can be relied upon as guides to the reactions of Xenophanes' original audience is a significant issue which surfaces in the interpretation of six different fragments.

In the study which follows I have attempted to provide the basic information needed in order to assess Xenophanes' achievements as a philosopher. Included are the Greek texts of the surviving fragments of Xenophanes' poetry, English translations, notes on the translations, commentaries on the fragments, and an English translation of all the ancient testimonia included in the A (life, writings, and teaching) section of Diels-Kranz (D-K). In accordance with the aims of this series I do not attempt to establish a new text for the fragments, although textual problems are discussed when they have a bearing on philosophical questions.[7] Commentaries on each of the fragments deal with questions of doctrine rather than translation, discuss differences in interpretation, and – at least in most cases – argue in favour of a preferred view. The commentaries also seek to provide a context for individual remarks by exploring interconnections between different aspects of Xenophanes' thinking. Chapters 1–4 in part 2 contain discussions of the philosophical importance of Xenophanes' teachings (on moral values, the nature of the divine, nature, and human knowledge) and part 3 includes an introduction to the ancient testimonia.

While I have followed the numbering of the fragments as they appear in Diels 1901 and in D-K, I have grouped them for discussion in part 2 according to subject-matter:

Chapter 1, On Men and Morals: fragments 1, 2, 3, 4, 5, 6, 8, and 22

Chapter 2, On the Divine: fragments 7, 10, 11, 12, 14, 15, 16, 17, 23, 24, 25, and 26

Chapter 3, On Nature: fragments 19, 27, 28, 29 and 33, 30, 31, 32, and 37

Chapter 4, On Human Understanding: fragments 18, 34, 35, 36, and 38

I have chosen not to provide separate discussions of fragments 9, 13, 20, 21, 39–42, and 45. Most of these are really only reports concerning Xenophanes' age and unusual terms found in his writings (there are no fragments bearing the numbers 43 and 44 in D-K's listing).

Since many of the intended readers of this book will not know ancient Greek, I have employed transliterated Greek terms and phrases in the notes and commentaries, except when quoting directly. Greek script is used extensively in the notes on translation, but a transliterated form of the Greek term or phrase under discussion appears at the outset of the note to aid the reader in making the transition to the use of the transliterated form.

My hope is that this material will enable students coming to the Presocratics for the first or second time to sense in Xenophanes an original intelligence worthy of study and that some portions of my account will be of use to other specialists in the field.

NOTES

References to scholarly studies are made by the author's name, with the full citation given in the Select Bibliography at the back of this volume. When more than one work by an author is listed, the individual items are identified by the date of their publication. Frequently mentioned reference works are cited by abbreviations of their authors' names. For a list of these, see the Abbreviations preceding the Preface. The fragments of Xenophanes are referred to by number only (1, 2 ...), whereas the testimonia relating to Xenophanes contained in D-K are referred to by the letter A and number (A1, A2 ...). References to material in other chapters of D-K follow the usual format; D-K 23 B12, for example, would refer to fragment 12 of Epicharmus contained in chapter 23 of volume 1 of D-K.

1 Cherniss 1970, 18
2 Reginald E. Allen, ed. *Greek Philosophy: Thales to Aristotle*, 2nd ed. (New York 1985)
3 Cf. Hussey: 'But Xenophanes ... was not an original or systematic thinker. There is nothing to suggest he tried to improve the Milesian framework ... His own views were in certain crucial places vague and incoherent, if we may trust Aristotle' (33). For some reasons not to trust Aristotle, see the concluding essay of chapter 2.
4 Barnes 1, 82
5 Osborne, esp. 1–32
6 For two critiques of Osborne's thesis, see the reviews by Barnes (1988, 327–44); and Mourelatos (1989, 111–17).
7 The fragments have most recently been edited, with translation and commentary, by Ernst Heitsch (1983). The most accessible edition of Xenophanes' poems for readers of English is Edmonds *Greek Elegy and Iambus* (see Bibliography).

Xenophanes of Colophon

INTRODUCTION

Xenophanes is reported to have been the son of Dexius, Dexinos, or Orthomenes (A1, A6) and to have come from the small (now non-existent) Ionian town of Colophon. By his own reckoning (fragment 8) he lived into his nineties, spending much of his life as a bard or travelling poet 'tossing about' the Greek world from Ionia to Sicily to the Italian mainland (A1). His birth date has been set as early as 620 BC and as late as 540 BC but most modern studies opt for a date sometime in the fourth decade of the sixth century, that is, 570–560 BC. Any earlier date is difficult to square with the reports of his contact with the court of Hieron, the tyrant of Syracuse who reigned from 478 to 467 BC. Ancient accounts of Xenophanes' personal qualities emphasize his critical spirit (A1, A19–22, A24, A25), a quality for which at least three fragments provide direct evidence (fragment 7 – against Pythagoras, and fragments 11 and 12 – against Homer and Hesiod). Other fragments reveal his sense of piety (fragment 1), concern for the welfare of his city (fragments 1–3), and seriousness about matters of personal conduct (fragments 1, 3, 5, 22, 38). In combining a pious attitude toward the gods with an outspoken reminder of service to his city, a rejection of false values, and a repudiation of false claimants to wisdom, he most closely resembles the gadfly to the Athenians who was born at about the time of his death. There is no mention of a wife or family life but Xenophanes is reported to have outlived his sons (A1).

Many later authors associated him with Elea, as either the author of a poem on the founding of the city (A1), the founder of Eleatic philosophy (A8, A30, A36), or the teacher of Parmenides of Elea (A2, A30, A31). It is sometimes conjectured that Xenophanes began his study of philosophy with the Pythagoreans. There is no clear evidence of either of these philosophical points of view in the surviving fragments, although Xenophanes' one, greatest, motionless god bears an obvious resemblance to Parmenides' 'being.' A reported connection with Anaximander is unconfirmed by other evidence and an association with the Athenians Boton and Archelaus (A1) probably stemmed from a confusion of Xenophanes with Xenophon.

The Xenophanes who emerges from the fragments (as well as from many testimonia) is an Ionian *physiologos* or 'natural philosopher,' imbued with the spirit of Ionian *historiē* or 'inquiry' that was aptly summarized by Russell (p. 73): 'it was not only scientific, it was imaginative and vigorous and filled with the delight of adventure. They were interested in everything – meteors and eclipses, fishes and whirlwinds, religion, and morality; with a penetrating intellect they combined the zest of children.' In fragments 27 and 28 Xenophanes continues the Ionian debate about the shape and location of the earth; in fragments 29 and 33 he gives his answer to the question raised by the Milesian philosophers about the basic substance or *archē* of all existing things; and in fragments 30–32 he discusses many phenomena (sea, winds, rain, clouds, sun, rainbow) previously studied by the Ionians. The testimonia provide evidence of the travel and firsthand observation characteristic of Ionian *historiē* and fragment 18 is perhaps best understood as an expression of his confidence in Ionian-style inquiry.

In his elegiac poems (fragments 1–9), Xenophanes touches on topics characteristic of the poetry of his time: on the gods and how they ought to be honoured, on personal excellence and the well-being of the city, on moderation in the pursuit of wealth and pleasure, on proper conduct at symposia, and so on. But in his satires or *silloi* (fragments 10–22), in other fragments, and in many of the views credited to him in the testimonia he explores new territory, attacking many conventional religious ideas and offering physical explanations for phenomena long regarded as rich in religious or spiritual importance. What men call, think of, or regard as a god, or goddess, or in some way as divine – this is really only a cloud, or vapour, or movements or collections of clouds, and so on. Other fragments (esp. fragments 34–36, 38, cf. A1, A25) display an unprecedented degree of interest in how much can be known by mortal men and whether those popularly regarded as paragons of wisdom really deserve that status.

In general, Xenophanes' 'teaching style' varies with the subject-matter: in the symposiac poems he preaches with moralistic fervour; in the *silloi* he chides and corrects; in his theological comments he asserts rather than argues; and in his epistemological remarks he offers only veiled hints as to the basis for his sweeping claims. Although some fragments (fragments 2, 15, 30, 34, and 38) contain logical connectives (*gar, touneken*, etc.) and take the form of a hypothetical argument, on the whole Xenophanes offers little by way of argument in support of specific conclusions. It is only when individual remarks are set in relation to one another that the depth of his thinking becomes evident: his explanations of natural phenomena coalesce into a coherent scientific theory (see the conclusion of chapter 3, following); his remarks on the accuracy and origins of religious conceptions coalesce into a sustained critique of the possibility of knowledge of religious matters (see chapter 2); and his comments on the limits of human knowledge (fragments 34–36, 38) put both of these lines of inquiry into perspective. The demythologized naturalism of his scientific outlook neatly complements his denaturalized theology. Thus, in spite of the non-argumentative character of most of the fragments, a philosophy of considerable complexity emerges from the corpus as a whole.

That philosophy, I would argue, rests on four basic claims:

1 The measures of personal excellence are piety in thought and deed (fragment 1), service to the city (fragment 2), and a life of moderation, avoiding the pursuit of unlimited wealth and useless luxuries (fragments 3, 4, 5, 22).
2 There is one divine being of exceptional goodness, power, and cognitive capacity who affects the cosmos as a whole through the exercise of his thought alone (fragments 23–26); but this is not well understood by believers and the poets from whom they get their ideas on such matters (fragments 10–12, 14–17).
3 The whole natural cosmos should be understood as a product of the operations of earth and water (fragments 29, 33), with all natural processes starting from and ending in the earth (fragment 27), especially in the sea (the source of all forms of moisture [fragment 30], including the clouds, which constitute the sun [fragment 31], the rainbow [fragment 32], and other celestial bodies).
4 The certain truth about the gods and the basic principles of nature cannot be known by anyone (fragment 34), but our accounts should be accepted as true opinion about how things really are (fragment 35); and our way of inquiring into nature has resulted in a number of discoveries – even if human opinion is shaped by the events experienced during the brief span of a lifetime (fragments 18, 19, 36, 38).

Apart from the reported (but uncertain) relationship with the philosophers of Elea, Xenophanes appears to have attracted few devotees to his philosophy. Euripides imitated his comments on the topic of divine majesty and the excessive honours accorded to victorious athletes (see part 3, imitation 2). Empedocles is reported to have admired Xenophanes (A5), but also to have dismissed his theory of the earth's 'unlimited' depth (A47). Timon of Phlius commended Xenophanes as a fledgling sceptic (A35) and the poet Epicharmus borrowed his satirical style as well as a few of his values (D-K 23 B12, B36, B38, B44a). But Xenophanes had an impact on subsequent philosophy even when he was not mentioned by name. His attacks on the honours accorded to athletes, the pursuit of useless luxuries, and poetic misrepresentations of the gods, especially his call for restraints to be placed on these forms of expression, all reappear as elements in Plato's philosophy (in the *Republic*; see chapter 1, following). In his attack on the possibility of certain knowledge, or claim of universal *dokos* or opinion (fragments 34, 35), Xenophanes posed a challenge to philosophical understanding to which virtually all his successors, at least until the time of Aristotle, fashioned some response (see chapter 4, following). Nevertheless, neither Socrates, nor Plato, nor Aristotle spoke of him as a significant thinker.

As one might expect for so diverse a thinker, Xenophanes' verses and opinions were preserved for posterity by persons with widely differing interests. The most extensive selections of his poetry were quoted by Athenaeus in his gastronomical encyclopaedia (fragments 1–3, 5, 6, 22, imitation C2). The remarks on god's nature were quoted by early Christian writers (fragments 14–16, 23 by Clement) as well as interpreters of early Greek philosophy (fragments 11, 12, 24 by Sextus Empiricus; fragments 25 and 26 by Simplicius). His chief epistemological comment (fragment 34) was multiply quoted and interpreted by the sceptical philosophers. Several fragments dealing with the circumstances of his life and relations with other early figures (fragments 7, 8, 19, 20; A1, A2, A5, A18) are contained in the invaluable (if not always credible) biography by Diogenes Laertius. Three fragments (fragments 18, 27, 30) and a large number of opinions were preserved by Aëtius and other doxographers. Many of the fragments are brief snippets quoted by later authors, either for literary effect (for instance, fragment 35 from Plutarch) or in order to preserve already obsolete forms of speech (fragments 9, 10, 31, 36–42). Others are preserved in scholia (marginal notations in ancient manuscripts, in this case usually the Homeric epics) written by scholars for whom Xenophanes' epic diction triggered an association with an earlier passage (fragments 17, 21, 21a, 32, 45). A report from the rhetorician Pollux about Xenophanes' knowledge of early forms of coinage (fragment 4), a chronological statement by the author Aulus Gellius (fragment 13), and the quotation of a geophysical view from the mathematician Achilles Tatius (fragment 28) round out the usual collection of fragments (for a newly claimed fragment, see the commentary on fragment 23 in chapter 2). Seventy-four selections, the most extensive of which is the 'Xenophanes' section of the pseudo-Aristotelian treatise *On Melissus, Xenophanes, Gorgias* (MXG), make up the collection of ancient testimonia concerning Xenophanes' life, writings, and teaching.

Significant textual problems exist in eleven fragments (fragments 1, 3, 12, 15, 16, 17, 27, 30, 34, 35, and 37) and there are lacunae in several testimonia, the most serious in the *MXG* treatise. There has been an extended scholarly debate (with a generally negative outcome) concerning the existence of a Xenophanean didactic poem, *On Nature*.

Perhaps the greatest impediment to a consistent understanding of Xenophanes' philosophy is the frequent disparity between the opinions he expressed in his poems and those attributed to him in the testimonia. The Xenophanes who emerges there is quite often an Eleatic thinker: the senses are false, only reason can be trusted; what exists is 'the whole,' and this is god – motionless, changeless, rational, and perceptive in all his parts. Scholarly assessments of the credibility of these reports of Xenophanes' opinions are sharply divided (see the commentary on fragment 23 in chapter 2 and the introduction to part 3). I have found the efforts to interpret the fragments from the point of view of the Eleatic theory embedded in the testimonia generally unconvincing and have come to share the widespread suspicion that later theories were retroactively attributed to him as the putative founder of Eleatic philosophy. When the doctrines ascribed to Xenophanes by the testimonia appear in conflict with those expressed in his own words it is only reasonable to side with the latter. Nevertheless, for all we know, Xenophanes might have had his 'Eleatic period' and the fragments we know might all stem from other portions of his life. Since we do not know how the surviving fragments correspond to the course of his personal philosophical development, our interpretation must remain to some extent a matter of conjecture. In this too perhaps '*dokos* is allotted to all.'

PART 1   FRAGMENTS

Except where noted to the contrary, the text presented here follows that in Edmonds *Greek Elegy and Iambus,* vol. 1. To simplify identification I list Edmonds' fragments 4, 5, 6–6a, 7, 8, 9, 21a, 21b, and 42 by the numbers assigned to them in Diels (1901) and D-K (fragments 5, 6, 7, 8, 9, 4, 42, 21a, and 45 respectively). Edmonds' fragment 43 (Aristotle *Rhetoric* 1377a) appears as testimonium A14 in part 3, 'Sayings.' For other editions, see the citations for Diehl, Diels (1901), D-K, Untersteiner (1956), and Heitsch (1983) in the Bibliography. Six fragments are contained in the collection by Defradas (1962b), eight in Hudson-Williams, nine in Campbell (1967), fourteen in Moore, seventeen in KRS and West (1972), and eighteen in Wright (1985). Xenophanes' poetic techniques and skills are discussed by Adkins (1985), Campbell (1967, 1983), and Classen (in Boudouris). As is customary, a smaller font is employed in fragments 4, 13, 19, 20, 21, 21a, 39, 40, and 41 to indicate material which relates to Xenophanes' life and teachings but does not represent his actual words. The English translations of each of these 'fragments' are placed in brackets ([]).

Fragment 1

νῦν γὰρ δὴ ζάπεδον καθαρὸν καὶ χεῖρες ἁπάντων

καὶ κύλικες· πλεκτοὺς δ' ἀμφιτιθεῖ στεφάνους,

ἄλλος δ' εὐῶδες μύρον ἐν φιάλῃ παρατείνει·

κρητὴρ δ' ἕστηκεν μεστὸς ἐϋφροσύνης·

5 ἄλλος δ' οἶνος ἑτοῖμος, ὃς οὔποτέ φησι προδώσειν,

μείλιχος ἐν κεράμοις ἄνθεος ὀσδόμενος·

ἐν δὲ μέσοις ἁγνὴν ὀδμὴν λιβανωτὸς ἵησι,

ψυχρὸν δ' ἔστιν ὕδωρ καὶ γλυκὺ καὶ καθαρόν·

πάρκεινται δ' ἄρτοι ξανθοὶ γεραρή τε τράπεζα

10 τυροῦ καὶ μέλιτος πίονος ἀχθομένη·

βωμὸς δ' ἄνθεσιν ἂν τὸ μέσον πάντῃ πεπύκασται

μολπὴ δ' ἀμφὶς ἔχει δώματα καὶ θαλίη.

χρὴ δὲ πρῶτον μὲν θεὸν ὑμνεῖν εὔφρονας ἄνδρας

εὐφήμοις μύθοις καὶ καθαροῖσι λόγοις·

11 Fragments: Translation

Appearing below are translations of the material appearing on the facing pages. Because of variations between Greek and English word order the division of lines does not always correspond exactly to that of the Greek texts. Below each translation are chapter and page numbers for the related notes, commentaries, and essays in part 2 following. For translations of the A-testimonia and C-imitation sections of D-K, see part 3 following, pp. 196–222. For additional information on ancient sources and authorities, see pp. 225–33.

Fragment 1

For now the floor is clean as are the cups and hands of all.

One puts on the woven garlands;

another passes along a fragrant ointment in a bowl.

The mixing bowl stands full of cheer

5   and another wine, mild and flower fragrant in the jars, is at hand –

which says it never will give out.

In the midst frankincense gives forth its sacred scent,

and there is cold water, sweet and pure.

Golden loaves lie near at hand and the noble table

10 is loaded down with cheese and rich honey.

An altar in the centre is covered all about with flowers

while song and festive spirit enfold the house.

But first glad-hearted men must hymn the god

with reverent words and pure speech.

15 σπείσαντας δὲ καὶ εὐξαμένους τὰ δίκαια δύνασθαι

πρήσσειν – ταῦτα γὰρ ὦν ἐστὶ προχειρότερον –

οὐχ ὕβρις πίνειν ὁπόσον κεν ἔχων ἀφίκοιο

οἴκαδ' ἄνευ προπόλου μὴ πάνυ γηραλέος.

ἀνδρῶν δ' αἰνεῖν[1] τοῦτον, ὃς ἐσθλὰ πιὼν ἀναφαίνῃ,

20 ὥς οἱ μνημοσύνη καὶ τόνος ἀμφ' ἀρετῆς·

οὔτε μάχας διέπει Τιτήνων οὔτε Γιγάντων,

οὐδέ <τι> Κενταύρων, πλάσματα τῶν προτέρων,

ἢ στάσιας σφεδανάς· τοῖς οὐδὲν χρηστὸν ἔνεστι·

θεῶν <δὲ> προμηθείην αἰὲν ἔχειν ἀγαθόν.

Athenaeus *Scholars at Dinner* 11.462c

---

1 Edmonds (E): αἰνέω, suspecting the influence of πίνειν above, but αἰνεῖν is retained by Campbell, West, and Heitsch as an infinitive with imperatival force.

Fragment 2

ἀλλ' εἰ μὲν ταχυτῆτι ποδῶν νίκην τις ἄροιτο

ἢ πενταθλεύων, ἔνθα Διὸς τέμενος

πὰρ Πίσαο ῥοῆς ἐν Ὀλυμπίῃ, εἴτε παλαίων

ἢ καὶ πυκτοσύνην ἀλγινόεσσαν ἔχων,

5 εἴτε τὸ δεινὸν ἄεθλον ὃ παγκράτιον καλέουσιν,

ἀστοῖσίν κ' εἴη κυδρότερος προσορᾶν,

καί κε προεδρίην φανερὴν ἐν ἀγῶσιν ἄροιτο,

καί κεν σῖτ' εἴη δημοσίων κτεάνων

ἐκ πόλιος καὶ δῶρον ὅ οἱ κειμήλιον εἴη·

15 And having poured a libation and prayed to be able to do

what is right – for these are obvious –

it is not wrong to drink as much as allows any but an aged man

to reach his home without a servant's aid.

Praise the man who when he has taken drink brings noble deeds to
light,

20 as memory and a striving for virtue bring to him.

He deals neither with the battles of Titans nor Giants

nor Centaurs, fictions of old,

nor furious conflicts – for there is no use in these.

But it is good always to hold the gods in high regard.

See chapter 1, pp. 47–54 and 73–77.

Fragment 2

But if by swiftness of foot one were to gain a victory

or in the pentathlon, there by Pisa's stream in Olympus in

the sacred grove of Zeus, or by wrestling,

or again the painful art of boxing,

5 or the fearsome sport they call pankration,

he would appear more glorious to his townsmen

and win the front-row seat of honour at games.

And there would be food from the city's public stores

and a keepsake gift for him.

10 εἴτε καὶ ἵπποισιν, ταῦτά κε πάντα λάχοι,

οὐκ ἐὼν ἄξιος[1] ὥσπερ ἐγώ· ῥώμης γὰρ ἀμείνων

ἀνδρῶν ἠδ' ἵππων ἡμετέρη σοφίη·

ἀλλ' εἰκῇ[2] μάλα ταῦτα νομίζεται· οὐδὲ δίκαιον

προκρίνειν ῥώμην τῆς ἀγαθῆς[3] σοφίης.

15 οὔτε γὰρ εἰ πύκτης ἀγαθὸς λαοῖσι μετείη,

οὔτ' εἰ πενταθλεῖν, οὔτε παλαισμοσύνην,

οὐδὲ μὲν εἰ ταχυτῆτι ποδῶν, τό πέρ ἐστι πρότιμον

ῥώμης ὅσσ' ἀνδρῶν ἔργ' ἐν ἀγῶνι πέλει,

τοὔνεκεν ἂν δὴ μᾶλλον ἐν εὐνομίῃ πόλις εἴη·

20 σμικρὸν δ' ἄν τι πόλει χάρμα γένοιτ' ἐπὶ τῷ,

εἴ τις ἀεθλεύων νικῷ Πίσαο παρ' ὄχθας·

οὐ γὰρ πιαίνει ταῦτα μυχοὺς πόλιος.

Athenaeus *Scholars at Dinner* 10.413f.

---

1 E punctuates ἄξιος, ὥσπερ ἐγώ, and translates 'yet it would not be deserved as 't would be were it mine' (p. 195), but ἄξιος has more to do with personal worth than with prizes, hence 'not being worthy of these as I (would be worthy of them).'

2 E: εἰκῆ ; cf. LSJ s.v. εἰκῆ.

3 E: ἠγαθέης, suspecting influence from πύκτης ἀγαθὸς in the next line, but a 'capable' or 'serviceable' expertise fits the context better than a 'most holy' one.

10 And even if he were to win with horses he would get all these,

not being as worthy of them as I.

For our expertise is better than the strength of men and horses.

But this practice makes no sense nor is it right

to prefer strength to this good expertise.

15 For neither if there were a good boxer among the people

nor if there were a pentathlete or wrestler

nor again if there were someone swift afoot –

which is most honoured of all men's deeds of strength –

would for this reason a city be better governed.

20 Small joy would a city have from this –

if someone were to be victorious in competing for a prize on Pisa's
banks –

for these do not enrich a city's treasure room.

See chapter 1, pp. 55–61 and 73–77.

Fragment 3

ἁβροσύνας δὲ μαθόντες ἀνωφελέας παρὰ Λυδῶν,
ὄφρα τυραννίης ἦσαν ἄνευ στυγερῆς,
ἤϊσαν εἰς ἀγορὴν παναλουργέα φάρε' ἔχοντες
οὐ μείους ὥσπερ χίλιοι εἰς ἐπίπαν,
5 αὐχαλέοι χαίτῃσιν ἀγαλμένοι εὐπρεπέεσσιν
ἀσκητοῖς <τ'> ὀδμὴν χρίμασι δευόμενοι.

Athenaeus *Scholars at Dinner* 12.526a

Fragment 4

εἴτε Φείδων πρῶτος ὁ Ἀργεῖος ἔκοψε νόμισμα ... εἴτε Λυδοί, καθά φησι
Ξενοφάνης.

Pollux *Vocabulary* 9.83 (Edmonds fragment 9)

Fragment 5

οὐδὲ κεν ἐν κύλικι πρότερον κεράσειέ τις οἶνον
ἐγχέας, ἀλλ' ὕδωρ καὶ καθύπερθε μέθυ.

Athenaeus *Scholars at Dinner* 11.782a (Edmonds fragment 4)

Fragment 3

And having learned unprofitable luxuries from the Lydians,

as long as they were free of hateful tyranny,

they used to go into the agora wearing robes all of purple,

not less than a thousand in all,

5 boastful, exulting in their gorgeous long-flowing hair,

drenched in the scent of prepared unguents.

See chapter 1, pp. 61–65 and 73–77.

Fragment 4

[Whether Pheidon of Argos first struck coinage ... or the Lydians, as Xenophanes says.]

See chapter 1, pp. 65 and 73–77.

Fragment 5

Nor would one when mixing in the drinking cup first pour in the wine, but water and then on top, the wine.

See chapter 1, pp. 66 and 73–77.

Fragment 6

πέμψας γὰρ κωλῆν ἐρίφου σκέλος ἤραο πῖον
ταύρου λαρινοῦ, τίμιον ἀνδρὶ λαχεῖν,
τοῦ κλέος Ἑλλάδα πᾶσαν ἐφίξεται οὐδ' ἀπολήξει
ἔστ' ἂν ἀοιδάων ᾖ γένος Ἑλλαδικόν.

Athenaeus *Scholars at Dinner* 9.368e (Edmonds fragment 5)

Fragment 7

Νῦν αὖτ' ἄλλον ἔπειμι λόγον, δείξω δὲ κέλευθον.

καί ποτέ μιν στυφελιζομένου σκύλακος παριόντα
φασὶν ἐποικτῖραι καὶ τόδε φάσθαι ἔπος·
Παῦσαι μηδὲ ῥάπιζ', ἐπεὶ ἦ φίλου ἀνέρος ἐστὶν
ψυχή, τὴν ἔγνων φθεγξαμένης ἀΐων.

Diogenes Laertius *Lives of the Philosophers* 8.36 (Edmonds fragment 6, 6a)

Fragment 6

For you sent the thigh of a young goat and won a fat leg
of a fatted bull, a thing of honour to fall to a man
whose fame will reach all Greece and never cease
so long as a Greek sort of song shall be.

See chapter 1, pp. 67–69.

Fragment 7

Now I will come to yet another account, and I will show the way.

And they say that once as he was passing by a puppy being beaten,
he felt compassion and said this:
'Stop, don't beat it, since in truth it is the soul of a friend
which I recognized upon hearing it cry out.'

See chapter 2, pp. 78–81 and 114–19.

Fragment 8

ἤδη δ' ἐπτά τ' ἔασι καὶ ἐξήκοντ' ἐνιαυτοὶ
βληστρίζοντες ἐμὴν φροντίδ' ἀν' Ἑλλάδα γῆν·
ἐκ γενετῆς δὲ τότ' ἦσαν ἐείκοσι πέντε τε πρὸς τοῖς,
εἴπερ ἐγὼ περὶ τῶνδ' οἶδα λέγειν ἐτύμως.

Diogenes Laertius *Lives of the Philosophers* 9.19 (Edmonds fragment 7)

Fragment 9

ἀνδρὸς γηρέντος πολλὸν ἀφαυρότερος

Etymologicum Genuinum s.v. γῆρας (Edmonds fragment 8)

Fragment 10

ἐξ ἀρχῆς καθ' "Ομηρον ἐπεὶ μεμαθήκασι πάντες

Herodian *On Doubtful Syllables* 296.6

Fragment 8

Already there are seven and sixty years

tossing about my counsel throughout the land of Greece,

and from my birth up till then there were twenty and five to add to
these,
if I know how to speak truly concerning these things.

See chapter 1, pp. 69–71.

Fragment 9

... much feebler than an aged man.

Fragment 10

Since from the beginning all have learned according to Homer ...

See chapter 2, pp. 81–82 and 114–19.

Fragment 11

πάντα θεοῖς ἀνέθηκαν "Ομηρός θ' 'Ησίοδός τε,
ὅσσα παρ' ἀνθρώποισιν ὀνείδεα καὶ ψόγος ἐστίν,
κλέπτειν μοιχεύειν τε καὶ ἀλλήλους ἀπατεύειν.

Sextus Empiricus *Against the Professors* 9.193 (= *Against the Physicists* 1.193)

Fragment 12

ὡς¹ πλεῖστ' ἐφθέγξαντο θεῶν ἀθεμίστια ἔργα,
κλέπτειν μοιχεύειν τε καὶ ἀλλήλους ἀπατεύειν.

Sextus Empiricus *Against the Professors* 1.289

1 Following Diels, Heitsch; E: οἵ; mss ὅς

Fragment 13

alii Homerum quam Hesiodum maiorem natu fuisse scripserunt,
in quibus Philochorus et Xenophanes, alii minorum.

Aulus Gellius *Attic Nights* 3.11

Fragment 11

Homer and Hesiod have attributed to the gods

all sorts of things which are matters of reproach and censure among men:

theft, adultery, and mutual deceit.

See chapter 2, pp. 82–85 and 114–19.

Fragment 12

... as they sang of numerous illicit divine deeds:

theft, adultery, and mutual deceit.

See chapter 2, pp. 83–85 and 114–19.

Fragment 13

[Some record that Homer was older than Hesiod, among whom are

Philochorus and Xenophanes, others that he was younger.]

Fragment 14

ἀλλ' οἱ βροτοὶ δοκέουσι γεννᾶσθαι θεοὺς
τὴν σφετέρην ἐσθῆτα <τ'> ἔχειν φωνήν τε δέμας τε.

Clement *Miscellanies* 5.109

Fragment 15

εἰ <δέ> τοι <ἵπποι> ἔχον χέρας ἢ βόες ἠὲ λέοντες
ἢ γράψαι χείρεσσι[1] καὶ ἔργα τελεῖν ἅπερ ἄνδρες,
ἵπποι μέν θ' ἵπποισι, βόες δέ τε βουσὶν ὁμοίας[2]
καί <κε> θεῶν ἰδέας ἔγραφον καὶ σώματ' ἐποίουν
τοιαῦθ' οἱόνπερ καὐτοὶ δέμας εἶχον ἕκαστοι.

Clement *Miscellanies* 5.110

———
1 E, following Diels: χροίῃσι, mss χείρεσσι
2 E reads ὁμοῖα (mss ὁμοίας) and transposes the line to final position.

Fragment 16

Αἰθίοπές τε <θεοὺς σφετέρους> σιμοὺς μέλανάς τε
Θρῇκές τε γλαυκοὺς καὶ πυρρούς <φασι πελέσθαι>·

Clement *Miscellanies* 7.22

Fragment 14

But mortals suppose that gods are born,

wear their own clothes and have a voice and body.

See chapter 2, pp. 85–89 and 114–19.

Fragment 15

But if horses or oxen or lions had hands

or could draw with their hands and accomplish such works as men,

horses would draw the figures of the gods as similar to horses, and

the oxen as similar to oxen,

and they would make the bodies

of the sort which each of them had.

See chapter 2, pp. 89–94 and 114–19.

Fragment 16

Ethiopians say that their gods are snub-nosed and black;

Thracians that theirs are blue-eyed and red-haired.

See chapter 2, pp. 90–94 and pp. 114–19.

Fragment 17

ἑστᾶσιν δ' ἐλάτης <Βάκχοι> πυκινὸν περὶ δῶμα.

Scholium on Aristophanes *Knights* 408

Fragment 18

Οὗτοι ἀπ' ἀρχῆς πάντα θεοὶ θνητοῖς ὑπέδειξαν,
ἀλλὰ χρόνῳ ζητοῦντες ἐφευρίσκουσιν ἄμεινον.

Stobaeus *Physical Selections* 1.8.2

Fragment 19

δοκεῖ δὲ κατά τινας πρῶτος ἀστρολογῆσαι καὶ ἡλιακὰς ἐκλείψεις καὶ τροπὰς
προειπεῖν ... ὅθεν αὐτὸν καὶ Ξενοφάνης καὶ Ἡρόδοτος θαυμάζει.

Diogenes Laertius *Lives of the Philosophers* 1.23

Fragment 17

... and bacchants of pine stand round the well-built house.

See chapter 2, pp. 95–96 and 114–19.

Fragment 18

Indeed not from the beginning did gods intimate all things to mortals, but as they search in time they discover better.

See chapter 4, pp. 149–55 and pp. 182–86.

Fragment 19

[According to some accounts (Thales) seems to have been the first to study astronomy and to foretell solar eclipses and the solstices ... for which reason both Xenophanes and Herodotus admire him.]

See chapter 3, pp. 120–24 and 145–48.

Fragment 20

καὶ ἐπανελθὼν ἐπ' οἴκου μετ' οὐ πολὺ μετήλλαξεν, ὥς φησι Φλέγων, βιοὺς ἔτη ἑπτὰ καὶ πεντήκοντα καὶ ἑκατόν ... ὡς δὲ Ξενοφάνης ὁ Κολοφώνιος ἀκηκοέναι φησι, τέτταρα πρὸς τοῖς πεντήκοντα καὶ ἑκατόν.

Diogenes Laertius *Lives of the Philosophers* 1.111

Fragment 21

ὁ Σιμωνίδης διεβέβλητο ἐπὶ φιλαργυρίᾳ ... χαριέντως δὲ πάνυ τῷ αὐτῷ λόγῳ διέσυρε ... καὶ μέμνηται ὅτι σμικρόλογος ἦν. ὅθεν Ξενοφάνης

κίμβικα

αὐτὸν προσαγορεύει.

Scholium on Aristophanes *Peace* 697

Fragment 21a

τὸ

῎Ερυκος

παρὰ Ξενοφάνει ἐν ε' Σίλλων.

Scholium on Homer *Oxyrhynchus Papyri* 1087.40 (Edmonds fragment 21b)

Fragment 20

[And returning home, (Epimenides) shortly after passed away, at the age according to Phlegon, of a hundred and fifty-seven ... as Xenophanes of Colophon says, he heard it said (that Epimenides lived for) a hundred and fifty-four years.]

Fragment 21

[Simonides was accused of avarice ... he (Aristophanes) very wittily ridiculed (them) in the same account ... and records that he (Simonides) cared about petty expenses, because of which Xenophanes calls him skinflint.]

Fragment 21a

[The word *Erykos* (D-K: a town or mountain in Sicily = Eryx) is found in the fifth book of Xenophanes' *Silloi*.]

Fragment 22

πὰρ πυρὶ χρὴ τοιαῦτα λέγειν χειμῶνος ἐν ὥρῃ
ἐν κλίνῃ μαλακῇ κατακείμενον, ἔμπλεον ὄντα,
πίνοντα γλυκὺν οἶνον, ἐπιτρώγοντ᾽ ἐρεβίνθους·
'τίς πόθεν εἶς ἀνδρῶν, πόσα τοι ἔτε᾽ ἐστί, φέριστε;
πηλίκος ἦσθ᾽ ὅθ᾽ ὁ Μῆδος ἀφίκετο;'

Athenaeus *Epitome* 2.54e

Fragment 23

Εἷς θεὸς ἔν τε θεοῖσι καὶ ἀνθρώποισι μέγιστος,
οὔτι δέμας θνητοῖσιν ὁμοίϊος οὔτε νόημα.

Clement *Miscellanies* 5.109

Fragment 24

οὖλος ὁρᾷ, οὖλος δὲ νοεῖ, οὖλος δέ τ᾽ ἀκούει.

Sextus Empiricus *Against the Professors* 9.144 (= *Against the Physicists* 1.144)

Fragment 22

One ought to say such things as these, beside a fire in wintertime,

lying fully fed on a soft couch,

drinking sweet wine and eating chick-peas for dessert:

'Who among men are you and what family are you from?,' 'How old
are you, good sir?,'
and 'What age were you when the Mede came?'

See chapter 1, pp. 71–73.

Fragment 23

One god is greatest among gods and men,

not at all like mortals in body or in thought.

See chapter 2, pp. 96–102 and 114–19.

Fragment 24

... whole he sees, whole he thinks, and whole he hears.

See chapter 2, pp. 102–6 and 114–19.

Fragment 25

ἀλλ' ἀπάνευθε πόνοιο νόου[1] φρενὶ πάντα κραδαίνει.

Simplicius *Commentary on Aristotle's Physics* 23.19

———
1 E: *νοῶν*. The *νόου* of the mss, though difficult, is not impossible. See note on the translation of *νόου* in fragment 25 in chapter 2 following.

Fragment 26

αἰεὶ δ' ἐν ταὐτῷ μίμνει κινούμενος[1] οὐδέν,
οὐδὲ μετέρχεσθαί μιν ἐπιπρέπει ἄλλοτε ἄλλῃ·

Simplicius *Commentary on Aristotle's Physics* 23.10

———
1 E: *κινεύμενος*, mss *κινούμενον* and *κινούμενος*

Fragment 27

ἐκ γαίης γὰρ πάντα καὶ εἰς γῆν πάντα τελευτᾷ.

Theodoretus *Treatment of Greek Conditions* 4.5

Fragment 25

... but completely without toil he shakes all things by the thought of
his mind.

See chapter 2, pp. 106–10 and 114–19.

Fragment 26

... always he abides in the same place, not moving at all,
nor is it seemly for him to travel to different places at different times.

See chapter 2, pp. 110–14 and 114–19.

Fragment 27

... for all things are from the earth and to the earth all things come
in the end.

See chapter 3, pp. 124–28 and 145–48.

Fragment 28

γαίης μὲν τόδε πεῖρας ἄνω παρὰ ποσσὶν ὁρᾶται
ἠέρι προσπλάζον, τὸ κάτω δ' ἐς ἄπειρον ἱκνεῖται.

Achilles Tatius *Introduction to the Phaenomena of Aratus* 4.34.11

Fragment 29

γῆ καὶ ὕδωρ πάντ' ἐσθ' ὅσα γίνοντ' ἠδὲ φύονται.

Philoponus *Commentary on Aristotle's Physics* 1.5.125

Fragment 30

πηγὴ δ' ἐστὶ θάλασσ' ὕδατος, πηγὴ δ' ἀνέμοιο·
οὔτε γὰρ <ἦν ἄνεμός κεν>[1] ἄνευ πόντου μεγάλοιο
οὔτε ῥοαὶ ποταμῶν οὔτ' αἰ<θέρος> ὄμβριον ὕδωρ,
ἀλλὰ μέγας πόντος γενέτωρ νεφέων ἀνέμων τε
καὶ ποταμῶν.

Geneva Scholium on *Iliad* 21.196 (= fragment 32a of Crates of Mallus)

1 Supplemental material supplied by E; mss ἐν νέφεσιν ἔσωθεν, which makes the line neither metrical nor intelligible. See the notes on translation on fragment 30 in chapter 3 following.

Fragment 28

This upper limit of the earth is seen here at our feet,

pushing up against the air, but that below goes on without limit.

See chapter 3, pp. 128–31 and 145–48.

Fragment 29

All things which come into being and grow are earth and water.

See chapter 3, pp. 131–34 and 145–48.

Fragment 30

The sea is the source of water and of wind,

for without the great sea there would be no wind

nor streams of rivers nor rainwater from on high;

but the great sea is the begetter of clouds, winds,

and rivers.

See chapter 3, pp. 134–37 and 145–48.

Fragment 31

ἠέλιός θ' ὑπεριέμενος γαῖάν τ' ἐπιθάλπων

Heraclitus *Homeric Allegories* 44.5

Fragment 32

ἥν τ' Ἶριν καλέουσι, νέφος καὶ τοῦτο πέφυκε,
πορφύρεον καὶ φοινίκεον καὶ χλωρὸν ἰδέσθαι.

Scholium BLT on *Iliad* 11.27

Fragment 33

πάντες γὰρ γαίης τε καὶ ὕδατος ἐκγενόμεσθα.

Sextus Empiricus *Against the Professors* 10.314 (= *Against the Physicists* 2.314)

Fragment 31

... the sun both passing over the earth and spreading warmth over its
                                                                surface ...

See chapter 3, pp. 137–39 and 145–48.

Fragment 32

And she whom they call Iris, this too is by nature a cloud,

purple, red and greenish-yellow to behold.

See chapter 3, pp. 139–44 and 145–48.

Fragment 33

For we all come into being from earth and water.

See chapter 3, pp. 131–34 and 145–48.

Fragment 34

καὶ τὸ μὲν οὖν σαφὲς οὖτις ἀνὴρ ἴδεν[1] οὐδέ τις ἔσται

εἰδὼς ἀμφὶ θεῶν τε καὶ ἄσσα λέγω περὶ πάντων·

εἰ γὰρ καὶ τὰ μάλιστα τύχοι τετελεσμένον εἰπών,

αὐτὸς ὅμως οὐκ οἶδε· δόκος δ' ἐπὶ πᾶσι τέτυκται.

Sextus Empiricus *Against the Professors* 7.49.110
———
1 E: γένετ' as in Plutarch; corrected to ἴδεν (in Sextus) following Snell
  1924

Fragment 35

ταῦτα δεδοξάσθω μὲν ἐοικότα τοῖς ἐτύμοισι.

Plutarch *Table Talk* 9.7.746b

Fragment 36

ὁππόσα δὴ θνητοῖσι πεφήνασιν εἰσοράασθαι

Herodian *On Doubtful Syllables* 296.9

Fragment 34

... and of course the clear and certain truth no man has seen

nor will there be anyone who knows about the gods and what I say
about all things.
For even if, in the best case, one happened to speak just of what has
been brought to pass,
still he himself would not know. But opinion is allotted to all.

See chapter 4, pp. 155–69 and 182–86.

Fragment 35

Let these be accepted, certainly, as like the realities (but ...)

See chapter 4, pp. 169–76 and 182–86.

Fragment 36

... however many they have made evident for mortals to look upon.

See chapter 4, pp. 176–79 and 182–86.

Fragment 37

καὶ μὴν[1] ἐνὶ σπεάτεσσι τεοῖς καταλείβεται ὕδωρ·

Herodian *On Peculiar Speech* 30

———

1 E: ἀγνὸν; mss καὶ μὴν

Fragment 38

εἰ μὴ χλωρὸν ἔφυσε θεὸς μέλι, πολλὸν ἔφασκον
γλύσσονα σῦκα πέλεσθαι.

Herodian *On Peculiar Speech* 41.5

Fragment 39

συκάμινα· ταῦτα δὲ καὶ μόρα Αἰσχύλος ὠνόμασεν, τὰ ἄγρια οὕτως ὀνομάσας τὰ
ἐκ τῆς βάτου. τάχα δ' ἄν τις καὶ κεράσια φαίη,

    κερασόν

τὸ δένδρον ἐν τῷ Περὶ Φύσεως Ξενοφάνους εὑρών.

Pollux *Vocabulary* 6.46

Fragment 37

... and indeed in certain caves water drips down ...

See chapter 3, pp. 144–45 and 145–48.

Fragment 38

If god had not made yellow honey, they would think
that figs were much sweeter.

See chapter 4, pp. 180–82 and 182–86.

Fragment 39

[Mulberries: These are called *mora* by Aeschylus, who gives the name
of *sukamina* to the wild variety, the fruit of the bramble. They might
also be called *kerasia*, for we find *kerason* – 'cherry tree' – in Xenophanes' *On Nature*.]

Fragment 40

βρόταχον

τὸν βάτραχον ᾿Ιωνες . . . καὶ παρὰ Ξενοφάνει.

Etymologicum Genuinum, s.v. βρόταχος

Fragment 41

σιλλογράφος δέ τις τὸ σι μακρὸν γράφει τῷ ῥῶ, δοκεῖ μοι, τοῦτο μηκύνας τάχα.
σιλλογράφος νῦν ὁ Ξενοφάνης ἐστὶ καὶ ὁ Τίμων καὶ ἕτεροι.

Tzetzes on Dionysius Periegetes, 940

Fragment 42

καί <κ᾿> ἐπιθυμήσειε νέος νῆς ἀμφιπόλοιο.

Herodian *On Peculiar Speech* 7, 11 (Edmonds fragment 21a)

Fragment 45

ἐγὼ δ᾿ ἐμαυτὸν ἐκ πόλιος πόλιν φέρων ἐβλήστριζον·

Scholium on Hippocrates *On Epidemics* 1.13.3; Erotian, *Glossary to Hippocrates* 102.19 (Edmonds fragment 42)

Fragment 40

[... Ionians use the word *brotachon* – 'frog'; it is found also in Xenophanes.]

Fragment 41

[... a certain writer of *silloi* writes the syllable *si-* long, lengthening it perhaps, in my opinion, in light of the *rho*. The writers of *silloi* are Xenophanes, and Timon, and others.]

Fragment 42

... and a young man would desire a young serving girl.

Fragment 45

I tossed about, bearing myself from city to city.

See chapter 1, pp. 69–71.

PART 2   INTERPRETATION

1

On Men and Morals

Fragment 1

[Seeing, then, that your banquet, as Xenophanes of Colophon says,
'is full of all kinds of pleasure':]
For now the floor is clean as are the cups and hands of all.
One puts on the woven garlands;
another passes along a fragrant ointment in a bowl.
The mixing bowl stands full of cheer
5   and another wine, mild and flower fragrant in the jars, is at hand –
which says it never will give out.
In the midst frankincense gives forth its sacred scent,
and there is cold water, sweet and pure.
Golden loaves lie near at hand, and the noble[1] table
10 is loaded down with cheese and rich honey.
An altar in the centre is covered all about with flowers
while song and festive spirit enfold the house.
But first glad-hearted men[2] must hymn the god
with reverent words and pure speech.[3]
15 And having poured a libation and prayed to be able to do
what is right – for these are obvious[4] –
it is not wrong to drink as much as allows any but an aged man
to reach his home without a servant's aid.
Praise the man who when he has taken drink brings noble deeds

to light,

20 as memory and a striving for virtue bring[5] to him.
He deals[6] neither with the battles of Titans nor Giants
nor Centaurs, fictions of old,[7]

nor furious conflicts – for there is no use in these.
But it is good always to hold the gods in high regard.[8]

Athenaeus 11, 462c (for full citation of this and subsequent fragments see Greek texts above).

NOTES

1 γεραρή (gerarē): The meaning of the epithet is unclear. LSJ offers 'table of honour,' corrected in the Supplement to 'lordly,' 'splendid.' 'Princely feast' (Hudson-Williams), 'worthy table' (D-K: 'würdige Tisch'), and 'stately' (Moore) are also possible. Heitsch's 'festliche' ('festive'), and Reinhardt's 'reicher' ('rich,' 'abundant') are less obvious choices. Marcovich (1978, 5) suggests that 'the table has the epithet "reverend" ... because it holds bread – the holy geras of Demeter,' but gerarē (like the noble deeds mentioned at line 19) contributes to Xenophanes' description of the dinner as 'a noble occasion' (cf. geras: 'gift of honour,' 'noble privilege,' and our expression, 'a table fit for a king').

2 εὔφρονας ἄνδρας (euphronas andras): The meaning of euphrōn (lit. 'well in one's phrēn') ranges across qualities of cheerfulness, merriment, graciousness, and soundness or reasonableness of mind. If we opt for either of the last two (e.g., Reinhardt's 'rechtgesonnene' – 'right-minded'), the remark is a platitude. If (following Defradas 1962b, 76n) we keep the connection with the conviviality of the occasion (i.e., the θαλίη just mentioned at 1.12, and the εὐφροσύνης at 1.4) the comment has more force: (even) at moments of great merriment it is incumbent on men to hymn the god in appropriate language (cf. the similar conclusion stated at 1.24: 'it is good always (αἰὲν) to hold the gods in high regard'). Adkins (1985, 181) comments: 'to advise drinkers who are euphrones in the usual sense to behave piously and decorously is perfectly comprehensible.'

3 μύθοις ... λόγοις (muthois ... logois): The later connotation of muthos as fictional account is not obligatory here; muthos is often just the spoken word (e.g., Iliad 3.76: μῦθον ἀκούσας). While some contrast between muthos and logos seems intended there is no consensus on what that contrast might be. Bowra (1953) translates 'reverent stories' and 'clean subjects' (similarly Heitsch: 'ehrfurchtsvollen Erzählungen und reinen Themen'), but Marcovich's suggestion that 'muthos refers to the content of the paean, logos to the verbal expression' (1978, 9) is not unreasonable in light of the close connection between logos and

legein (saying). It is also possible that the contrast concerned only different forms of expression: (individually) reverent words and (collectively) reverent stories.

4 ταῦτα ... προχειρότερον (*tauta ... procheiroteron*): Neither the meaning of προχειρότερον nor the antecedent referents of ταῦτα can be fixed with certainty. LSJ gives 'obvious' and takes the ταῦτα to refer back to the prayers of line 15; similarly, Denniston: (sc. *euxasthai*: 'for this in truth ...'). Many others have taken the ταῦτα to refer to the just or right acts one is praying to be able to do, but then it is difficult to see how *these* could be either easy, obvious, or 'nearer to hand' for us to do. Adkins (1985, 181–82), realizing that 'it is not plausible to say that justice is easier than *hubris*, and *procheiroteron* cannot mean preferable' proposes that we read προτιμότερον instead.

I am inclined to take ταῦτα as referring back to the activities of drinking a libation and praying mentioned in the previous line. These are *procheiroteron* – 'obvious' in the sense of 'obviously correct,' since such libations would be a proper way to behave (cf. *Odyssey* 3.45ff.: 'And when you have poured libations and prayed, *as is fitting* ...' (σπείσῃς τε καὶ εὔξεαι, ἢ θέμις ἐστί).

West (1974) reads ὕβρεις for ὕβρις at 1.17, and takes τὰ δίκαια δύνασθαι πρήσσειν as antithesis to οὐχ ὕβρεις, hence what lie 'nearer to hand' are τὰ δίκαια, not evil deeds. Heitsch also takes ταῦτα to refer to the preceding τὰ δίκαια, and understands πρήσσειν (τὰ δίκαια) and οὐχ ὕβρις to complement one another (94). But one would normally suppose just the opposite to be the case (cf. Hesiod *Works* 288: 'the road to badness is smooth and very nearby'), and the separation of οὐχ ὕβρις or ὕβρεις from πίνειν at 1.19 would impart too strong a meaning to Xenophanes' remark: not 'it is not wrong to drink as much ...' but instead 'drink as much ...,' etc.

5 Cf. Adkins (1985, 183): 'In 20, the general sense is clear, but the text is very doubtful. It is impossible to be confident that any of the suggestions best represents what Xenophanes wrote.' My translation requires that we supply an unstated verb ('brings' or its equivalent) paralleling *anaphainei*, with 'him' (*hoi* – 3rd sing. pers. pron.) as its indirect object.

6 διέπει (*diepei*): Lit. 'manage' or 'conduct' (διέπω). My translation follows a suggestion made by Heitsch: 'er nicht etwa handelt von Kämpfen ...' ('he will not deal with battles'). Adkins (1985, 183–84) opts for a more literal interpretation, understanding Xenophanes here and at 1.19 (ἀναφαίνῃ) to be discouraging misconduct like that of the gods

described by the poets. The phrase πλάσματα τῶν προτέρων, however, points toward understanding 'the battles' as referring to those described by the poets rather than to any which Xenophanes' hearers are supposed to avoid (similarly Defradas 1962b, 78n: 'he does not organize battles' – as did Hesiod). Roth (120) points out that the similar verb *diatithenai* acquires a specific meaning of 'recite' as well as 'arrange' (e.g., Plato *Charmides* 162d), and he suggests a similar dual meaning for *diepein*. While the possibility cannot be excluded, there is not a single use of *diepein* where 'recite' would be the only possible meaning.

7 τῶν προτέρων (*tōn proterōn*): 'Of men of former times.' Cf. Hesiod *Theogony*, 629ff.; *Odyssey* 21.295–304; Theognis, 542.

8 προμηθείην (*promētheiēn*): LSJ cites Herodotus 1.88 'to hold in great *consideration,*' and for *promētheomai,* Herodotus 2.172; 9.108 'show regard or respect for.' Fränkel (1973, 327n.), emending θεῶν to χρεών, translates 'one should always have a good purpose before one's eyes' which is both unduly sceptical about προμηθείην and a radical measure for so prosaic a conclusion. It is preferable to take the αἰὲν with ἔχειν immediately following it rather than with ἀγαθόν; Xenophanes need hardly argue that it is *always good* to honour the gods (when could it not be?), but he can reasonably argue that is good to honour them always, as in D-K: 'aber der Götter allzeit fürsorglich zu gedenken, das ist edel' ('but taking care to be mindful at all times of the gods, that is noble'). Priam displays a similar piety upon learning that the gods have protected Hector's body from complete destruction: 'it is good indeed to give fitting gifts to the immortals, for never did my son ... forget within our halls the gods who inhabit Olympus' (ἀγαθὸν ... θεῶν, *Iliad* 24.425ff.).

COMMENTARY ON FRAGMENT 1

The basic features of Xenophanes' sympotic poem are clear enough: the poet describes a banquet scene brimming with good food and drink, piety, and festive spirits, and calls for conduct that befits both the occasion and the gods, whom we must hold always in high regard. The specific details of the highly descriptive first half of the poem (lines 1–12) can also be accounted for on the basis of similar depictions of other festive occasions (e.g., *Odyssey* 9.5–11, 203–11). But in many other respects – the meaning of the moral injunctions that make up the second half (lines 13–24), the relation of these to the preceding description, the rationale behind Xenophanes' moralizing – considerable doubt and uncertainty remain. It is highly likely however that the poem is more than a few 'cheerful lines' which 'scarcely goes beyond the limits of conventional piety' (Guthrie, 361). Before we try to assay the quality of Xenophanes' thought we must first recognize the various respects in which our understanding of the fragment is incomplete.

Line 1 Since νῦν γὰρ δή is an unlikely opening for an elegiac poem (Denniston cites this passage as an example of δή emphasizing the connective γάρ), Athenaeus' quotation of the poem may not be complete. His introduction ('seeing that your banquet, as Xenophanes of Colophon says, 'is full of all kinds of pleasures') suggests a possible content for the original lines. Adkins (177) suggests another: 'Let us begin our drinking party. We have what we need; for ...,' etc. The use of θεὸν at 1.13 and θεῶν at 1.24 does serve (as Marcovich and Ziegler noted) to frame the second half of the poem, and in any case the entire presentation embodies a single coherent idea: even on occasions of great conviviality men must be mindful of the gods and do what is right.

The appearance of καθαρὸν in the poem's opening line (with its recurrence at 1.8 and 1.14) sets a tone of uncommon purity or cleanliness (in surroundings, person, utensils, drink, deed, and word). The description of the physical circumstances (in lines 1–12) seems to parallel and prepare the way for the injunctions to personal decency (in lines 13ff.), but the precise nature of the relationship between the two parts is not certain. Bowra (1960, 122) suggests that Xenophanes 'saw a connection between the outward circumstances and the spirit which was to pervade the occasion ... outward purity imposed an obligation of inward purity on the guests.' But Xenophanes may have thought that 'cleanliness was next to godliness' in some sense without supposing that being *katharos* in the first respect mandated or 'imposed' being *katharos* in the second. It is possible that the need for physical cleanliness was merely *analogous* to the importance of spiritual purity. It might also be thought that cleanliness in both respects was of moral importance without supposing that they were interrelated or mutually implicative. I am inclined to think that the opening description has a propaedeutic purpose: by calling attention to the spiritual qualities already acknowledged to be present in such a setting Xenophanes prepares the ground for the call to piety and right conduct to follow. While *theos* itself does not appear until near the midpoint, the repeated references to pure, sacred, and wholesome qualities establish a climate in which a call for further piety is entirely natural. In setting the scene as he has, Xenophanes gives voice to a conventional piety but is also attempting to deepen his audience's understanding of the demands of true piety.

Line 3 The 'fragrant ointment' mentioned here (with the similar references to flowers and fragrances at 1.6, 1.7, and 1.11) helps to create the image of convivial celebration, but it is not obvious how we are able to reconcile this positive portrayal of the use of fragrances with the negative remarks about 'prepared fragrances' in fragment 3.6.

Line 15 The phrase 'praying to be able to do what is right' marks a turning point in the poem – from the demands of piety per se to the demands of piety in or through right conduct. The novelty of the prayer, asking not simply for success or for divine intervention but for the power to act rightly, has been noted (Fränkel, 327; Marcovich 1978, 8; Reinhardt, 128ff; von Fritz 1894–1963, 1547). While *aretē* is not mentioned explicitly until 1.20 it has been in the background of the occasion since the outset (for instance, in the placing of the garlands, the 'noble' table, the wholesome food and drink, and now in the prayer for a *dunamis* to do what is right – an implicit request for *aretē*; cf. Plato's *Meno* 77b). The scope of the prayer is unclear: either for the power to do rightly the remaining tasks of the occasion (οὐχ ὕβρις πίνειν, αἰνεῖν, ἐσθλὰ πιὼν ἀναφαίνῃ, ἔχει προμηθείην, etc.) or to do what is right in all one's daily conduct.

Line 17 A call for moderation in drinking is not novel (cf. Theognis 467–96, 505; Anacreon 356a 5–6), but the index for wanton behaviour – not being able to get home on one's own – is unusual. In what may be a paraphrase of Xenophanes' own words, Athenaeus (in a comment following fragment 3) states that 'so enfeebled were they [the Colophonians who practised Lydian ways] by constant drunkenness (ἄκαιρον μέθην) that some of them never saw the sun rise or set' (526a). If Xenophanes had spoken elsewhere against excessive drinking it would be appropriate for him here, in a bibulous setting, to explain how one could drink without offence. The same index of propriety or impropriety appears in Heraclitus' fragment 117: 'a man when he is drunk (μεθυσθῇ) is led by a beardless boy, stumbling, and not knowing where he goes, having his soul moist.' Plato perpetuates the idea in his description of Socrates' legendary feats of self-control (*Symposium* 176c, 223d): having 'drunk his companions under the table,' Socrates 'spent the rest of the day as usual, then, toward evening, made his way home.' Xenophanes' comment about excessive drinking, like these later philosophical remarks, evaluates behaviour from the perspective of creating and preserving *sōphrosunē*. For Plato's differentiation between decent and indecent celebration, see *Republic* 363c–d, 372b–d, 420e, 586a; *Laws* 637a–e, 639d–42a, 671c–72a.

Lines 19–22 Xenophanes calls upon his audience to praise 'this one' (τοῦτον – presumably either himself or anyone else who tells a tale) who is enabled by memory and a striving or 'intensity' for virtue to bring noble deeds to light while avoiding the old fictions about divine warfare. While the targets of his rebuke almost certainly include Homer and Hesiod (cf. fragments 11, 12), the rationale lying behind the rebuke is harder to pin down. Bowra's suggestion, 'because they introduce an element of discord into a harmonious occasion' (1953, 10), is inadequate; Xenophanes is himself prepared to be controversial (cf. his attack on athletic claims to virtue in fragment 2), and a concern for merely polite behaviour fails to do justice to the moral seriousness that pervades the second half of the poem. Marcovich proposes that at bottom there is a 'theological reason: such stories about the gods are sheer lies ... Xenophanes the religious reformer is speaking' (1978, 13). This is undoubtedly correct, but it may not go far enough. There are many false or erroneous things said about the gods (cf. fragments 13–16); why then are tales of divine warfare singled out here for special condemnation? There seems to be something especially pernicious about these *plasmata* of old, beyond the mere fact of their falsity. Eisenstadt (1974, 142–50) claims that the stricture against telling these stories was based on a 'homeopathic sociology': they 'exacerbated violent tendencies in an inebriated audience' (147). But I doubt that Xenophanes' real concern lay in curbing rowdy behaviour at parties. What we can see generally in fragment 1, and will see elsewhere, is his concern with virtue or moral excellence – how to exhibit and preserve it, and how to present it in our songs and stories. The best explanation of this censure of stories of divine misconduct is that they are not only bad religion, they are also bad paradigms for moral education and civic training. A concern with moral education is probably inherent in Xenophanes' characterization of Homer as 'educator of all' (in fragment 10), and it is reflected here in his urging not only to avoid some subjects but also to bring 'noble deeds' (ἐσθλὰ) into view. The comparison with Plato's attack on poetry (drawn by Diels, Eisenstadt, Marcovich, and many others) provides a significant clue to Xenophanes' thinking here because the parallels are so close and so extensive (see fragments 2, 3, 22, and chapter 2 following). 'We can admit no poetry into our city,' says Plato 'save only hymns to the gods and praises of good men (ὕμνους θεοῖς καὶ ἐγκώμια τοῖς ἀγαθοῖς),' *Republic* 607a. Stories of divine enmities are contrary to the well-being of a state not so much because they *incite* violence but because they tend to legitimize it (cf. *Republic* 378b and *Euthyphro* 6a), and undercut a society's efforts to inculcate right conduct, especially in children (*Republic* 378c–e). The scene described in fragment 1 closely resembles the wholesome family dinner Plato describes at the outset of his account of the ideal city: 'they will serve noble cakes and loaves (μάζας γενναίας καὶ ἄρτους) on some arrangement of reeds or clean leaves. And recline on rustic beds strewn with bryony and myrtle they will feast with their children, drinking of the wine, garlanded, and singing hymns to the gods in pleasant fellowship' (372b).

Line 23 'Furious conflicts' may refer either to the divine warfare already mentioned or to the kind of civil strife recounted by Alcaeus in his *stasiōtika*. Since the next line provides a concluding call to pay due honour to the gods, the former option is more likely. The stated reason for this prohibition – there is nothing *chrēston* in them – is significant (as both Bowra and Marcovich have argued) since it reveals Xenophanes' concern for what is 'useful,' that is, beneficial to the city or community at large. 'Civic utility' becomes a frequent index for personal excellence in later writers (cf. *Republic* 380c: 'the saying of such things would be neither holy nor profitable to us'). Xenophanes' use of *chrēston*, especially in light of its parallel with the 'noble deeds' (*esthla*) called for in 1.19 above, is an important indication of his interest in 'the public good' (cf. fragment 2 on *eunomiē* following). What would be particularly unhelpful about such stories is their potential to undermine the idea of a group loyalty or 'common good' (cf. *Republic* 378b-c).

Line 24 The poem ends with *agathon* (or *agathēn*), which is an appropriate ending for a progression from a description of material circumstances to the spiritual qualities conveyed by them to the demands of moral seriousness the latter give rise to. This progressive elevation of sentiment, aptly symbolized by the upward progression from the floor (1.1) to table (1.9) to house (1.12) to human excellence (1.20) to respect for the gods (1.24) gives the poem its didactic character; it is an exercise in moral sensitizing, even 'consciousness raising' beyond the level of conventional entertainment and piety with which it began. For this reason it is difficult to accept the suggestions that Xenophanes composed his poem for a Pythagorean or Parmenidean circle of associates (see Defradas 1962a, 344–65; and Herter, 33–48). While the poem might have been repeated in any number of settings, it seems to have in mind as an intended audience those who do not yet sense fully the demands of goodness or excellence in their own conduct. Xenophanes' close circle of philosophical associates (assuming that he had one) is not especially likely to fit this description.

Fragment 2

[These (sentiments) Euripides (see part 3, imitation C2) took from
the elegies of Xenophanes who spoke as follows:]
But if by swiftness of foot one were to gain a victory
or in the pentathlon, there by Pisa's stream in Olympus in
the sacred grove of Zeus, or by wrestling,
or again the painful art of boxing,
5   or the fearsome sport they call pankration,
he would appear more glorious to his townsmen
and win the front-row seat of honour at games.
And there would be food from the city's public stores
and a keepsake gift for him.
10 And even if he were to win with horses he would get all these,
not being as worthy of them as I.
For our expertise[1] is better than the strength of men and horses.
But this practice makes no sense[2] nor is it right
to prefer strength to this good expertise.
15 For neither if there were a good boxer among the people
nor if there were a pentathlete or wrestler
nor again if there were someone swift afoot –
which is most honoured of all men's deeds of strength –
would for this reason a city be better governed.[3]
20 Small joy would a city have[4] from this –
if someone were to be victorious in competing for a prize on
                                     Pisa's banks –
for these do not enrich a city's treasure room.

Athenaeus 10.413f.

NOTES

1 σοφίη, ἀγαθῆς σοφίης (*sophiē, agathēs sophiēs*): 'Knowledge,' 'skill,' even
  'wisdom' are also possible here (and at line 14 below). The expansion
  in the meaning of *sophiē* from the original (at least Homeric) meaning
  of 'craft' or 'skill' (*Iliad* 15.412 where a shipwright is said to be
  well-versed in all kinds of *sophiē*) to a more comprehensive exercise
  of intelligence properly termed 'wisdom' is summarized in Guthrie
  2, 27–34; but it should be noted that the broader sense of *sophiē*
  parallels the narrower 'skill' sense rather than *replaces* it (cf. Aristotle,
  Nicomachean Ethics 1141a12, where the ascription of *sophia* to an artist
  (Pheidias) is distinguished from the use of *sophia* designating 'the

supreme science'). As a representative sampling: for 'skill'/'art'
– Campbell, Bowra, Edmonds, Guthrie; 'knowledge'/'wisdom' –
Adkins, Jaeger, Marcovich, D-K (wissen); Heitsch opts for both: 'un-
sere Kunst und Kenntnis' ('our skill and knowledge'). For a discussion of the specific form of skill, expertise, or knowledge involved,
see Jaeger (1945), 172–74; Bowra (1953), 16–20; Marcovich (1978),
21–22; Adkins (1985), 194–95 and the following comments on line
12. My choice of 'expertise' attempts to capture something of the
honorific quality of *sophiē* (as Aristotle suggests, it is an ἀρετὴ τέχνης,
'excellence in an art').

2 εἰκῇ μάλα ταῦτα νομίζεται (*eikēi mala tauta nomidzetai*): Lit. 'these are
very rashly practised as a custom' (cf. Heraclitus, fragment 47: 'let us
not converse εἰκῇ about the greatest things'). *Nomidzō* can also mean
'consider,' 'think,' 'believe' (LSJ II), but it commonly designates what
is customary practice (cf. *nomos*). It is more likely that Xenophanes
is criticizing an unreflective form of behaviour than a way of thinking (hence Campbell [1967]: 'this practice is completely haphazard');
similarly Heitsch: 'willkürlich ist dieser Brauch' – 'this custom is arbi-
trary.'

3 μᾶλλον ἐν εὐνομίῃ πόλις (*mallon en eunomiēi polis*): Lit. 'a city more in
the condition of being well-ordered.' As Campbell (1983, 59) explains,
eunomiē involves 'both the existence of good laws and the readiness
of the citizens to obey them'; cf. Solon, fragment 3, and Aristotle *Politics* 1294a1–7.

4 σμικρὸν ... πόλει ... γένοιτο (*smikron ... polei ... genoito*): dative
of possession (D-K: 'hätte die Stadt davon' – 'would the city have').
Xenophanes has just contrasted the goodness of the athlete (*agathos,
protimon*) with the benefits that accrue (or fail to accrue) to the city.
Here the joy that a city has (or fails to have) is contrasted with the
victory achieved by an individual (*tis*).

COMMENTARY ON FRAGMENT 2

Xenophanes' famous comment on the honours accorded to Olympic
victors continues the practice evident in fragment 1 of combining detailed description of current practice with a strongly worded admo-
nition to his audience to reflect upon the priorities reflected in their
practices. The thesis of fragment 2 has a double focus: the preferen-
tial treatment accorded to victors in the games at Olympia is a rash
or unwise practice and it is wrong for any to place greater esteem
on feats of strength than on Xenophanes' own expertise. These strong

words on athletic boosterism mark Xenophanes as a person of uncommon independence of thought; only Tyrtaeus (for militaristic reasons) and Euripides (in the *Autolycus* passage mentioned by Athenaeus in his introduction to this fragment; see imitation C2) expressed similar reservations. In a general way, the point of Xenophanes' teaching seems clear: 'Only a useful wisdom (such as my own) can bring about good government (on which the well-being of the city depends): no athlete's strength can' (Marcovich 1978, 19; a conclusion adopted by Adkins 1985, 198 and Heitsch, 110). But we have as yet no satisfactory answers to the more specific questions this explanation raises: which aspect of Xenophanes' teaching would have been especially conducive to good government? Why couldn't the celebration of athletic victories promote civic well-being? How, in fact, could Xenophanes say that 'small joy' came to the city through such victories when just the opposite seems to have been the case?

The answer Jaeger gave to the first question (that Xenophanes was alluding to his scientific outlook) surprised Jaeger himself (1945, 173) and it has found few supporters since. Bowra's specific diagnosis of the evil of athletics (it encourages *hubris* in the athletes by suggesting that they can rise above their social station; 1960, 132) goes beyond what Xenophanes actually says (see the critiques by Adkins 1985, 197–98 and Marcovich 1978, 20–21). Eisenstadt's 'homeopathic' alternative (1970, 68ff.) is also unsatisfactory; as Marcovich explained (21), swiftness of foot does not suggest any disturbing effect on the passions of the audience. Defradas (1962b, 80n) took Xenophanes to be claiming a superior value for his skill as poet and interpreter of the gods. I suspect that Xenophanes' attempt to preserve *eunomiē* (e.g., in fragment 1) provides the key to the solution (see the notes following on lines 15–23).

Lines 1–5 This opening description of the Olympic events (footrace, pentathlon, wrestling, boxing, pankration) is noteworthy for its evaluative neutrality. As Adkins argues (1985, 190, against Campbell 1983, 59), an expression of sarcasm or contempt for the athletic competitions or competitors themselves is hard to detect, nor would sarcasm suit Xenophanes' objective – which is not to denigrate athletic excellence but to demand equal or superior honour for himself. The adjectives ἀλγινόεσσαν (painful) and δεινὸν (fearsome, terrible) are evidence that Xenophanes understood the dangers inherent in ancient athletic competition, especially in the pankration, a combination of boxing, wrestling, kicking, twisting and strangling. As Marcovich noted (1978, 23), the listing of events follows the chronological order of their adoption in the games rather than the sequence of their occurrence; when combined with the listing in reverse order (15–17) the events provide a chiastic scheme for the entire presentation. Additional positive epithets (ἀγαθὸς, πρότιμον) appear without challenge, which suggests that a view often expressed about Xenophanes' attitude toward athletics – that he disparaged or denigrated them (cf. Snell 1953, 177; Guthrie 1, 364) – is too strong. The problems lay neither in the competitions themselves nor in an athlete's claim to his *aretē*, but rather in the city's excessive way of honouring them – and in not recognizing the greater importance of their poetic advisers.

Lines 6–10 'He would appear more glorious' is ambiguous: either 'more glorious than he was before' (D-K: 'glorreicher anzuschauen *als zuvor*'), or 'more glorious than others' (Defradas, Marcovich), or 'more glorious than he – Xenophanes.' 'Than others' is probably the right choice here; being more glorious than he was before is not obviously offensive (he did after all *win*) and 'more glorious than Xenophanes' muddies the presentation – Xenophanes' personal statement, οὐκ ἐὼν ἄξιος ὥσπερ ἐγώ, has greater force as his first evaluative statement following the entire descriptive section (lines 1–10).

Lines 7–9 Xenophanes lists the special honours accorded to the victorious athlete: he is given the front-row ('VIP') seats, he is fed from the city's public food supplies, and he is given a keepsake gift in recognition of his victory. As Fränkel noted, what all this represents is 'the granting of official distinctions' (329), an ancient equivalent of the presidential phone call and invitation to the White House. This élitist treatment (a feature which may be relevant to Xenophanes' comment about *eunomiē* at 2.19) explains the way in which the athlete is regarded as *kudroteros*.

Line 10 The sense of εἴτε καὶ ἵπποισιν is unclear: either 'if (he) also (won) with horses' or 'even if (he won) with horses' all these honours would fall to him. The context supplies conflicting considerations: (1) coming after the listing of honours accorded to other athletes, a separate mention of the victorious charioteer suggests a distinct level of esteem and since it was after all the horses that did the running (Fränkel 1925, 336n), we might attribute a negative twist to the comment: *even if* with horses, he would still get the honours, etc; (2) coming just before the main statement of Xenophanes' claim to honour (οὐκ ἐὼν ἄξιος ὥσπερ ἐγώ) we cannot suppose that the charioteer is being especially disparaged – for that would undercut the force of Xenophanes' own claim.

While I am inclined to think that 'even if' is the correct translation (in light of the four-line separation from the last mention of an athlete), I do not think the charioteer is being singled out as unusually undeserving. The contrasting claim (οὐκ ... ἐγώ) is after all best understood as a contrast between Xenophanes and each and every one of the athletes mentioned earlier; he is not claiming here to be superior just to the charioteer, but to them all, as is clear from the generality of his supporting reason: his *sophiē* is better than the strength of *men and horses*. The issue is discussed at length by Fränkel 1925, 335–37; Marcovich, 1978, 17–18; and Heitsch, 106.

Lines 11–14 Xenophanes' *sophiē* is 'better than' strength. Not only does this not imply that strength is a bad thing, but in order for Xenophanes' *sophiē* to be of great value it is necessary that we regard it as better than something already regarded good. The claim has a traditional 'brains are better than brawn' quality to it (cf. Nestor's claim that *mētis* is *ameinōn* than strength at *Iliad* 23.315), but Xenophanes gives it a personal twist – 'our' *sophiē*, the expertise he would be understood to have to offer (cf. the similar phrase 'my *phrontis*' in fragment 8 following). The following assertion – it would not be *dikaios* to esteem strength more highly than his 'good *sophiē*' – repeats his claim of superior value, but in a way that links that claim to the civic considerations to follow; his *sophiē* is both *agathē* and *ameinōn and* it is *dikaios* – just or right – to so regard it.

Lines 15–23 That neither claim (*ameinōn, dikaios*) would be obviously valid in the minds of Xenophanes' audience is indicated by the length of the explanation or argument he supplies. The 'argumentative' character of Xenophanes' presentation is reflected in his extensive use of causal or explanatory connectives (γὰρ at 2.15 and 2.22 and τοὔνεκεν at 2.19). Though stated in a compressed format the argument makes an interesting case for the superiority of Xenophanes' *sophiē* by contrasting the private or personal nature of the good achieved in athletic competition with the civic character of Xenophanes' expertise. The argument proceeds by constructing a hypothetical 'best case' scenario: suppose you had a *good* athlete, suppose even that you had a *good* athlete of the *best* type of athlete, even so it would not be by reason of this athlete that the city would be in better condition. This first 'premiss' in effect claims that the goodness of an athlete and the goodness of a city are separate categories. The second 'premiss' (lines 20–23) completes the argument by asserting that the joy which a city has in such victories is 'small,' that is, small in relation to the joy a city has when it prospers, because athletic honours do not of themselves 'enrich the treasury,' a synecdoche for 'make the city prosperous.' Having relegated athletic victories and excellence to the 'private sector' and having ranked the value of private gains in general below the level of the value of civic contributions, Xenophanes' conclusion (οὐδὲ δίκαιον ...) stated at the outset can be reasonably drawn: it is not right to place (private) achievements above the (public) good he himself has provided. The ordering of civic good above a personal or private good would likely have been accepted by Xenophanes' audience. Aristotle, at the outset of his *Nicomachean Ethics*, includes this sentiment among the moral commonplaces with which moral philosophy must operate: 'the good of the city appears [φαίνεται – a term which marks this as one of the moral *phainomena*] to be greater and more final both to have and to preserve; for though it is worthwhile to attain the good for an individual it is finer and more god-like to do it for the people and the city' (1094b7ff.). In a passage reminiscent of Xenophanes, Plato explains that the guardians of his ideal state will be more deserving of honours and public support than the victors at Olympia (*hoi olympionikai*): 'their victory is nobler (καλλίων) and their public support more complete (τελεωτέρα) for the victory they have won is the salvation of the entire state (*Republic* 465d6–8).

What would be controversial in Xenophanes' argument would be the relegation of athletic honours to a strictly personal status and the (unexplained) characterization of his *sophiē* as 'good' (*agathos*) with the implication that it (and not athletic achievement) led to greater *eunomiē*. In support of the former Xenophanes may have already provided a hint that the civic pride created through Olympic victories can easily be offset by resentment and disharmony (cf. Alcibiades' attempt to discount the envy in his fellow citizens created by his victories at Olympia in Thucydides 6.16.1ff.). In support of the latter claims Xenophanes must have regarded it as relevant that his teaching about *aretē* (e.g., in fragment 1) included discouraging behaviour that was inimical to *eunomiē*, that is, discouraging the retelling of the old stories about divine *staseis* or civic discord among the gods (1.23), criticisms of tasteless (and potentially destructive) displays of wealth (fragment 3), as well as a call for encomia of good men that would naturally serve to promote the good order of a city (cf. Plato's parallel conclusion: 'we should be justified in not admitting the mimetic poet into the well-ordered city' – εὐνομεῖσθαι πόλιν, *Republic* 605b). Euripides' conclusion in the *Autolycus* passage that imitates Xenophanes' fragment 2 (see imitation C2 in part 3) contains a call to honour that *sophrōn* and *dikaios* man who 'through his words liberates the city from evil deeds, ridding it both of battles and civil strife' (μάχας ... στάσεις). In short, Xenophanes must have believed that his *sophiē* – his expertise as a moral and spiritual adviser to his fellow citizens – could help to produce and preserve *eunomiē* in a city as athletic competition – even at its highest levels of achievement – never could, because his words could help to bond the citizens together in harmony. This dual thesis about *eunomiē*, both that the granting of official privileges to victorious athletes tends to work against it and that his own *sophiē* works to promote it, represents the heart of Xenophanes' teaching here in fragment 2.

Fragment 3

[The Colophonians, as Phylarchus says, being originally austere in their habits, ran aground on a luxurious lifestyle when they made themselves friends and allies to the Lydians, walked about with their hair decked out with gold ornament, as Xenophanes also says:]
And having learned unprofitable luxuries from the Lydians,
as long as they were free of hateful tyranny,
they used to go into the agora[1] wearing robes all of purple,
not less than a thousand in all,[2]
5 boastful, exulting in their gorgeous long-flowing hair,[3]
drenched in the scent of prepared unguents.[4]

Athenaeus 12.526a

NOTES

1 εἰς ἀγορὴν (*eis agorēn*): 'into the agora' – either the open 'market place' or the 'assembly,' the gathering together of the citizens for the purpose of conducting the city's affairs. The latter option (adopted by Fränkel 1925 and Defradas 1962b) gives Xenophanes' criticism a pointed meaning: while the Colophonians spent their time during their assemblies delighting in their Lydian fripperies their city was fated for conquest. The former, adopted by Bowra (1941), pp. 121–23 and Heitsch ('Marktplatz'), is supported by the paraphrases by Theopompus (*astupolein*, fragment 117 Jacoby) and Cicero (*in forum, Republic* 6.2) and has a natural enough sense: in parading about in public the Colophonians displayed their decadent values.

2 εἰς ἐπίπαν (*eis epipan*): Heitsch: 'im ganzen' ('on the whole'), but also 'in all' (Edmonds), or perhaps 'on average' (Bowra, citing Herodotus 2.68.5, etc.). See commentary following on line 4.

3 ἀγαλμένοι (*agalmenoi*): from ἀγάλλω – 'glory in,' 'exult in'; mss: ἀγαλλόμενοι, ἀγάλλομεν. Hudson-Williams, following a conjecture by Hermann, proposes χαίτης ἐν ἀγάλμασιν (εὐπρεπέεσσιν), 'boastful of their gorgeous ornamented long hair' (104). The change, as Bowra notes, may not be absolutely necessary, but there is a mention of 'hair decked out with gold ornament' in the summary by Phylarchus and hair ornaments of gold would qualify as 'useless luxuries.' A similar critique of Samian luxuries by Asius of Samos (which may have been known to Xenophanes) makes reference to the use of gold ornaments as well as elaborate hair arrangements (Athenaeus 12.525e). Heitsch reads ἀγαλλόμενοι ('glorying') but translates 'verzierten' ('ornamented').

4 ἀσκητοῖς ... χρίμασι (*askētois ... chrimasi*): The adjective *askētos* (from *askeō* – 'prepare') connotes preparation or artful fashioning – as in the 'fashioned bed' (ἀσκητὸν λέχος) of Odysseus (*Odyssey* 23.189). D-K and Heitsch translate 'künstlich bereitete Salben' ('artificial or synthetic prepared oils').

COMMENTARY ON FRAGMENT 3

Bowra comments: '... these lines are in their own way as interesting as anything else that [Xenophanes] wrote ... on examination they raise more questions than are usually found in them' (1941, 119). The then unraised questions which Bowra proceeded to discuss concerned mainly historical details ('What period of Colophonian history was Xenophanes discussing?,' 'Who were the Colophonian "thousand"?,' and so on), but Bowra also raised (though he did not conclusively answer) what might fairly be regarded as the fundamental question about fragment 3: 'What was the ultimate basis for Xenophanes' attack on the Colophonians' lifestyle?' We should set aside what to a modern ear (or eye) might first be suggested by the specifics of lines 5 and 6: mention of features of personal dress and hygiene notwithstanding, Xenophanes was not expressing a merely personal aesthetic reaction; he was instead concerned about the values and priorities reflected in behaviour.

Line 1 'Unprofitable luxuries' is not redundant. The luxuries Xenophanes mentions in lines 3–6 (purple garments, perhaps ornamented or coiffured hair, perfumes) would probably be recognized by his audience as examples of Lydian luxuries, but we cannot assume that the mere listing would have provoked a negative response. As Bowra (1941, 123–24) explains, the term ἁβροσύνας (corrected by Schneider from the manuscripts' ἀφροσύνας) was used both before and after Xenophanes' time without an inherently pejorative overtone.

The characterization of these 'Lydian ways' as anōpheleas 'unprofitable,' 'useless' is not easily explained. Why should Xenophanes have been so offended by fancy dress? For Fränkel (1925, 337; 1973, 328) the remark reflects the *economic* point of view that surfaced at the end of fragment 2 (οὐ . . . πιαίνει. . . μυχοὺς πόλιος). But this explanation could not account for Xenophanes' mention of 'boastfulness' (αὐχαλέοι), or for the unattractiveness of the description ἀσκητοῖς . . . δευόμενοι. Recognizing the importance of these Bowra opted for the moral that Theognis drew from the collapse of Colophon: ὕβρις καὶ Μάγνητας ἀπώλεσε καὶ Κολοφῶν' (1103–4), that is, 'pride goeth before the fall.' But this requires further qualification: would Xenophanes have allied himself with the ancient concept of divine *nemesis* for *hybris*? While there was almost certainly *some* connection between Colophonian behaviour and the fall of the city (for instance, the mention that that behaviour occurred 'while without hateful tyranny,' and the claims made by both Athenaeus and Theopompus that these luxuries led to problems) a divine punishment for *hybris* committed may carry implications that would be out of place in Xenophanes' thinking. Hesiod's description of Zeus' punishment of *hybris*, for example, imagines that Zeus arranges to punish evil-doers across a broad range of disasters (*Works* 238ff.) and employs a small army of 30,000 'spirit-watchers clothed in mist' to keep tabs on evil-doers all over the world (248–255). Is it conceivable that the Xenophanes who developed the austere conception of the divine in fragments 24 and 26 and a demythologized cosmology would have allied himself with such a view by attributing the collapse of Colophon to divine punishment for *hybris*?

I suspect that Xenophanes regarded the fall of the city as related to personal *hybris* in perfectly natural ways, as Solon had warned of the civic consequences of the excessive pursuit of wealth and pleasure (4.1–10) and Plato would later regard personal tastes to be a matter of political concern in the establishing of the ideal state (*Republic* 372c ff.): the pursuit of 'useless' luxuries (that is, those that do not serve *basic needs*) can create a taste for luxury and a consequent pursuit of wealth to satisfy it which will in time undermine the well-being of a city. It may be, as Heitsch contends, that the impetus to tyranny resided in the resentment caused by *public display* of wealth of the privileged class (116), but other fragments (1, 4, 5, 22) give evidence that Xenophanes' interest in wholesome and moderate desires was as basic a concern in his view of *eunomiē* as it would become in Plato's. Among the symptoms of a 'luxury-fevered' city listed by Plato: elaborate furnishings for dinners, painted goods, embroidered clothing, gold and ivory ornamentation, imitative artists, performers, contractors and 'the manufacture (σκευῶν) of all sorts of articles, especially those that have to do with women's adornment' (373a–b). Fully in pursuit of such fineries a city must of necessity arm itself (to protect its wealth, invade adjoining territory) or it will be overrun by other cities with their own lavish lifestyles and armies to support them (373d). We need not attribute to Xenophanes Plato's distinctive conception of pleasure (like an itch made worse by scratching, a desire for pleasure is only heightened by being satisfied) in order to see an overlapping of concerns. The contrast between the unattractiveness of the artificial items in fragment 3 and the attractiveness of the wholesome food and drink in fragment 1 suggests that Xenophanes shared Plato's preference for simple fare, for what Epicurus would call the 'necessary, natural pleasures' (*Principal Doctrines* 29); cf. Lucretius, *On the Nature of Things* 2.24ff.: 'few things at all are needful for the body's nature' (included among those things we can do without: silver and gold decoration, embroidered and purple fabrics, riches, high birth, kingship). Xenophanes' rebuke may therefore have had less to do with divine punishment and tasteless public displays and more to do with the harmful and perfectly predictable natural consequences of an artificial and luxurious lifestyle. It seemed clear to Theopompus in any case that 'this lifestyle' (τοιαύτην ἀγωγήν) was the cause of their 'becoming involved with tyranny and civil divisions which destroyed the city' (Athenaeus 12.526c).

For the behavioural connotation of *mathontes*, see the discussion of *manthanein* in the commentary on fragment 10.1 (chapter 2 following).

Line 2 The period when Colophon was 'free of hateful tyranny' is almost certainly before 546 BC when Colophon fell to Harpagus the Mede, but there may have been an earlier tyranny as well to which Xenophanes is referring.

Line 3 'This [purple], as everyone knows, was at that time a colour rare even for princes and very much desired. For purple [or purple shell] was reckoned as equivalent to its weight in silver' (Theopompus in Athenaeus 12.526c). Herodotus (1.50.1) reports that the offerings of Croesus to Apollo at Delphi included purple garments as a token of Lydian wealth. For an account of the increasing status of purple garments see Meyer Reinhold (1970).

Line 4 The political significance of the group described here as 'not less than a thousand' is a matter of some dispute. It has been taken by many to be a reference to a ruling élite (= The Thousand), as on occasion an ancient city might be entrusted to such a group (cf. Heraclides Ponticus, fragment 39: χιλίοις παρέδωκε τὴν πολιτείαν). Others assume that it is merely a reference to a large number of rich Colophonians. Some specification of the size of the crowd would have been required in any event to make clear that the luxurious lifestyle was widely practised. For, the 'ruling élite' view, see Fränkel 1925, 338; Wilamowitz 1913, 284; Untersteiner 1956, 118; and for the opposing view, Bowra 1941, 123; Heitsch, 114.

Fragment 4

[Whether Pheidon of Argos first struck coinage or Demodice the Cymean, the wife of Midas the Phrygian (she was the daughter of Agamemnon, king of the Cymeans), or Erichthonius and Lycus did it for the Athenians, or the Lydians, as Xenophanes says.]

Pollux 9.83

COMMENTARY ON FRAGMENT 4

Xenophanes' interest in the inception of coinage might have stemmed from his concern about Lydian wealth and its corrupting influence on the citizens of Colophon. Aristotle (*Politics* 1257) observed that the invention of coinage transformed the nature of commerce from a barter system to retail trade with an unlimited potential for the accumulation of wealth. If Xenophanes had a desire to limit the consumption of goods to those which met 'necessary, natural' desires or needs – and thereby to avoid a corrupting pursuit of wealth and luxury – he might well have had a special reason to be interested in the origins of coinage and disposed (as Plato was in the *Laws*, 741ff.) to curtail or eliminate its use.

Herodotus (1.94) comments that the Lydians 'first used coinage struck from gold and silver,' but this might have meant only that they were the first to coin (and use) a dual, that is, bimetallic currency (see Milne, 85–87).

Fragment 5

[It was the custom to put water into the cup first, after that the wine; compare Xenophanes:]
Nor would one when mixing in the drinking cup first pour in the wine,

but water and then on top, the wine.

Athenaeus 11.782a

COMMENTARY ON FRAGMENT 5

The practice mentioned by Athenaeus was at least as old as the Homeric epics: 'And as often as they drank that honey-sweet red wine he would fill one cup and pour it over (ἀνὰ) twenty measures of water and a fragrance would rise from the mixing-bowl ...' (*Odyssey* 9.208–9). But Xenophanes himself might have been endorsing rather than just describing the procedure (cf. Hesiod *Works* 595–96, Anacreon 409), that is, this is how one would mix the wine – if one were to act rightly. Theophrastus' explanation of the practice suggests a link between the procedure and a moderation of one's desire more in keeping with the values evinced in Xenophanes' fragment 1 and elsewhere: 'They did not pour the water on the wine, but rather the wine on the water in order that they might use a drink that was more diluted (ὑδαρεστέρῳ) and having obtained satisfaction from this they would have less desire for the remainder' (Athenaeus 782b). Strictly speaking, a 'more watery' wine would be a function not of the sequence of pouring the water and wine, but the relative proportions of each in the mixture. If, however, the objective of the procedure were to produce a mixture that was more water than wine it would only be prudent to pour in first the fluid taking up the greatest volume. To do otherwise would be to risk exceeding the capacity of the container during the mixing process and ending up with too strong a mixture. If Xenophanes is not merely mentioning or describing this ancient custom but actually endorsing it, fragment 5 would reflect the earlier call for moderation in drinking (fragment 1) and the criticism of the excessive drinking of the Colophonians contained in Athenaeus' remark following fragment 3.

It is, however, possible that in its original context the remark was not intended to be about drinking at all, but merely an example of a proper procedure, that is, 'first things first' (cf. Heitsch, 116–17; and Aristotle *Politics* 1262b15ff., where a weak mixture of wine and water is merely a simile for the 'diluted' personal relationships under discussion).

Fragment 6

[Xenophanes, the Colophonian, says in the elegies:] For you sent
the thigh of a young goat and won a fat leg
of a fatted bull, a thing of honour to fall to a man
whose[1] fame will reach all Greece and never cease
so long as a Greek sort of song shall be.[2]

Athenaeus 9.368e

NOTES

1 τοῦ κλέος (*tou kleos*): 'whose fame,' referring either to the man who re-
ceives the honour or to the honour itself. In general one would expect
men to be more famous than prizes, but Edmonds translates 'a gift
whose fame, etc.' and supplies a metaphorical sense to the 'fat leg of
a bull': 'a poem or book of poems by the author.'
2 γένος Ἑλλαδικόν (*genos Helladikon*): Edmonds, Heitsch, Hudson-
Williams, and West: 'so long as a Greek sort of song shall be,' but
if one accepts D-K's reading of the genitive form Ἑλλαδικῶν, then the
songs are being characterized as Greek, rather than the *sort*.

COMMENTARY ON FRAGMENT 6

The brevity and obscurity of fragment 6 have spawned diverse, speculative and not entirely satisfactory interpretations. Edmonds (197) supposed that the occasion for the poem was the presentation of a gift of
poems (the 'rich leg of a fatted bull' of 6.1–2), but failed to explain
why this should be made in response to the sending of a goat thigh.
Wilamowitz (1926) and Defradas (1962b) understood the occasion as an
interchange of gifts between friends or lovers and sensed a mocking
tone. D-K suggested that fragment 6 contained an 'attack on a singer
such as Simonides' and cited the characterization of Simonides in fragment 21 as 'skinflint' (κίμβικα). Similarly, Reinhardt (135) saw fragment
6 as a 'falling out against a colleague' reflecting Xenophanes' characteristic concern with fame, reward, and honour. Characterizing these as
'pure supposition,' Heitsch (117) regarded the fragment as supporting
a general statement which can no longer be reconstructed.

It is perhaps worth noting that several features of fragment 6 echo
the attack on public honours for athletes in fragment 2. On this reading
fragment 6 would have a suitably caustic tone: 'You (the athlete) sent
(i.e., for sacrifice) a thigh of a goat; you won (as a prize) the fat leg of a

bull, quite an honour for someone whose fame will spread throughout Greece and will last so long as there are Greek songs.'

Line 1 Wilamowitz interpolated a pronoun ('mir') as an indirect object for πέμψας but that is not required by the sense (cf. *Odyssey* 16.83: πέμψω καὶ σῖτον). Since the thigh of a goat is a suitable object for sacrifice (cf. *Iliad* 1.40–41: πίονα μηρί᾽ ἔκηα / ταύρων ἠδ᾽ αἰγῶν; *Iliad* 24.34; *Odyssey* 17.241; *Odyssey* 21.265–66 – where a sacrifice is performed to open the archery contest), one could take the comment as referring to the kind of sacrifice made at the games for the sake of a victory (cf. Plato *Laws* 950e).

Line 2 That the 'leg of a bull' is a prize won as an honour is suggested both by *timion* and *ērao* (*aeirō*) (cf. *Odyssey* 24.33: μέγα κλέος ἤραο) and confirmed by the awarding of such prizes in the games, both for athletic contests (Pausanias 1.16) and other competitions (Simonides, fragment 174: 'Fifty and six, Simonides, were the bulls and the tripods you won'). So far, then, 'you' might mean either Simonides or the victorious athlete, but three other considerations point toward the latter: (1) These prizes would qualify as examples of the *kudroteros* treatment of athletes described in fragment 2, especially 2.14: 'there would be food for him.' (2) The τίμιον ἀνδρὶ λαχεῖν 'thing of honour for a man to obtain' moreover parallels the 'ταῦτά κε πάντα λάχοι of 2.10, 'he would obtain all these.' (3) In his imitation of fragment 2 Euripides describes the athlete as 'one who is a slave to his jaw and defeated by his belly' and criticizes those Greeks who award athletes 'the honour of the useless pleasures of a feast' (see imitation C2). We can, moreover, hardly suppose that Xenophanes (the guest poet) would be in any position to complain about the practice of 'free meals for poets.'

Line 3 The *kleos* involved has been understood as the fame of the poet whose works will be recited throughout Greece so long as songs are sung, but it is just as easily the subject of the song (for instance, the victorious Olympian athlete) whose *kleos* will be preserved. Simonides had already created such songs and they would qualify as yet another case of the *kudroteros* treatment of athletic heroes which Xenophanes complains about in fragment 2.

Line 4 'So long as there would be Greek songs' calls attention to the extent of the poet's influence over time. If fragment 6 does represent a continuation of the criticism voiced in fragment 2, then we are being given an additional directive concerning the contents of our songs and celebrations: neither retelling the old divine battles and furious conflicts nor (now) memorializing in song someone who has already received back more than he contributed.

Fragment 8

[He (Xenophanes) had a very long life, as indeed he himself says:]
Already there are seven and sixty years
tossing about[1] my counsel[2] throughout the land of Greece,[3]
and from my birth up till then there were twenty and five to add
                                                                      to these,
if I know how to speak truly concerning these things.

Diogenes Laertius 9.19

NOTES

1 βληστρίζοντες (blēstridzontes): 'tossing about.' The term is used by Hippocrates (*Concerning the Sacred Disease* 3.7; *Epidemics* 1.26) to describe an invalid tossing on his sickbed. Cf. fragment 45. The sense in which the *years* are or have been tossing Xenophanes' *phrontida* about is unclear, as is the precise meaning of *phrontida*, but the general sense of the remark is that he has spent sixty-seven years as an itinerant poet and thinker from the time he first left Colophon.

2 φροντίδα (phrontida): LSJ proposes 'care, anxiety' (s.v. φροντίς, 2c), similarly, D-K – 'Sorge' ('cares, sorrows'), but there are few cares or sorrows on display in the surviving fragments and testimonia. Xenophanes did express (in fragment 2) his annoyance with the skewed priorities of his fellow citizens, his disapproval of their public celebrations and displays (in fragments 1–3) and disagreement with their beliefs about the gods (in fragments 11–17), reactions that might be captured by 'concerns,' 'thoughts,' or 'reflections' (as Heitsch translates: 'Nachdenken'). If we opt for 'thought' or 'reflection' we will need also to select the particular shading that will best fit the context here in fragment 8. Did Xenophanes, for example, have in mind 'thoughts' as occurrent events in one's mental life (cf. Simonides 85.10: 'when men are enjoying life *they never have a thought* about illness yet to come') or might he have meant 'thoughts' in a more abstract sense (as Edmonds proposed: one's writings or philosophical opinions on a subject, as in 'Hume's thoughts on causality')?

Xenophanes' phrase 'my *phrontis*' is reminiscent of his ἡμετέρη σοφίη – 'our expertise' in fragment 2. There, so I have argued,

Xenophanes staked his claim to honours equal to those accorded to victorious athletes on the wise counsel he had provided to his fellow citizens. *Phrontis* is used in just this sense in Aeschylus' *Persians* (140–43), first performed in 472 BC, or about the time fragment 8 would have been composed (φροντίδα κεδνὴν καὶ βαθύβουλον / θώμεθα; Smyth translates: 'But come ... let us devise some sage and deeply-pondered counsel'). Since counsel (on the nature of the gods, on right conduct and on how best to gain an understanding of the mysteries of nature) was in fact Xenophanes' stock-in-trade, *phrontis* in this sense would have been an entirely appropriate term for him to use in referring to his life's work.

3 ἀν' Ἑλλάδα γῆν (*an' Hellada gēn*): 'up and down the length of Greece' would be an odd way to describe a career that moved mainly from East to West. Homer speaks of there being 'many maidens ἀν' Ἑλλάδα τε Φθίην τε, i.e., 'throughout Hellas and Phthia,' *Iliad* 9.395; similarly Heitsch: 'durch das hellenische Land' ('throughout the Greek nation'). Cf. GG, sec. 1210b.1

COMMENTARY ON FRAGMENT 8

The importance of this quatrain has been thought to lie almost entirely in its utility for determining the date of Xenophanes' birth. Strictly speaking these lines provide no more than a two-part summary of his life (sixty-seven years in 'tossing about' plus another twenty-five before then), but they become of historical importance if we assume that the point of division represents Xenophanes' departure from Colophon upon the conquest of the city by the Mede Harpagus in 546/5 BC. But, unless we suppose that Xenophanes talked about his age so that later historians might gain a foothold for their chronology, we must still wonder why he bothered to make these comments. The lack of a surrounding context may forever preclude a certain answer.

Line 1 Diogenes Laertius' brief introduction provides what is perhaps our only clue: Xenophanes' comments confirm that he was *makrobiōtatos* – 'very long-lived.' If we remember an older remark of Mimnermus of Colophon: 'Would that I without any sickness, without any trouble or sorrow, could at three-score years come to the end of my days' (6), we might suspect an element of boasting in Xenophanes' claim, '*already* (ἤδη) sixty-seven years, etc.' It might also have served Xenophanes' purpose as an adviser to his fellows to remind them of his length of life, as old age had served others before him (cf. Nestor's claim: γέρας ἐστὶ γερόντων, *Iliad* 4.321ff.).

Line 2 The striking expression 'tossing about' (βλήστρίζοντες) may have evoked in Xenophanes' audience the idea of the overseas travels he had made (for instance, in D.L. 9.2.18: 'He was banished from his native city and lived at Zancle in Sicily ... he also lived at Catana'). Cf. the dual meaning of *saleuō* – 'to toss or roll about' (LSJ II), especially of ships at sea, but also because of sickness or old age (e.g., Plato *Laws* 923b).

Lines 3–4 It should not be surprising that Xenophanes would express some uncertainty about the exact length of this first period of his life, as Thesleff explains (5): 'I find it rather natural that a nonagenarian who has spent his life abroad since he was a youth, who has no registration offices to consult and no identity cards to carry in his pocket, would forget in what year exactly he was born.' Xenophanes' expression of some uncertainty in this connection provides some reason to think that (at least in this late period of his life) his 'scepticism' was the usual 'retail' sort rather than the 'wholesale' or 'philosophical scepticism' often found in fragment 34 (see the commentary on fragment 34 in chapter 4 following).

Fragment 22

[Xenophanes the Colophonian in the *Parodies*:]
One ought to say such things as these,[1] beside a fire in wintertime, lying fully fed on a soft couch,
drinking sweet wine and eating chick-peas for dessert:
'Who among men are you and what family[2] are you from?,' 'How
old are you, good sir?,'
and 'What age were you when the Mede came?'

Athenaeus 2.54e

NOTES

1 τοιαῦτα λέγειν (*toiauta legein*): either 'saying' things (i.e., words) of such a sort, or 'speaking about' things (i.e., subjects) of such a sort. If we suppose the former we should understand Xenophanes to be specifying which words ought to be spoken following the dinner. If

the latter, we should understand him to be directing what topics or subject matter should supply the evening's entertainment. The former appears more likely: we have been given specific examples of questions (τίς, πόθεν, etc.) to ask, Xenophanes has elsewhere not hesitated to prescribe the sort of words to be used on such occasions (fragment 1.16: θεὸν ὑμνεῖν ... μύθοις καὶ ... λόγοις), and directions for verbal behaviour at symposia would not have been peculiar to Xenophanes (cf. Phocylides, fragment 14: 'At the symposium while the cups pass round, one ought to chat pleasantly (χρὴ ἡδέα κωτίλλοντα) as one sits drinking the wine').

2 πόθεν (pothen): D-K: 'von wem bist du,' Heitsch: 'von wem stammst du' ('from whom ...'); as Heitsch explains 'pothen is not the place, but parents and family' (143); cf. Odyssey 17.373 and 19.162: εἰπὲ τεὸν γένος ὁππόθεν ἐσσί.

COMMENTARY ON FRAGMENT 22

We may reasonably suppose that these hexameters were created for the purpose of leading off the after-dinner entertainment, confirming the statement by Diogenes Laetius (9.18) that Xenophanes 'recited his own poems' (without implying that he was a rhapsode devoted to the recitation of Homer). Homeric phrases occur at several points in the poem (for instance, the opening πὰρ πυρί as the line opening at Odyssey 7.154; τίς πόθεν εἰς ἀνδρῶν as at Iliad 21.150, Odyssey 1.170, etc.; and τίς ... φέριστε as at Iliad 6.123, etc.); but this would serve to enhance the stylishness of the presentation. It is uncertain whether these lines were meant to serve a larger didactic purpose.

Lines 1–3 Guthrie (1, 361) suggests that this opening description contains an implicit moral about polite conduct: 'only when [the stranger] is fed, over the nuts and wine, is it proper for the questions to begin,' but this equates 'what one ought to say over dessert' with 'what one ought to say only over dessert.' Xenophanes might, however, have been implicitly commending the entire situation, that is, this is how one ought to live – 'sitting by the fire, etc.,' in much the same way as the glowing description of the banquet scene in fragment 1 endorses a certain way of celebrating. The general atmosphere of moderate tastes and seemly conversation anticipates Plato's description of the lifestyle of the citizens of the 'healthy city' at Republic 372c–d.

Lines 4–5 Heitsch reads fragment 22 in the light of Eumaeus' invitation to Odysseus to reminisce about hard times, 'taking delight in each other's grievous woes, as we recall them to mind' (*Odyssey* 15.399–400). Bowra, similarly regarded these questions as well suited to the evening's entertainment by evoking memories of the 'old days' in Colophon (1960, 109), but as both Fränkel (325) and Heitsch (142) observed, each of the questions is well suited to Xenophanes talking about *himself*: his travels 'throughout the Greek land,' his great age, his views on the old Colophonian lifestyles, and so on. Reinhardt (136) notes that Xenophanes has adapted an old Homeric device (τίς πόθεν, etc.) used to introduce accounts of heroic exploits to a new use-personal self-expression. If the intention of these lines was to invite the audience to inquire about Xenophanes' past (as opposed to encouraging them to ask questions of one another) they might well have served as preliminaries to a statement of Xenophanes' own views on the nature of *aretē*, and so forth, or a detailing of the contributions on which his own claim to *aretē* would be based.

We cannot, however, completely exclude the possibility that these lines were meant as an encouragement to the audience to reflect upon and speak about their own actions (or those of others known to them) 'when the Mede came.' Certainly the contrast between the comfort and coziness of the situation (warmth in wintertime, soft couches, full stomachs, sweet wine and dessert) and the starkness of the question 'where were you, etc.' lends itself to such an interpretation. If Xenophanes were encouraging his fellows to recount stories about their exploits when the Medes conquered Colophon, the practice would fit the description of praiseworthy conduct given in fragment 1: 'praise the man who when he has done with drink, brings noble deeds to light (ἐσθλὰ ... ἀναφαίνῃ).'

CONCLUSION

If we take moral philosophy to involve an engagement with moral *theory* (with, for example, providing an analysis of the meaning of the terms of our moral vocabulary, or the nature of ethical reasoning, or the foundations of moral values) then we ought to regard Xenophanes as more moralist than moral philosopher. For this reason it would be fair to find 'nothing particularly philosophical' in the fragments so far considered, and to classify them as didactic poetry in the tradition of Hesiod Theognis and Solon (Barnes 1, 22). Is *aretē* acquired by nature, or practice, or is it a form of knowledge which can be taught? Are actions 'just' or 'unjust' in themselves, or do justice and injustice vary from city to city? Is a life marked by self-restraint and respect for the rights of others really in one's best interest? Is there a single, supreme human good around which we may organize all our energies and activities? Can we achieve happiness in the form of a self-sufficient way of life or must happiness rest to some degree on external (hence accidental) circumstances of possessions, family, and friends? On these central issues in classical moral philosophy, Xenophanes (at least in the surviving fragments of his teachings) had nothing to say. Indeed, since many of these issues were largely created by the sceptical challenges of the sophists, it is fair to say that these issues hardly existed at all in the minds of Xenophanes and his contemporaries.

But this does not make Xenophanes' remarks about men and morals in his own time devoid of philosophical interest; later philosophers both moralized and theorized and the values they espoused on more than one occasion echoed sentiments found first and distinctively in Xenophanes' teachings. As we have noted, his call for strictures on poetic accounts of divine conduct, concern for *eunomiē* in the city, criticism of the pursuit of wealth and luxury, and esteem for statesmanlike *sophiē*, all foreshadow the values which underlie Plato's account of his ideal city in the *Republic*, book 2. Like Socrates, and very much in the spirit of Aristotle's 'great-souled' man, Xenophanes claims recognition of his worth as well as honour for his *sophiē* that exceeds the honours accorded to Olympian victors (*Apology* 37a; *Nicomachean Ethics* 1124a). Like philosophers of almost any era he encourages his fellow citizens to reflect on their customs and priorities and to pursue a life of moderation free of desires for worthless possessions. Although he cannot be supposed to have spoken of the *psuchē* in the relevant sense of that term,[1] he was clearly engaged in the Socratic enterprise, endeavouring to convince his fellow citizens 'to care not for bodies or possessions, but for the highest welfare of their souls' (*Apology* 30b). Like Socrates and Heraclitus before him, Xenophanes does not hesitate to excoriate the leading poets of Hellas and to deny them their popular status as sources of moral knowledge and guidance.

---

1 According to Diogenes Laertius, Xenophanes 'was the first to declare that ... the soul is breath (ἡ ψυχή πνεῦμα),' 9.19, and fragment 7 claims to be recognizing the *psuchē* of a friend in a barking dog. The latter may be alluding to Pythagorean beliefs about the transmigration of the soul and in any case these allusions do not provide us with the conception of the soul as the vital, unitary force in one's personal existence, the seat of consciousness, valuation and action (virtually identical with the person) that we hear about from Socrates and, to a less obvious extent, from Heraclitus. See Nussbaum, 1–16, 153–70; and Snell 1953, 8–22.

On occasion Xenophanes employs a technique unusual among poets,[2] couching his instruction within the terms of a hypothetical argument or 'thought experiment.' We have encountered it on one occasion during his critique of the awarding of public honours to the victors at Olympia (fragment 2.15–19):

... for neither if there were a good boxer among the people, nor if there were a pentathlete, or wrestler, nor again if there were someone swift afoot – which is most honoured of all men's deeds of strength – would for this reason a city be better governed.

Xenophanes assesses the potential value of athletic prowess by extending it to its furthest extent – a victorious athlete of the finest sort – and then observing that, even in the optimal case, this excellence could not of itself help to produce or preserve *eunomiē*, the characteristic quality of the healthy city. The line of argument serves to separate athletic excellence from civic well-being and to subordinate the former, as a whole, to the latter. The same pattern of argument occurs in four other fragments:

Fragment 15: 'But if horses or oxen or lions had hands [their gods would resemble horses and oxen and lions].'
Fragment 30: 'without the great sea there would be no wind ... nor streams ... nor rainwater ...'
Fragment 34: 'For even if, in the best case, one happened to speak just of what has been brought to pass, still he himself would not know.'
Fragment 38: 'If god had not made yellow honey, they would think that figs were much sweeter.'

Each observation begins from an 'if,' or hypothetical state of affairs and draws an appropriate conclusion. On two occasions (fragments 2 and 34), the argument takes the form of a 'best case scenario' in order to

2 But not uncommon for a philosopher. Cf. Heraclitus, fragments 5, 7, 15, and Parmenides, fragments 8, 20–22, 33, etc. The construction of hypothetical arguments is of course most characteristic of Eleatic philosophy; cf. Zeno's arguments at Aristotle *Physics* 233ff., Philolaus (D-K 44 B2) and Gorgias (D-K 82 B3). The similarity in style of presentation is not enough to confirm the traditional view of Xenophanes as the founder of Eleatic philosophy, but it does serve to distinguish him as a poet with a penchant for an 'if-then' or 'as if' mode of thinking. The use of the 'thought experiment' was, so far as I know, first noted by Fränkel (331, 333) with reference to fragments 15 and 38.

heighten one's awareness of the differences between the two matters under discussion (athletic glories and civic well-being; correct assertion and genuine knowledge). On three other occasions (fragments 15, 30, and 38) the thought-experiment serves to establish a previously unnoticed connection (between the personal attributes of a believer and those of his divinities; between the sea and various meteorological phenomena; and between the qualities we experience and the realities we believe there are). In these respects Xenophanes' poems do more than moralize and entertain; they explore unnoticed connections and distinctions between various matters and offer a deeper understanding to his audience of how things are structured. It is didactic poetry that probes beneath the surface, or beyond custom, and recommends a new understanding through persuasion on rational grounds. Because of these affinities with the teachings and techniques of subsequent philosophers it is appropriate to think of Xenophanes as a kindred spirit to Heraclitus and Parmenides rather than to lump him together with contemporaries such as Ibycus, Anacreon, and Simonides, in whom the philosophical muse appears not to have stirred at all.

Considered simply as moralist, Xenophanes may be regarded as both a revisionist and a revolutionary, imbued with existing moral sentiments across a wide range of topics, but prepared to challenge conventional wisdom and social practice in order to satisfy more fully the demands of justice or excellence rightly understood.[3] As fragment 11 ('Homer and Hesiod have attributed to the gods all which are matters of reproach and censure among men ...') reveals, he concurs in the conventional disapproval of theft, adultery and deceit. His call for moderation in drink and avoidance of excessive wealth and useless luxuries was already a poetic commonplace (cf. Anacreon 356a; Theognis 145, 331, 335; Solon 4; etc.), but his call for seemly behaviour at feasts goes beyond conventional piety (hymn the gods with pious words, pray for the power to act rightly, and so on) to point to the full requirements for *aretē* and remind his audience of the importance of the survival of the *polis*. In these two areas only (as far as we know) was he willing

---

3 Adkins (1960, 74) claimed that the undeniable importance of the *aretē* of the soldier for the survival of the city-state 'doubtless prevents Xenophanes from maintaining that his political skill is *aretē* without qualification,' but it is difficult to take 'not being as *axios* as I' at 2.11 as anything other than an unqualified claim to *aretē* based on his *sophiē* – even if Xenophanes wished to grant the existence of *aretai* of other sorts. If this is correct then Xenophanes' teachings form a part of the process of 'deliberate reorganization and redefinition of the moral vocabulary' taking place during the sixth and fifth centuries (see MacIntyre, 126ff.).

to deviate radically from the common view, repudiating old accounts of divine misconduct as both morally offensive and politically harmful, and demanding that his expertise be valued above the excellence represented by the strength of men and horses. His premiss for these radical demands, the overriding importance of a healthy, stable *polis*, would become an axiom of moral philosophy in the classical period.

2

On the Divine

Fragment 7

[Concerning his (Pythagoras') having become another person at
another time Xenophanes bears witness in an elegy, the beginning
of which is 'Now ... way.' That which he says of him (Pythagoras)
goes as follows, 'and ... hearing it cry out':]
Now I will come to yet another account,[1] and I will show the way.[2]
[What he says of him goes as follows:]
And they say that once as he was passing by a puppy being beaten,
he felt compassion and said this:
'Stop, don't beat it, since in truth[3] it is the soul of a friend
which I recognized upon hearing it cry out.'

Diogenes Laertius 8.36

NOTES

1 λόγον (*logon*): Heitsch takes λόγος here and at 1.14 to mean 'Thema'
   ('subject'), but λόγος is commonly an 'account,' 'story,' or 'report'
   (as D-K translates: 'Rede'), and here: what people say or have said
   about Pythagoras. The passage abounds in references to λόγοι in this
   sense: D.L.'s προμαρτυρεῖ ('bears witness') and φησιν ('he says'), and
   Xenophanes' own φασιν ('they say'). Cf. the similar reference to the
   λόγοι told to Hecataeus: 'I write these things as they seem to me true.
   For the λόγοι of the Greeks are in my judgment many and ridiculous'
   (fragment 1). Both αὖτε ('again,' 'next') and ἄλλον ('another') suggest
   that this is but one of several stories being told, hence 'yet another.'

2 κέλευθον (*keleuthon*): Either the path or way taken (e.g., Parmenides fragment 1.11: the paths taken by day and night), or the passage or journey itself (e.g., *Iliad* 11.504), but also metaphorically a 'way of life' (e.g., Empedocles fragment 115.8 ἀργαλέας βιότοιο ... κελεύθους). Since Plato refers to a Pythagorean τρόπος τοῦ βίου (*Republic* 10.600b), we may at least conjecture that δείξω δὲ κέλευθον means 'I will show the way of life' (of Pythagoras and his associates).

3 ἐπεὶ ἦ (*epei ē*): Denniston: 'ἦ ... is used in a manner similar to δή'; i.e., as a particle of emphasis: 'in fact,' 'of course,' 'certainly' (LSJ, s.v. δή, II, and ἐπεί B, 5)

COMMENTARY ON FRAGMENT 7

We may take two points of interpretation as fairly well settled: in this fragment Xenophanes alludes to a belief in metempsychosis or the transmigration of the soul and, second, his story is intended as ridicule. It does not follow from just these, however, that metempsychosis was the specific target for Xenophanes' ridicule, nor can we be entirely sure how much of the story was fact and how much fiction.

Lines 1–3 It is not completely certain that μιν here actually refers to Pythagoras, but fragment 7 is almost universally regarded as among the best pieces of evidence we have concerning this semi-legendary figure. Kahn comments, 'If there is anything about Pythagoras that we know with reasonable certainty, it is that he taught his disciples a new view of the human soul as deathless, hence divine, and capable of passing into other animal forms' (1974, 121–22).

It does not seem far-fetched that Pythagoras should have spoken on some occasion about the mistreatment of an animal, in the light of reported Pythagorean 'kinship' doctrines (e.g., Porphyry *Life* 19, D-K 14 A8a; D.L. 8.13, etc.) or that Pythagoras might have claimed a previous existence for himself or others (cf. Empedocles' fragment 117: 'For already have I once been a boy, and a girl, and a bush, and a fish that jumps from the sea as it swims').

Lines 4–5 There is a consensus that these lines contain a large element of mockery or ridicule: 'mocked by Xenophanes ... for his extravagant theory of metempsychosis' (KRS), 'sarcastic anecdote' (Fränkel), 'scandalized tone' (Burkert), 'ridiculous' (Bowra 1960), 'a jest' (Barnes), 'ridicule his doctrine of transmigration' (Guthrie), 'an anecdote caricaturing Pythagoras and the belief in immortality' (Kahn), and so on. The humour has been supposed to be evident on its face (Fränkel, 272: 'To pay serious attention to a puppy and treat it as an incarnation of a human soul seemed ... the height of absurdity'; cf. Bowra 1960, 114–15; Heitsch, 120).

But we should be cautious in judging Xenophanes' intent on the basis of our own sense of the ridiculous, and in inferring that metempsychosis was the particular object of his barb. It was Plato, no less, who espoused as a hypothesis that the soul is 'born many times' (*Meno* 81c) in order to explain how knowledge (of at least some sorts of truths) was possible, and appended to his rational defence of just conduct the extraordinary myth of Er, according to which the souls of men descend into wild and domestic animals (*Republic* 10.620d; cf. *Phaedo* 81e–82b). We need not suppose that Plato was committed to the truth of these stories in all their details in order to grant to them some degree of respectability.

Xenophanes' criticism may in fact have been directed not at the doctrine or theory of metempsychosis itself but rather at the preposterous idea that a particular dog can be known (ἔγνων) to be the *psuchē* of a dear friend based on the sound of its voice. Before we conclude that Xenophanes must also have been hostile to metempsychosis we should remember that the view of the soul which D.L. attributed to *him* (A1: that he was the first to regard the *psuchē* as *pneuma* – breath) not only implies the existence of the *psuchē* in men and animals but also resembles the *pneuma*-based view of *psuchē* which Aristotle attributes to 'some Pythagoreans' (*On the Soul* 404a17). But it could well have disturbed Xenophanes that anyone would have dared to go beyond these speculations about the nature of *psuchē* in general to claim to possess knowledge of individual *psuchai* and their present and former identities. This caricature would focus Xenophanes' disapproval on Pythagoras' claims to a special wisdom (cf. Pythagoras' claim to knowledge extending over twenty human lifetimes: Empedocles, fragment 129), just as Heraclitus rebukes Pythagoras for his *polumatheiēn* and *kakotechniēn* (fragment 129).

On this reading, Xenophanes' target was not the doctrine of metempsychosis per se but rather Pythagoras' extraordinary claim to insight: when to all the world the puppy sounds like a yelping puppy, to Pythagoras it is 'in truth' identical with the soul of a dear friend. The 'extravagance,' as KRS calls it, of such a claim would be epistemic rather than metaphysical. As Reinhardt (141) explained, to give credence to such a claim as Pythagoras' we would have to throw out everything we are told by reason, appearance, and experience, jettisoning our acquired sense of the differences between men and animals, our normal assumption about what a person's voice sounds like, and so forth. The genius

of Xenophanes' caricature lies in its ability to isolate Pythagorean char-
latanry from any reasonable point of view – without ever expressly
saying that this is what must be done.

Fragment 10

Since from the beginning all have learned according to Homer ...

Herodian 296.6

COMMENTARY ON FRAGMENT 10

Line 1 Diels proposed that what all have learned according to Homer
is τοὺς θεοὺς κακίστους εἶναι ('that the gods are very wicked'), but a
broader moral may have been intended. As Heitsch (p. 124) notes, a
few decades later Herodotus (2.53) would attribute to Homer and Hesiod the creation of an entire system of religious belief. Plato (*Republic*
10.606c) would voice a broader concern about Homer as 'educator of
all Hellas,' and the evidence of the other fragments points toward this
same concern: Xenophanes shows his displeasure not only with beliefs
about the gods in mortal form (fragment 14), and with attributions
to the gods of improper conduct (fragments 11–12), but also with the
impact on personal virtue and the social fabric of the city of ancient
poetic fictions about divine battles and conflicts (fragment 1). On this
reading Xenophanes' attack on Homer as an all-purpose authority and
source of wisdom parallels the criticism of the popular poets made by
Heraclitus (fragments 42, 56, 57, 104, A22).

It is not clear whether ἐξ ἀρχῆς, 'from the beginning,' refers to the
beginning of the whole of Greek culture or to the beginning of an
individual's education. When in fragment 18 Xenophanes asserts that
'not ἀπ' ἀρχῆς have the gods revealed all things to mortals ...' he has
in mind 'men' in the plural, hence 'from the beginning' would mean
'from the outset of human experience.' Yet *archē* can also be used to
refer to the beginning of an individual life (cf. Gorgias, fragment 11a
(29): διὰ παντὸς ἀπ' ἀρχῆς εἰς τέλος), and it was instruction at the earliest stages of an individual's life that most concerned Plato (*Protagoras*
325c).

We may gain some slight leverage on this last issue by taking into
account a feature of the early use of *manthanein*. It is natural, indeed un-
avoidable, that we should take πάντες μεμαθήκασι as 'all have learned,'
but we cannot assume that Xenophanean 'learning' would correspond
in every respect with our conception of how or what one routinely

learns. Xenophanes' use of the term retains one important feature of its use in the Homeric epics; namely, a close connection with action or behaviour, with an implicit idea of 'learning through repeated action or becoming accustomed.' Homer speaks, for example, of μανθάνειν ἔμμεναι ἐσθλὸς / αἰεί – 'learning to be valiant always' (*Iliad* 6.444–5) and in each of its occurrences in the epics the verb involves acquiring a habit of temper or conduct. It is in precisely this vein that Xenophanes spoke of his fellow Colophonians as 'having learned (μαθόντες) useless luxuries from the Lydians' (fragment 3). On the two occasions of its use in Parmenides' poem, *manthanein* (unlike *punthanesthai*) is linked to mortal *doxa*, that is, the beliefs which custom and experience have created in mortal men (1.31, 8.52), and Heraclitus' statement that 'having learned, they do not know' (fragment 17: οὐδὲ μαθόντες γινώσκουσιν ...) can be naturally read as a contrast of beliefs acquired through customary practice with a philosophical insight into the nature of things acquired through inquiry and reflection.

Thus, while it is true that *manthanō* will later encompass various kinds of learning (for instance, when Plato speaks of the soul as μεμαθη-κυίας ... ἅπαντα in its previous existence, *Meno* 81d), there is no reason to assume an equally broad meaning for the use of the term here in Xenophanes. (For a discussion of the evolution in the meaning of *manthanō*, see Snell 1973/78, esp. 38–40).

When, therefore, Xenophanes says that 'all μεμαθήκασι according to Homer' he is probably best understood as complaining (in a Platonic vein) about the extent of Homer's influence on customary thought and conduct as well as about his status as authority on the behaviour, epithets, and other attributes of the gods. Understood in this way it would be entirely natural (though not quite mandatory) for us to understand the *archē* under discussion as the earliest stage of an individual's life, the critical formative period for values and attitudes toward others.

Fragment 11

[Hence Xenophanes' refutation of Homer and Hesiod:]
Homer and Hesiod have attributed to the gods
all sorts of things which are matters of reproach and censure among
men:
theft, adultery, and mutual deceit.

Sextus Empiricus 9.193

Fragment 12

[Homer and Hesiod, according to Xenophanes the Colophonian:]
... as they sang of numerous illicit divine deeds:
theft, adultery, and mutual deceit.
[For Cronus, in whose time they say was the happy life, castrated his father and swallowed his children, while his son, Zeus, after removing him from his kingdom 'threw him under the earth ...'
(*Iliad* 14.204) etc.]

Sextus Empiricus 1.289

COMMENTARY ON FRAGMENTS 11–12

Some have supposed that Xenophanes' comments on poetic attributions of disgraceful behaviour to the gods must have been related in some way to the rejection of theistic anthropomorphism represented by fragment 23 ('not at all like mortals in body nor in thought') and fragment 14 ('but mortals suppose that the gods are born, wear their own clothes and have a voice and body'). Thus Fränkel (330): 'Xenophanes is not content simply to reject; he exposes thoroughly and methodically the anthropomorphic fallacy that makes such errors possible'; see also Heitsch, 126; Jaeger 1947, 47. But a belief in the moral excellence of the gods sits rather uncomfortably with a conviction of their dissimilarity to human beings. The attribution of moral attributes to the divine might well qualify as a form of anthropomorphism itself in so far as it would imply shared moral traits as well as other attributes (choice, action, interpersonal relations) necessary for their possession. Gilbert Murray once observed that Xenophanes' 'nor in thought' in fragment 23 'reminded one of the medieval Arab mystic who said that to call God "just" was as foolishly anthropomorphic as to say he had a beard' (69). Fragments 11 and 12 suggest that Xenophanes himself would deny that the gods committed theft, adultery, and mutual deception, but whether his denial should be taken to mean that the gods respected one another's property and marriage vows, and valued interpersonal honesty – or (as Aristotle argued at *Nicomachean Ethics* 1178b8ff.) that they could not be supposed to be either adulterous or faithful, and so on – is difficult for us to say. On the character of Xenophanes' critique of belief in anthropomorphic gods see the commentary on fragments 15 and 16 following.

Lines 1–2 The most plausible diagnosis for the grounds of Xenophanes' reproof, I believe, is a doctrine of divine perfection. Xenophanes does not, in any of the surviving fragments, actually commit himself to such a view, but that thesis is attributed to him by Simplicius (A31: τὸ δὲ πάντων κράτιστον καὶ ἄριστον θεός; cf. MXG 927b27, 'when he calls him most powerful and best [δυνατώτατον καὶ βέλτιστον λέγειν].' A belief in the inherent goodness of god or the gods was widely shared by the Greek philosophers (including Euripides, 'the philosopher of the Stage,' fragment 292.7: 'if gods do anything evil, they are not gods'; Democritus, fragment 714: 'the god is in all things good'; Plato *Republic* 379b: 'And is not God of course good in reality and always to be spoken of as such?'; Aristotle *Metaphysics* 1072b25–29: 'God is a living being, eternal, most good'). Both Euripides (in the *Heracles* 1341ff.) and Plato (in *Republic* 379b; cf. also *Euthyphro* 5e–6a) voice disapproval of misrepresentations of the gods that may have been modelled on Xenophanes' attack on the poets. We have, moreover, already seen Xenophanes' assertion that it is *agathon* to hold the gods in high regard at all times (fragment 1.24), which implies at least a high degree of moral excellence on the part of the recipients of that esteem. The call to *prometheie* in fragment 1 also confirms a suggestion made by Heitsch that Xenophanes' use of *anethekan* bears a touch of sarcasm: most men honour the gods by 'offering' or 'dedicating' (ἀνατίθημι, LSJ II; cf. Hesiod *Works* 658: 'a tripod which I dedicated [ἀνέθηκα] to the Muses'); Homer and Hesiod on the other hand 'pay tribute' to the gods by 'attributing' all sorts of things that are matters of shame and reproach.

Line 3 (12.1–2) It is perhaps worth noting that Xenophanes singles out for mention forms of misconduct involving the institutions of property and marriage, that is, crimes against organized society. We should not suppose that Xenophanes was not offended by Homer's depiction of Apollo on a nine-day killing spree (*Iliad* 1.44–50) or of Poseidon's intention of inflicting κακὰ πολλά on Odysseus (*Odyssey* 5.286–90, 339–40), or that he was unaware of a whole variety of ways in which men supposed that the gods could be envious, jealous, or the source of undeserved sufferings (see, for example, the accounting by K.J. Dover, 75–81). But these forms of wickedness are not explicitly mentioned. The poets' accounts are therefore deplorable on three counts: they misrepresent the gods, they dishonour them, and they also threaten to do damage to men as they must live with one another in cities. By appearing to sanction acts of theft, infidelity, and dishonesty, the poets undermine the mutual trust and honesty essential to a healthy society. Seen in this light, fragments 11 and 12 display the concern with 'civic utility' that surfaced in Xenophanes' criticisms of the poets' fictions of old in fragment 1, and reinforce the impression that his attitude toward poetry was mainly *moralistic*: the poets claim to teach men how they ought to live, bringing into their accounts various supporting ideas about the gods and claiming a divine sanction for their poetic inspirations.

Fragment 14

[And again:]
But mortals suppose[1] that gods are born,[2]
wear their own clothes[3] and have a voice and body.

Clement 5.109 (following fragment 23)

NOTES

1 δοκέουσι (*dokeousi*): while δοκέω can also mean 'seem' or 'appear to one' and 'they seem to have begotten gods' (Edmonds) is a possible translation, I am inclined to prefer 'mortals suppose (or assume, etc.)' since mortal conceptions about the gods are implicitly under discussion in several other fragments (16, 17, 18, 23, 26, 34) and 'mortal opinions' are a natural subject for philosophical interest (cf. Parmenides, fragment 1.30: βροτῶν δόξας; Heraclitus, fragment 17.1–2: πολλοί ... δοκέουσι).

The etymology of δοκέω (from δέχομαι 'take,' 'receive'; Chantraine, s.v. δοκάω) suggests an element of choice or will in Xenophanes' remark: men 'take' the gods to have a certain nature, but this is a fact about men without any implication about what is either likely to be true or actually the case (for a discussion of this feature of δοκ- words see Mourelatos 1970, 194ff.). Etymologically the English 'assume' would be the closest parallel to *dokeō* (from *ad,* 'to,' and *sumere,* 'to take'), but an element of personal choice, or at least action, would also be present in 'suppose,' 'imagine,' or 'conjecture.'

2 It has occasioned some concern that the first line of this doublet is in iambic trimeter, inviting suggestions such as γεννᾶσθαι ὁμοίως for the sake of metrical regularity (cf. Wright 1985, 47), but the combination of iambic trimeter with hexameter has been defended by Wilamowitz (1962), Heitsch, and others (see Heitsch, 127).

3 τὴν σφετέρην ἐσθῆτα (*tēn spheterēn esthēta*): 'clothing of their own,' but not necessarily 'mortal clothing' as is commonly assumed (e.g., KRS: 'clothes ... like their own'; Nahm: 'man's clothing,' etc.). σφετέρους

(θεούς) appears in (Diel's reconstruction of) fragment 16 and means 'their own gods,' i.e., the Ethiopians' gods, but neither the meaning of σφετέρην nor the grammar of fragment 14 dictates that 'their own clothing' must mean 'clothing of mortals' rather than 'clothing of the god's own.' For a discussion of the latter possibility, that Xenophanes is attributing to mortals a belief in *divine* clothing, voice, and body, see the following commentary.

COMMENTARY ON FRAGMENT 14

With fragment 14 we reach one on Xenophanes' central concerns: mortal conceptions of the divine. No less than eight fragments (15–18, 23, 26, 32, and 34) touch on the issue, some of them among the most widely known of his teachings.

Line 1 We may infer here that Xenophanes is concerned not simply with what men think or suppose to be true about the gods, but also with whether these conceptions are faithful to the reality of god's nature. This dual concern is suggested at the outset by *alla* (but): 'but mortals suppose ...,' a contrast which would make sense if fragment 14 followed a statement about the nature of the divine, as in Clement's arrangement where it follows fragment 23: 'one god ... similar to mortals in neither body nor thought,' 'but mortals suppose ... etc.'

The poets had spoken of 'the birth of gods' in individual as well as in group terms. Homer, for example, spoke of gods born at particular moments (cf. *Iliad* 13.355, where Zeus is said to have been born of Cronus before Poseidon) and also of the whole race of gods as sprung from 'Oceanus and mother Tethys' (*Iliad* 14.302–3). Hesiod spoke of the race of the gods as begotten of Earth and Heaven, as well as of others born from these first gods (*Theogony* 45–46). But when Xenophanes speaks of what *brotoi* assume (as opposed to what the *poētai* say), and links being born with wearing clothes and having a voice and body, he is best understood as referring to popular beliefs about the gods as individuals, so individual in fact that gods could have legends about events attendant at their birth (for instance, Heracles' strangling of the snakes as a one-day-old) and individual birth-dates (cf. Hesiod *Works* 771: 'the seventh day of the month, on which Leto gave birth to Apollo'; 804: 'on a fifth, they say, the Erinues assisted at the birth of Horcus (oath),' etc.). We can well imagine that these popular ideas would have struck someone of intelligence as unsuitable to the grandeur of 'one god, greatest among gods and men' (fragment 23), but it would also be interesting to know whether there was something especially problematic about the particular attributes mentioned here in fragment 14.

For the first of these attributes, 'not being born,' there are unfortunately all too many possible explanations. Jaeger, for example, took Xenophanes to be following out the details of Anaximander's conception of the *apeiron*, that is, as incapable of generation and destruction (1947, 47). KRS suggests that the denial of anthropomorphic qualities was intended to follow from certain facts about the tendencies among believers to paint the gods in their own image, showing that 'such assessments are subjective and without value' (169). The first of these merely speculates, the second goes so far as to attribute to Xenophanes the famous 'genetic fallacy,' inferring the falsity of a belief from its disreputable origins (for a discussion of this second issue, see the commentary following on fragments 15 and 16).

Aristotle reports 'a saying of Xenophanes': 'that to assert that the gods had birth is as impious as to say that they die; the consequence of both is that there is a time when the gods do not exist' (*Rhetoric* 1399a). This suggests a line of argument against divine births based upon a traditional way of thinking of the gods as 'those who are forever' (e.g., Homer *Iliad* 1.290; Hesiod *Theogony* 21, 33, 105, etc.: αἰεὶ ἐόντες): men think of the gods as existing forever, but when (as in Hesiod's *Theogony*) they imagine successive generations of the gods they imply facts about gods which are, strictly speaking, incompatible with belief in their eternality. So understood, Xenophanes is merely drawing out in an explicit fashion a latent contradiction which had either gone unnoticed or, if noticed, had received insufficient consideration at the hands of the poets (cf. Heitsch, 128).

Could Xenophanes have supposed himself to have refuted a belief in divine births by simply reminding his audience that the gods are supposed to be *aiei eontes*? Would not an adherent quickly reply that what they had meant by *aiei eontes* was simply *athanatoi*, that is, that (once the gods were born) they lived forever after? If so, Xenophanes would have needed additional considerations related to god's true nature in order to make his point. We may accept Aristotle's report of what Xenophanes said as entirely accurate, but we need not believe that Xenophanes regarded the mere accusation of impiety as constituting a persuasive *argument* against the idea of divine births.

Some have found a significant parallel between Xenophanes' thoughts here about the gods and Epicharmus' comments about the birth of Chaos (Jaeger 1947, 213n40; Barnes 1, 87) but Epicharmus talks about problems in the idea of being *first*-born. The criticism can be generalized to work against all divine births only with considerable supplementation (for one 'undeniably contorted' attempt to do so, see Barnes 1, 86-89).

But we have at least one supporting concept behind the rejection of divine births in a quality alluded to in fragments 25 and 26: divine invariability. That god (or perhaps just the 'one god' of fragment 23) constantly occupies the same place is made clear by 'always remaining in the same, not moving, etc.' and that he is unchanging in other respects is at least suggested by fragment 25, beginning 'but far removed from toil' (ἀλλ᾽ ἀπάνευθε πόνοιο). As we have noted, Plato (in *Republic* 2) develops a number of Xenophanean ideas about the nature of the divine – and how it must be represented. Among his proposals about god is just this claim of 'invariance in form': μένει ἀεὶ ἁπλῶς ἐν τῇ αὑτοῦ μορφῇ (381c9). If variability in form were precluded by the very nature of the divine, there clearly could not have been a time in the past when a god did not exist (or if there had been such a time he would not now exist). Once we accept the idea of divine invariance, we must extend the period of the gods' existence indefinitely far back into the past as well as 'deathlessly' into the future.

Line 2 So invariant a being would necessarily have little involvement with such short-term conditions as wearing clothes or manifesting a voice and physical form; these would imply processes such as 'manufacturing *epea*' (cf. Homer's depiction of speech as production of *epea* from the *phrēn*, as moulded by the tongue and teeth, *Iliad* 2.213; 4.350; 20.248) and the processes of nutrition and growth implied by having a *demas* (literally, 'build'; cf. *phuē* and the cognate process verbs *demō* and *phuō*). In each of these respects, mortal conceptions would draw divine beings down into a setting of natural change and processes incompatible with their invariant form of existence.

It was a feature of Greek popular religion that the gods were thought to make themselves manifest to men through certain distinctive traits. These included exceptional beauty, unblinking eyes, a special fragrance as well as special clothing, voices, and exceptional stature. Homer speaks of the 'ambrosial raiment' woven for Aphrodite and in the same verse speaks of the special *ichor* which flows through her bloodless veins (*Iliad* 5.338). When she appears before Anchises (*Hymn to Aphrodite* 85ff.) she is said to be remarkable for her 'appearance, size, and shining garments.' Elsewhere she miraculously rises to the height of the ceiling when she discloses her true identity (*Hymn to Aphrodite*

173), as does Demeter on occasion (*Hymn to Demeter* 1.187–88). Ovid retains the idea of larger-than-lifesized gods stooping to enter into the homes of mortals (*Metamorphoses* 7, 'Baucis and Philemon'). 'Larger than life' describes both the Homeric gods (e.g., Poseidon at *Iliad* 13.18–39) and the representations of them fashioned by the artists (e.g., Pheidias' enormous statues of Athena Parthenos and Zeus). That the gods were assigned special voices we may infer from those occasions in Homer's stories when the gods must assume mortal speech in order to avoid recognition, as well as from that one occasion described in *Iliad* 20, when the combined sound of the gods' voices is so great it threatens to shatter the earth and expose the nether regions to plain view (20.45ff.; for additional details see Mussies, 1–18, and Verdenius 1949, 294–98).

When Xenophanes criticizes mortals for believing that the gods have 'their own' clothing, voice, and body, he may therefore have had under his critical fire this particular belief in special, divine clothing, voice, and bodily size. Since these features were tied to other beliefs about miraculous epiphanies and revelations from the gods, fragment 14, when given this special focus, would serve to reinforce the denial of knowledge through divine revelation contained in fragment 18 and complement his naturalistic explanations of Iris (fragment 32) and the Dioscuri (according to A39).

On either construal, however, fragment 14 makes the same basic point: mortal conceptions of the gods reduce them to humankind (if not necessarily to human scale) and ascribe to them transitory and natural qualities which are strictly incompatible with their true nature (cf. also the mortal/immortal sayings of A13).

Fragment 15

[And again:]
But if horses[1] or oxen or lions had hands
or could draw[2] with their hands and accomplish such works[3] as
men,
horses would draw the figures of the gods as similar to horses,
and the oxen as similar to oxen,
and they would make the bodies
of the sort which each of them had.

Clement 5.110 (following fragment 14)

Fragment 16

[The Greeks suppose that the gods have human shapes and feelings, and each paints their forms exactly like their own, as Xenophanes says:]
Ethiopians say that their gods are snub-nosed and black;
Thracians that theirs are blue-eyed and red-haired.

Clement 7.22

NOTES

1 The text as printed by Edmonds contains several supplements proposed by various editors: ἵπποι (15.1) proposed by Diels, κε (15.4) by Sylburg, and ἕκαστοι by Herwerden. Heitsch rejects ἵπποι, regarding the ἵπποι in line 3 as an equivalent replacement for the λέοντες of line 1 (for this and a discussion of other textual uncertainties, see Heitsch, 129–30).

2 γράψαι (*grapsai*): often translated as 'paint' (e.g., by Nahm, Edmonds) or equivalent expressions (Diels, Heitsch: 'malen.' Either is acceptable (cf. Theodoretus *Treatment of Greek Conditions* 3.73: μέλανες καὶ σιμοὺς γράφειν; Empedocles fragment 23; LSJ, s.v. γράφω I, etc.). 'If horses ... had hands or could draw ...': imperfect indicative (with the infinitive) implying that the condition is not or was not fulfilled (GG, sec. 1407).

3 ἔργα τελεῖν (*erga telein*): Taken alone, ἔργα τελεῖν could mean either 'to produce works' (that is, works of art or products of some kind), as at *Odyssey* 6.234, where ἔργα τελείει refers to the products of a metalworker's skill; or 'to perform actions,' as at *Odyssey* 17.51, where ἔργα τελέσῃ refers to the 'deeds of revenge' (ἄντιτα ἔργα) requested of Zeus. The text provides two parallel phrases in lines 2 and 4: γράψαι χείρεσσι καὶ ἔργα τελεῖν ἅπερ ἄνδρες (15.2), and ἰδέας ἔγραφον καὶ σώματ' ἐποίουν (15.4). If the ἰδέας are the one-dimensional products of drawing, then the σώματα would be the three-dimensional products of the other activity, hence 'accomplish such ἔργα as men' would mean 'make the same sorts of objects men make,' perhaps statues or figurines representing the gods such as those commonly left as votive offerings for the gods.

COMMENTARY ON FRAGMENT 15–16

There is a deceptive simplicity in these famous remarks. Fragment 16 (on Diels' imaginative reconstruction) says only that Ethiopians say their gods have certain attributes while Thracians say their gods have others. It is also evident (though not said) that the attributes assigned by each group are identical to their own typical features. Fragment 15 generalizes (see Denniston's note on the generalizing force of τε at 15.3) that various kinds of animals would depict their gods as similar to themselves, if they could, each assigning to the gods bodies like the ones they themselves had. Clement restates Xenophanes' conclusion as the intended moral: 'each paints their forms exactly like their own' (7.22). At least superficially, these are comments on the diversity of belief and on a certain propensity of believers to attribute to gods qualities which the believers themselves possess. We are not told whether these considerations should serve to *undermine* these beliefs, either by having proved them false or having subjected them to ridicule, although they are commonly read in this way ('to render the anthropomorphic view wholly ridiculous, he crosses the boundary between man and beast,' Fränkel, 330–31; cf. KRS, 169, 'a *reductio ad absurdum* that animals would also do the same'; Guthrie 1, 372, 'heap further ridicule,' etc.), perhaps in the same vein as Rupert Brooke's 'fish god' (from 'Heaven,' 1913):

And there (they trust) there swimmith One
Who swam ere rivers were begun,
Immense, of fishy form and mind,
Squamous, omnipotent and kind ...

Lines 1–2 (16) Since each of the attributes mentioned here is a bodily trait, we may be fairly sure on the basis of fragments 14, 15, and 23 that Xenophanes regarded these Ethiopian and Thracian conceptions of the gods to be in error: men think that the gods have a *demas* like that of mortals but gods (or at least the one greatest god) are not at all like mortals in *demas*. But it is more difficult to determine whether fragments 15 and 16 were intended to serve as *arguments* in support of an attack on such conceptions (for instance, by showing the inherent absurdity or inconsistencies of such conceptions) or merely to provide *examples* of such views of the divine, or to help explain their *origins*.

As is the case of Xenophanes' caricature of Pythagoras in fragment 7, it is not always clear when we are dealing with ridicule rather than with simple dissent. To some ears fragment 16 appears to sound a note of ridicule in its enumeration of crudely physical attributes assigned to the gods by distant and perhaps less advanced peoples. Yet Homer had spoken of Zeus' 'shaggy locks and dark eyebrows' (*Iliad*

1.528–30), 'dark-haired Poseidon' (*Iliad* 13.563), and a 'blue-grey eyed' Athena (*Iliad* 1.206 and elsewhere) whose skin could darken on occasion (μελαίνετο ... χρόα, *Iliad* 5.354). If, moreover, Xenophanes had intended to criticize the inconsistencies of religious conceptions he would need to supply differing views of a single trait (not the four different traits mentioned here: nose, eyes, skin colour, hair colour). In the next century Herodotus would describe many different conceptions of the gods held by people in different parts of the world, all within a context of tolerant acceptance of diversity (cf. Herodotus' famous comment at 2.3, declining to adjudicate among different systems of belief: 'all men have equal knowledge of the gods'). Writing as Xenophanes did for an audience of believers who found their gods everywhere and in all shapes and sizes, it would take more than the varying physical features mentioned in fragment 16 to qualify as caricature or ridicule. If there is a degree of ridicule present in fragment 16 it would lie in the happy coincidence explicitly stated in fragment 15 that the gods should happen to possess exactly those features the believers themselves possess.

Lines 1–5 (15) Fragment 15 explicitly states the 'isomorphism' thesis illustrated by the examples of Ethiopian and Thracian believers in fragment 16: each assigns to the gods the same sort of body they themselves have, here extended in Xenophanes' most imaginative 'thought experiment' (see the conclusion of chapter 1) to the hypothetical case of horses and oxen equipped with the capacities to fashion physical representations of horse and ox gods. Although this is never said in any surviving fragment, it is hard to avoid the conclusion that Xenophanes is offering a genetic explanation of religious conceptions; that is, proposing that people believe that the gods have certain specific traits *because* they themselves possess those traits. In a remark that may well have been a reminiscence of Xenophanes, Aristotle draws just this conclusion: 'wherefore men say that the gods have a king because they themselves either are or were in ancient times under the rule of a king. For they imagine not only the forms of the gods, but their ways of life to be like their own' (*Politics* 1252b23–26). So construed, fragment 15 asserts a causal connection between specific traits of believers and the attributes of the deities they worship, and the thought experiment would constitute an argument in support of this causal thesis by speculating about how non-humans would fashion their gods if they both had gods and the power to represent them in physical or at least visual form. If, for all sorts of creatures, the attributes of deities correspond with those of their believers, then the most plausible conclusion to draw is that these subjective circumstances causally determine these aspects of their religious beliefs.

Whether Xenophanes' genetic account was also meant to serve either as a reductio or in some other way to refute these beliefs is another, more difficult matter. The following considerations, while not conclusive, at least suggest that this was not the case: (1) Xenophanes elsewhere (fragments 14, 23, 24) provides argumentation sufficient to counter these beliefs. The same is almost certainly true for one of Xenophanes' *silloi* which has not survived but may be glimpsed lying behind the remark of Aristotle about divine kingship (the *Politics* passage just mentioned) and later imitations and testimonia:

But I do not think ... that one god is master over another. For god, if indeed he is truly a god, lacks nothing [Euripides, *Heracles* 1341–46; see imitation C1 in part 3, following].

For it is inherent in the nature of the divine not to be mastered [*MXG*, chapter 3.4; see part 3, A28].

He declares also that there is no one of the gods in single command over them, for it would be impious for any of the gods to be mastered; and not one is in any way in need of any of them [Pseudo-Plutarch *Miscellanies* 4; see part 3, A32].

On the model of Xenophanes' fragment 14, we may reasonably reconstruct something like the following *sillos* on 'divine kingship':

[ὡς μὲν βροτοὶ δοκέουσι, μετ' ἀθανάτοισι θεοῖσιν
δεσπόζει θεὸς ἀλκὶ· θεοί δ' ἄρα, εἴ τινες ὀρθῶς
οὔτε τῷ ἄρχοντ' οὔτε τοῦ αὖ ἐπιδευέες εἰσίν.]

[As mortals think, among immortal gods
a god rules by strength, but gods – if truly gods –
are neither subject to the rule of another, nor is any of them in need.]

Such a belief in divine kingship (cf. *Iliad* 2.203–4; Hesiod *Theogony* 506) would be *explained* by reference to a human institution, as Aristotle states, but *falsified* by reference to a more adequate conception of the nature of the divine, as Euripides, the *MXG* author, and Pseudo-Plutarch make clear.

(2) In order for Xenophanes to employ his genetic explanation of religious conceptions as an argument for their falsity he would need to

assume that the disreputable or irrelevant origins of a belief assured its falsity or, conversely, that all true beliefs had an appropriate causal nexus with the events or states of affairs they were about. But in fragment 34.3–4. Xenophanes is prepared to admit that someone could 'accidentally speak the truth,' that is, 'in speaking of what is brought to pass happen to hit right on it' as a matter of some coincidence (see note 5 on fragment 34 in chapter 4 following). Moreover, in characterizing Homer as an unreliable source for information about the gods (i.e., fragment 10), Xenophanes would be required to hold that *all* Homeric views about the gods were to be rejected as false, which seems too strong (cf. fragment 1.15–16 and *Odyssey* 3.45ff.). Fragments 15 and 16 are therefore better regarded as explanation than as attempted refutation: once we see how men have fashioned the gods as like themselves we can understand why they have done so (and – but not therefore – these conceptions are mistaken). It is, however, still possible that Xenophanes employed the genetic account in connection with a general critique of claims to religious *knowledge* (see Barnes 1, 140–43, and the conclusion of this chapter).

Line 5 (15) The appearance of *demas* here (and in fragments 14 and 23, with reference to other bodily features in fragment 16: *simous, melanas, glaukous, purrous*) raises the question of the overall consistency of Xenophanes' 'attack on anthropomorphism.' In general, a philosopher who both denounced anthropomorphism and affirmed his own belief in a god with personal qualities such as moral perfection (fragment 11), the ability to see, think, and hear (fragment 24), a *noos* and a *phrēn* (fragment 25), and the power to make yellow honey (fragment 38), would reasonably be accused of rank inconsistency.

We should note, therefore, that Xenophanes nowhere rejects anthropomorphic conceptions of the gods of any and all sorts. What fragments 15 and 16 discuss are ideas of the gods as *like* men in bodily form; what fragment 14 (implicitly) rejects is a conception of the gods as 'having their own clothes, voice, and body'; and what fragment 23 denies is that the one, greatest god is 'like mortals in either body or thought' (this last quality being explained in fragments 24 and 25). A Xenophanean comment on divine kingship would probably have denied that (as Aristotle put it) the gods enjoy a way of life *like* that of men. What Xenophanes asserts in these remarks is not the complete *incomparability* of gods and men, but rather their complete *dissimilarity*. It would not have confounded *this* critique of religious belief for him to have held that both men and gods had some (vastly different) kind of body, thought, way of life, or capacity for goodness and justice.

Fragment 17

['bacchants' ... the branches which the initiates carry. Xenophanes mentions in the *Silloi*:]
... and bacchants[1] of pine stand round the well-built[2] house.

Scholium on Aristophanes *Knights* 408

NOTES

1 Βάκχοι (*Bakchoi*): Following the emendation of Wachsmuth, which is warranted by the scholium: ' "Bacchus" was the name given not only to Dionysus but to all the participants in his rites, and even to the branches carried by the initiates.' The attribution of the name to the branches is repeated in the definitions given by Hesychius and the Suda (s.v. Βάκχος).

2 πυκινὸν ... δῶμα (*pukinon ... dōma*): LSJ (πυκνός III): 'well-built,' applied to things joined together. Since the branches 'stand round' the house, 'well-fenced' is also possible (cf. *Odyssey* 10.283: 'Your comrades in the house of Circe are penned like swine in closely fenced recesses (πυκινοὺς κευθμῶνας).'

COMMENTARY ON FRAGMENT 17

Line 1 Fragment 17 has generally been understood in the context of fragments 14–16, that is, as a continuation of the caricaturing of mortal conceptions of the gods. Guthrie's conclusion is representative: 'its purpose was to heap further ridicule ... now a god in vegetable form!' (1, 372; cf. Fränkel, 331, and Heitsch, 135). Bacchus, or Dionysus, is of course a natural target for an attack on the idea that a god can assume natural form; as the life-force in nature, the 'force that through the green fuse drives,' he is perhaps the paragon of the 'naturalized deity,' taking possession of his initiates during their moments of ritual ecstasy, coursing through all living things, even, as here, in the limbs or branches associated with him in story and pictorial representation.

But there is more to fragment 17 than simply a reference to a curious belief in a 'vege-morphic' deity: *these* bacchants stand about a 'well-built' or 'well-fenced' house. Nilsson (36–41) identifies the practice as a common folk superstition (known more generally as the May bough) in which green branches are cut and placed around the house in order to confer good luck and divine protection to the inhabitants (see also Farnell 5, 118–19; West 1971, 72–74).

Seen in this light, fragment 17 has less to do with Xenophanes' critique of representations of the gods as possessing a human or animal *demas*, and more to do with his belief in divine immobility (fragment 26) and cosmic causal role (in fragment 25). Xenophanes' god is not only not a man, or an animal, or a pine branch, he is also not the sort of being that could flit about from place to place to intercede in the course of natural events for the sake of the safety of a particular house or its inhabitants. Xenophanes offers similar criticisms of other popular ideas about manifestations of the divine: fragment 32 (on Iris-rainbow), A39 (on St Elmo's fire – the twin Dioscuri), A52 (against divination).

Fragment 23

[Xenophanes of Colophon, teaching that god is one and without body, asserts:]
One god is[1] greatest[2] among gods and men,
not at all like[3] mortals in body[4] or in thought.[5]

Clement 5.109

NOTES

1 Εἶς θεὸs (*heis theos*): It is notoriously uncertain whether fragment 23 contains three predicates (one, greatest, not like) or only two, with 'one' functioning as attribute (as above: 'one god is greatest among gods and men.' It is correspondingly uncertain whether Xenophanes is here (1) merely *mentioning* the one god who is the greatest, not at all like, etc.; or (2) *asserting* (by means of an assumed ἐστί) something about this god – i.e., (a) that such a god exists, or (b) that only such a god exists, or (c) that such a god is the greatest, or (d) that one god is the greatest; or (3) neither mentioning nor asserting anything about the existence, singularity, or greatness of god in so far as εἶs ...
νόημα may have formed part of some larger sentence asserting something else (e.g., as in fragment 25, that this god 'shakes all things'). I have opted for (d), following Stokes who cites *Iliad* 12.243 εἶs οἰωνὸs ἄριστοs as one of many examples of εἶs reinforcing a superlative (cf. also Lumpe, 27ff., and Hershbell, 125ff.). A concatenation of divine attributes cannot, however, be absolutely excluded (cf. *Iliad* 2.204–5: εἶs κοίρανοs ἔστω, / εἶs βασιλεύs; Heraclitus, fragment 67: ὁ θεὸs ἡμέρη εὐφρόνη, χειμὼν θέρος ...).

2 μέγιστος (*megistos*): While the superlative form of the adjective can serve merely as intensifier (e.g., 'very great'), this is unlikely here in conjunction with εἷς (cf. LSJ, s.v. εἷς, 1,b); hence 'one greatest,' 'one is greatest,' etc.

3 ὁμοίίος (*homoiios*): LSJ identifies this occurrence of ὁμοίίος with the more common adjective ὁμοῖος ('like'), in contrast with its use in Homer where it is applied only to war, strife, old age, and death, and appears to mean 'distressing.' The term occurs once in Hesiod (*Works* 182) and is thought to mean 'in agreement with' or 'like in mind and wish' (LSJ). οὔτι (neuter form of οὔτις used as adverb): 'by no means, not at all' (LSJ 2), hence 'not at all like.'

4 δέμας (*demas*): In light of the negative remarks about the idea of a divine δέμας in fragments 14–16 it would be reasonable to interpret 'not at all like mortals in body' as 'not having a body, at least a human frame, at all.' Xenophanes might well have chosen δέμας in light of traditional poetic comparisons of divine and mortal bodies (e.g., *Odyssey* 8.14: δέμας ἀθανάτοισιν ὁμοῖος; cf. 5.212; 8.305), as Deichgräber (27n) noted. δέμας is better rendered therefore as 'body' or 'bodily form' rather than the more general 'form' (Edmonds, Burnet) or 'Gestalt' (D-K, Heitsch). Whether Xenophanes' god is ἀσώματος, as Clement states, is another matter (see the following commentary).

5 νόημα (*noēma*): Like the English 'thought,' νόημα has several related senses: (1) a particular product of thinking (*Odyssey* 2.363–64); (2) the faculty or general capacity of thinking (*Iliad* 19.217–18); (3) an intention or purpose (*Iliad* 10.104–5). Since νόημα is coupled with δέμας, sense (2) makes the most natural reading, but Aeschylus' *Suppliants* 96–103 (which echoes Xenophanes fragment 25 in discussing how god accomplishes his intentions in ways men cannot) shows that (3) is not impossible. Since νόημα in sense (2) above is equivalent to νόος, 'mind' (Edmonds) is also appropriate, but 'Einsicht' (Heitsch) is too narrow (see the commentary following on fragment 25).

COMMENTARY ON FRAGMENT 23

The ideal commentary on fragment 23 would do three things: establish whether Xenophanes here espoused monotheism, explain how the 'one greatest god' alluded to in line 1 related to the physical universe, and last, explain how this god was 'not like mortals in δέμας or νόημα.' But since the centuries have seen a plethora of stoutly argued and generally incompatible answers on each of these points, the ideal commentary may be out of reach. Not all the competing accounts, however, are equally compelling, and at least some aspects of this difficult fragment can be clarified.

Line 1 Barnes was certainly correct in pointing out (1, 89–92) that Xenophanes had available to him the makings of an argument for monotheism based on the commonly ascribed attribute *kratistos* – 'strongest.' Several ancient testimonia (A28, A31, A32) ascribe an argument along these lines to Xenophanes. Even the predicate *megistos* – 'greatest' – conjures up a superiority that would be hard to square with a restricted sphere of influence or shared authority (Fränkel, 331; cf. Zeller 1920, 648). There is, moreover, no obstacle in the path of a monotheist view in the phrase 'among gods and men.' Not only does the phrase, like other 'polar expressions,' not strictly imply the existence of items at both poles (following D-K, Burnet, KRS, among many), we may also discount the implications of the remark by regarding Xenophanes' comment as 'speaking with the vulgar'; that is, when he speaks of gods (in the plural), 'he means the gods of popular superstition' (Fränkel, 331). We may also sense some degree of emphasis on *heis* in its initial position (Guthrie 1, 374n). If, in addition, one assumes that the doxographic tradition beginning with Aristotle's 'he says the one is god' cannot be completely mistaken, then it becomes quite plausible to claim *some* degree of monotheistic tendencies in fragment 23.

But it is not a compelling interpretation. Other references to the gods (in the plural) cannot be so simply dismissed. Pace Guthrie (who followed Zeller, ibid., 648n), fragment 1 cannot be dismissed as a trivial concession to the customary deities by a genial *arbiter bibendi*. On the contrary, it is a thoughtful effort to bring out the full implications of religious piety and moral excellence, with a call for honour to the *gods* at its final and most serious point (see the commentary on fragment 1). Xenophanes does not, moreover, fault Homer and Hesiod for saying *that there are gods*, but for what they say those gods are like. We would moreover 'misinterpret by inference' (to use a phrase coined by R. Robinson) if we thought that Xenophanes must have espoused monotheism just because he had the logical ammunition required to demonstrate its truth. We may also reasonably doubt, as Stokes (following Freudenthal) observed, 'whether a convinced monotheist in an unreceptive polytheistic society would cloud the issue by a mention of plural gods which is at best ambiguous, in the very context where he is firmly stating his revolutionary view' (76). Even Guthrie, who defends the monotheistic interpretation, concedes that this is 'at the least a surprising carelessness' (1, 375). Finally, it must be counted something of a puzzle that Plato, who fully imbibed Xenophanes' view of divine perfection with its consequent strictures on poetic representations of the divine and developed them at length in *Republic* 2, should have remained so thoroughly indifferent to god's number, switching repeatedly from speaking of 'the god' to 'gods' to 'the gods' (e.g., ὁ θεός at 381b4, θεοί at 381c7, and οἱ θεοί at 381e8). The fragments warrant attributing to Xenophanes the novel idea of a single god of unusual power, consciousness, and cosmic influence, but not the stronger view that beyond this one god there could be nothing else worthy of the name.

Xenophanes does not say why he believes there is one greatest god, nor what that greatness would consist in, although a 'really big god' would fit poorly with the rejection in fragment 14 of the idea of god having a body (perhaps even an especially large body). 'Biggest' has, however, seemed appropriate to those who go on to identify Xenophanes' god with the physical universe (e.g., Havelock in Robb, 22; Hershbell, 130). Two distinct measures of greatness would, however, have naturally occurred to Xenophanes' audience: greatness in honour or glory (*kudos*) and in power (*kratos*). So Homer and Hesiod spoke of the gods, especially of Zeus, who was pre-eminent in both (cf. ὑπερμενής, *Iliad* 2.350; κράτος ἐστὶ μέγιστον, *Odyssey* 5.4; κύδιστε μέγιστε, *Iliad* 2.412 – all said of Zeus; κύδιστε, *Iliad* 4.515; *Odyssey* 3.378 – said of Athene; ὑπερμενεῖ *Theogony* 534; κράτεῖ τε μέγιστος, ibid. 49; κύδιστε μέγιστε, ibid. 548 – all said of Zeus). If Xenophanes had greatness of this sort in mind we would have to regard fragment 23 as more revisionist than destructive theology, beginning from an established conception of divine power but stripping it of its cruder features (that is, like Zeus in being greatest, in honour and power, among all other gods and men, but unlike men in various physical respects). That an early philosophical critique of religious belief could assume this revisionist character is clear from Heraclitus when he speaks of a god, identified as 'the one wise' who is 'both unwilling and willing to be spoken of by the name of Zeus' (fragment 32), and takes Zeus' traditional epithet and applies it to his ultimate force (fragment 53: 'Strife is father and king of all ...'). Signs of god's greatness are evident in several other fragments: he is exempt from the cycle of birth and death, perhaps because he is completely impassive in all respects (fragment 14); he is incapable of being moved about (fragment 26); and he is able to 'shake all things' through his *noos* and/or *phrēn* alone. Also, greatness in *kudos* would underlie the call for due homage (προμηθείη) to the gods in fragment 1 and the rejection of divine ἀθεμίστια ἔργα in fragments 11–12. Since

Xenophanes' god does play a causal role in 'shaking all things,' parallel to the cosmic role played by Zeus who likewise makes Olympus quake (ἐλέλιξεν, *Iliad* 1.530), we can at least conjecture that Xenophanes was led to assert the existence of one *greatest* god as an answer to the perennial question, 'What moves everything?' or in the terms of Homer's famous simile, 'Who is the god on whom hang all the other gods, goddesses, lands, and oceans?'

Line 2 Clement's introduction, διδάσκων ὅτι εἷς καὶ ἀσώματος shows that he took Xenophanes' god to lack a body, but few modern interpreters would agree (cf. Guthrie 1, 276; Jaeger 1947, 43; KRS, 172; and Stokes, 77, among others. Fränkel is an exception: 'he operates through his spirit only (to put it in modern terms) from somewhere outside space,' 331). There are of course some signs of a lack of at least mortal corporeality: fragment 14 seems to say that the gods no more have a *demas* than they have voices and wear clothes; fragment 24 attributes thought and perceptual awareness to god but not the usual organs of sense; fragment 25 speaks of god 'shaking all things' but through his *noos/phrēn*, not an obvious reference to physical organs. But fragment 26 insists that god 'remains unmoving in the same' (presumably 'place'), 'not changing position from one place to another,' and so on, which would be inconceivable as a description of a being existing in a completely non-spatial way. Complete incorporeality may therefore be regarded as highly unlikely, but as to exactly what kind of non-human body god might have, Xenophanes does not say.

Later writers provided two answers: god is spherical in form and he is identical with the physical universe. On this famous question in Xenophanean scholarship I would make the following six defensible, but hardly definitive, general comments.

(1) *Many* scholars have regarded the ancient testimonia affirming divine sphericity and identity with the physical universe as sufficiently well founded to establish, albeit with some reservations, these two elements as genuine Xenophanean ideas; among these are: Barnes, Bowra, Burnet, Deichgräber, Diels, Finkelberg, Guthrie, Reinhardt, Snell, and Zeller (for a recent defence of this view see the study by Finkelberg).

(2) *Many other* scholars regard the accounts contained in the testimonia as largely unworthy of credence, spawned in part by a confused assimilation of Xenophanes' philosophy with that of Parmenides, misled by superficial similarities between Xenophanes' god and Parmenides' one 'Being,' and relying on an overly optimistic reading of some cryptic comments by Plato (*Sophist* 242c–d) and Aristotle (*Metaphysics*

986b10ff.); among these are: Cherniss, Fränkel, Heidel, KRS, Jaeger, Lumpe, Untersteiner, Stokes, and myself (for a defence of this view see Stokes, 66–84, and the introduction to part 3 following).

(3) There is not a single clear indication within the extant fragments that Xenophanes regarded god as either spherical or identical with the universe. One can understand how several isolated comments might begin to suggest such views – or be retroactively interpreted in this light. If, for example, we believed (against various objections) that fragment 23 espoused a monotheistic creed, and if we thought that the *oulos* of fragment 24 referred to the 'whole universe' (as Plato speaks of τὸ ὅλον at *Gorgias* 508a), and if we took fragment 26 to be describing god as at the centre of all things in motionless equipoise (like Parmenides' 'Being' at 8.44–45), then we might begin to read the fragments as at least suggesting this idea. But they do not clearly say any of these things. The 'new Xenophanes fragment' claimed by Lebedev 1978/86 refers to 'all things full of god' (πάντα θεοῦ πλήρη), but the emendation of the manuscript's plural θεῶν ('gods') makes the claim problematic (for a defence of the original θεῶν see the discussion by Giangrande).

(4) The sphericity of the physical universe itself would be prima facie incompatible with the assertion in fragment 28 that while there is an upper limit to the earth, it stretches downward without limit (but see Guthrie, 381n), and the identification of god with the whole physical universe is prima facie incompatible with the assertion in fragment 25 that god shakes 'all things,' hence is non-identical with them, unless he shakes himself – in which case we need some explanation for 'not moving' in fragment 26 (but see also Guthrie, 382). Such an identification is also incompatible with the distinction voiced in fragment 34.1 between 'the gods' and 'all things' (θεῶν τε καὶ ἄσσα λέγω περὶ πάντων).

(5) A decision as to whether the testimonia do or do not accurately describe Xenophanes' thinking about god's physical features involves not only the evaluation of individual bits and sources of information, but also overall standards for credibility and plausibility. Those inclined toward a positive verdict generally recognize the gaps in our evidence, the possibility of error, and the need for an imaginative reconstruction. Those inclined toward a negative verdict tend to place greater weight on the possibility that the ideas of later thinkers were erroneously transferred to their forerunners, and the possibility that Aristotle, Theophrastus, and later writers misconstrued Xenophanes' meaning. Guthrie, amazingly characterizing the identification of Xenophanes' god with the whole world as 'inescapable' (1, 381), acknowledged that the 'whole nexus between Aristotle, Theophrastus and the

writer of *MXG* affords an illuminating insight into the growth of a myth of philosophical history' (369n). Reviewing that same nexus, Heidel (1943, 276–77) drew the opposite conclusion: the identification was based only on conjecture and an imagined connection between Xenophanes and Parmenides.

(6) In so far as the tradition rests on the assumption that Xenophanes' concept of god paralleled Parmenides' conception of 'Being' as spherical, the tradition almost certainly rests on a mistake. Parmenides does not say 'Being' or 'what is' is spherical, he says that it is perfect, fully formed or completed (τετελεσμένον ἐστί), 'in every way *resembling* (ἐναλίγκιον) the bulk of a well-rounded sphere, equally balanced in all ways from the centre' (fragment 8.42–44). What exists, in short, exists fully in every respect; 'slightly existing,' 'pieces of existence,' and so on, are incoherent ideas. *Like* a fully filled-out sphere which retains its circular form when viewed from any angle, 'what is' must be said to exist in every possible way, and never 'not be' in any respect. So Parmenides *analogizes* about 'what is' (and so Plato followed him in describing the ultimate realities which could never be not-X in any respect, e.g., *Symposium* 211; *Republic* 477; as elsewhere). See further, Mourelatos 1970, 124–30; Owen, 61–68.

The god of the doxographical tradition may therefore be fairly described as a later reconstruction of Xenophanes' theory based on an assumed correspondence between the views of Xenophanes and Parmenides – a correspondence which rests in part on an erroneous understanding of Parmenides and the loose identifications of Xenophanes as an Eleatic thinker by Plato and Aristotle (for further discussion of the Xenophanes testimonia on this topic see the introduction in part 3 following).

Line 2 The sense of 'not at all like mortals ... in thought' is explained by fragments 24 ('whole he thinks') and 25 ('completely without toil he shakes all things by the thought of his mind'). See note 5 above, note 2 on fragment 24, and notes 3 and 4 on fragment 25, following.

Fragment 24

[For if the divine exists, it is a living thing, and if it is a living thing, it sees whole:]
... whole[1] he sees, whole he thinks,[2] and whole he hears.

Sextus Empiricus 9.144

NOTES

1 οὖλος (*oulos*): The Ionic form for ὅλος, 'whole,' 'entire,' 'complete in all its parts' (LSJ 1); in Homer, 'a whole loaf,' 'a whole month,' etc. Alternative translations abound, some taking οὖλος as subject, and others as adverbial (= καθόλου). I understand the οὖλος as meaning the 'whole' of god and the point of the assertion to be that (since he has no δέμας such as men have) god has no separate organs of sense or thought, thus (as KRS translates) 'All of him sees, all thinks, and all hears.' Consequently, translations which convert activity verbs back into names of organs (e.g., Edmonds' 'all eye, all mind, all ear' or D-K's 'ganz Auge, etc.' seem to me headed in the wrong direction. Two of our ancient sources, Cyril and Irenaeus (see Heitsch, 54), mention sense-organs; the other five and Sextus do not. Diogenes Laertius' version, omitting οὖλος or ὅλον νοεῖν and adding μὴ μέντοι ἀναπνεῖν ('he does not however breathe') has given rise to the idea (KRS, 169) of a later interpolation by someone interested in Pythagorean ideas of a breathing universe – or perhaps is a sign of Xenophanes or D.L. attempting to distinguish Xenophanes' views from those of the Pythagoreans (see Diels 1901, 20n; Guthrie 1, 374n, Kahn 1960, 98n). The phrase might, however, have been triggered simply by the use of φρενί (in fragment 25), the organs of thought in the chest closely linked with breath, passions, speaking and receiving words, etc.; see Onians, 67ff.

2 νοεῖ (*noei*): The Greek verb νοέω is closely related to the noun νόος (later νοῦς) and cognate terms νόημα, νόησις, etc., and is perhaps best understood as referring to the whole range of activities engaged in by νόος (thinking, noticing, realizing, planning, paying attention, pondering, recognizing, knowing, etc.). Since the English verb 'to mind' has a more specialized meaning (to obey, heed, dislike, etc.), we lack an all-purpose term to characterize this wide range of mental activities. 'Think' is useful to some degree since it captures *some* functions of νόος and some uses of νοεῖν, but it misses others (notice, recognize, realize, etc.). Heitsch urges that νοεῖν be taken as 'mental or intellectual perception, recognition' ('geistig wahrnehmen, erkennen') rather than as 'think' ('denken'), and many have held that νοέω at this early period must be given a *cognitive* sense (implying knowledge of some sort): '*noein* ... could not, in and before [Parmenides'] time, convey the notion of imagining something non-existent, for it connoted primarily an act of immediate recognition' (Guthrie

2, 17, with similar claims by Mourelatos and others). Often cited
in defence is the pioneering study by von Fritz (1943, 79–93) in
which 'realizing the situation' was identified as the basic sense of
νοέω.

The wide variety of Homeric uses of νοέω however counts against
a restriction of its meaning to cognitive uses, and von Fritz's findings
have been oversimplified in the retelling (e.g., in Mourelatos 1970,
68, where the results of von Fritz's study are cited in an attempt to
establish that the νόος of Parmenides' poem must *always* be related in
some way to τὸ ἐόν). Von Fritz himself regarded 'realizing the situation' as a 'main' or 'fundamental' meaning of νοέω, but acknowledged
the existence of other senses (e.g., 'attitude,' 'plan,' even 'visualizing
situations and objects which are remote in space and time'). Quite
commonly in Homer aorist forms of νοέω mark an act of detection
or acute observation, detecting the presence of an enemy, recognizing the identity of an individual (cf. *Iliad* 4.200; 18.486; *Odyssey*
16.160; etc.). Often the central figures in Homer's story fail to realize
or understand the events taking place in their midst (e.g., the suit-
ors to Penelope: τὸ δὲ νήπιοι οὐκ ἐνόησαν, *Odyssey* 22.32), or to realize
the larger pattern of events lying both 'before and after' (οὐδέ τι οἶδε
νοῆσαι ἅμα πρόσσω καὶ ὀπίσσω, *Iliad* 1.342–44). Conversely, those who
excel in *noos* are those who can direct their minds πρόσσω καὶ ὀπίσσω
(Nestor, Halitherses, etc.), i.e., they can remember what has happened
in the past and foresee what is yet to come (cf. Theoclymenus' claim
at *Odyssey* 20.365–67). In all these, νοέω marks a cognitive achievement, either asserting that one knows, recognizes, or understands (or
denying it) or implying indirectly (i.e., through 'realizing,' 'noticing,'
'noting,' etc.) that one has come to know. Yet elsewhere νοέω can be a
matter of contriving, devising, or conceiving an idea or plan of some
sort (e.g., *Iliad* 7.358; *Odyssey* 2.122). On occasion, 'thinks' seems almost mandatory: 'As swiftly flies the νόος of a man who has travelled
over distant lands and νοήσῃ ["thinks," "imagines," but not "knows"]
in his heart (φρεσὶ) "would that I were here" or "would that I were
there"' *Iliad* 15.80–82). Thus, cognitive uses of νοέω stand alongside
ratiocinative, purposive, or intentional uses and cannot be rightly
regarded either as a sole or fundamental sense. οὖλος νοεῖ, in short,
is best understood neither simply as 'knows' nor simply as 'thinks,'
but rather as 'the whole exercises its νόος': knows, recognizes, understands, realizes, plans, foresees, conceives, devises, remembers,
thinks, imagines, intends, etc.

COMMENTARY ON FRAGMENT 24

Line 1 Exceptional awareness, like exceptional power, was ascribed to the deities of the Homeric-Hesiodic pantheon, especially to Zeus, occasionally to lesser deities, and routinely to the Muses invoked as the source of the singer's inspiration and knowledge of distant times, place, names, and events (e.g., *Iliad* 2.484–87). Zeus who 'well knows all things' (εὖ οἶδεν ἅπαντα, *Odyssey* 20.75) is a paragon of knowledge almost certainly because he is also 'far-seeing,' enjoying a synoptic view from his vantage point on Olympus (*Iliad* 8.51–52, cf. Hesiod *Works* 267: 'the eye of Zeus, seeing all things and noting all things – πάντα νοήσας). The sirens can offer Odysseus the promise of knowledge because they themselves 'know (ἴδμεν) all the toils that the Argives and Trojans endured in wide Troy, and we know (ἴδμεν) all things that come to pass upon the fruitful earth' *Odyssey* 12.189–91). The contrast between divine and mortal *noos* must be considered one of the leitmotifs of the Homeric epics (cf. Odysseus' famous speech to Amphinomous at *Odyssey* 18.130–37: '... such is the νόος of mortal man ...') and a cardinal measure of the gulf that separates mortals from the divine.

In light of Xenophanes' decision to deprive the gods of a *demas* like that of mortals and his insistence that one of the gods is greatest of all, it is not surprising that he should also provide a fresh conception of how such a being can have an awareness of how all things are. In this respect, Heitsch may be correct in regarding fragment 24 as the working through of a latent inconsistency in the older poetic accounts (153): a god of truly synoptic awareness would hardly achieve that state with the usual mortal organs of sense. On this reading, fragment 24 continues the revisionist program begun in fragments 11–12, 14–16, and 23, beginning with the essential traits of the gods of popular religion, but stripping away their unattractive, demeaning, or otherwise limiting attributes.

But we should not imagine that 'clarification and revision of prevailing religious sentiment' would have been one of Xenophanes' avowed purposes. He was perfectly prepared to jettison existing wisdom about the gods across wide areas of belief (for example, about the gods' behaviour); he showed no evidence of the Aristotelian notion that earlier thinkers have all grasped portions of the truth and must all be conserved within a truly adequate theory. On the contrary, his overriding objective (at least in fragments 23–26) appears to have been to provide an account of the divine truly reflective of its nature, previous conceptions of the gods notwithstanding. So while the notion of a god who thinks 'as a whole' may actually resolve certain inconsistencies in older views, that fact could not of itself serve to explain Xenophanes' support for the idea. We should, therefore, suppose that the idea met certain (unstated) theoretical demands imposed by the real nature of the divine. The idea of a body possessing full awareness in all of its parts might have rested on any or all of the following considerations: (1) only such a body would be compatible with an attribution of omniscience to the divine; or (2) only such a body could achieve the 'shaking of all things' ascribed to the deity in fragment 25; or (3) only such a body would be fully 'befitting' to the divine, just as only spatial immobility could befit such a being according to fragment 26.

An ascription of awareness throughout the whole (of god) is not synonymous with an ascription of complete knowledge or omniscience, but fragment 24 nevertheless points in this direction through the repetition of *oulos* with each separate verb of awareness. 'God sees and thinks and hears,' in short, is not merely a listing of separate facilities but an emphasizing of god's degree of awareness through duplication, a statement of the superior quality of god's awareness in the form of a quantitative summary (cf. Snell on the archaic style of substituting 'much' for 'very,' 1953, 18). Understood as an implicit assertion of divine omniscience, fragment 24 can be seen as a perpetuation of common beliefs in divine omniscience (Homer *Odyssey* 20.75; Hesiod *Works* 267; etc.), but, more important, as a function of the 'greatness' affirmed in fragment 23, especially – in light of the connection between god's *noos* and his shaking the world – 'greatness in power.'

Later writers who held that Xenophanes' god equalled 'the all' or 'the whole' would almost certainly have read fragment 24 as an assertion of *cosmic* sentience (and so three testimonia – A28, A33, A34 – report). Like other aspects of the doxographers' god, this reading of fragment 24, while at odds with other aspects of Xenophanes' teachings, cannot be absolutely ruled out. (For a recent defence of this version of Xenophanes' god, see Lebedev 1986, 13–15.)

Fragment 25

[And Xenophanes says that it thinks all things, saying:]
... but completely without[1] toil he shakes[2] all things by the
thought[3] of his mind.[4]

Simplicius 23.19

NOTES

1 ἀπάνευθε (apaneuthe): strengthened form of ἄνευ(θε): 'without,' hence 'completely without,' 'far from,' 'aloof,' etc., emphasizing the utter effortlessness of god's active impact on the world, an effect heightened by both φρενί and πάντα: he manages to move *everything* simply by thinking. Like fragments 23, 24, and 26, the particular attribution made by fragment 25 contributes to the overall claim to μέγιστος θεός, specifically (here): greatest in power. Cf. Aeschylus *Suppliants* 100: πᾶν ἄπονον δαιμονίων.

2 κραδαίναι (kradainei): Calogero proposed emending to κραάνει (κραίνω: 'accomplish'), which would give a natural reading: god accomplishes all things by his *noos/phrēn* (cf. *Suppliants* 96–103, and Zeus' assurance to Thetis that no word of his will remain unfulfilled (ἀτελεύτητον) when he nods his head, *Iliad* 1.526–7). But while κραδαίνω has evidently puzzled some (LSJ and Diels opted for 'swing') it is an apt expression for a deity in its meaning of 'shake' (cf. Poseidon's epithet 'earth-shaker' and Zeus' shaking of Olympus either by nodding his head (*Iliad* 1.530) or seating himself (*Iliad* 8.443), or Jehovah's promise (*Isaiah* 13.13; 2.19, etc.), 'I will shake the heavens, the earth shall be displaced.' Reinhardt (112–13n) usefully collected together texts in which κραδαίνω is a matter of cosmic shaking: Aeschylus *Prometheus Bound* 1045; Aëtius 3.15.4 (On Anaxagoras); Aristotle *On the Heavens* 290a22, etc. Guthrie's view (1, 383n, following Cornford) that the meaning of κραδαίνω is 'much the same as that of the κυβερναῖ ['guide'] of Anaximander and later Diogenes of Apollonia, and the οἰακίζει ['steer'] of Heraclitus (fragment 64)' is not compatible with the material assembled by Reinhardt; κραδαίνω does not appear to involve any element of intelligent oversight or guidance (although some causal role for intelligence is suggested by νόου φρενί).

3 φρενί (phreni): Dative singular form of φρήν: mind, heart, breast, intelligence, the seat of both thought and the emotions (commonly used in plural form φρένες, ἐνὶ φρεσί, etc.). The combination νόου φρενί causes difficulties since both terms can be used to designate a (or the) faculty of thought, hence 'by the mind of his mind.' Fränkel (331n) accepted this consequence and regarded the phrase as emphasizing god's sheer intellectuality, but most translators attempt to make some distinction between the two terms: 'mit des Geistes Denkkraft' (D-K); 'by the thought of his mind' (KRS); 'by the power of his mind' (Jaeger); 'durch eine Regung der Einsicht' (Heitsch); etc. Edmonds actually divides the two, emending to νοῶν, but 'perceiving

without toil' makes for an odd accolade for the divine (when had νοεῖν ever involved toil?). Von Fritz, emphasizing the role of the φρήν or φρένες in instigating action, translates 'by the active will (or impulse) proceeding from his all-pervading insight'; similarly, Marinone defines φρήν as 'facoltà o impulso volitivo' (64). Yet Heraclitus' fragment 104 ('what νόος or φρήν do they have? They believe the singers of the people and take the crowd as their teacher ...') reveals that νόος and φρήν can both designate a *functioning* faculty or achieved *state* possessed by the few who comprehend. Hence φρενί is perhaps best understood as 'by the intelligence' or 'by the active exercise of the thought' of his νόος. As E.L. Harrison noted, in Homer the φρήν is the locus of *processes* rather than *achievements* while just the opposite is true for νόος, which makes φρήν the more natural choice for the faculty which causes the cosmic shaking (75).

It is possible to take φρενί as a locative dative ('in the φρήν'), and ἐνὶ φρεσί is quite common in Homer. A locative as well as instrumental sense is assumed by Darcus (26), but that reading faces one serious difficulty. Xenophanes denies that god has a δέμας (fragment 14) and affirms that the *whole* of god sees, thinks, and hears (fragment 24); only with considerable risk of inconsistency can he here be asserting that god's mental activity is taking place in a locatable single organ of thought (hence, pace KRS, νόου φρενί cannot be 'obviously based' on the clearly locative νόει/νοέω φρεσί at *Iliad* 9.600, and 20.235). Darcus avoids this problem by accepting the later attribution of sphericity, noting that human φρένες are 'around the heart' (περί, ἀμφί), and conjecturing that god's *phrēn* surrounds the world, but this solution creates at least as many problems as it solves.

4 νόου (*noou*): Usually read as a possessive genitive 'by the φρήν of (belonging to) his νόος,' but since φρήν is never said to belong to anything (other than a person), it is more likely to be a genitive of source (cf. von Fritz: 'proceeding from his νόος'). Early use of νόος ranges across a spectrum of related senses (never clearly distinguished as such) from that of a 'faculty' or natural endowment of thought (or feeling, intention, etc.), naturally spoken of as 'mind' (cf. *Odyssey* 20.365–66), to that of a special kind of creative intelligence (cf. *Odyssey* 16.374; 19.325–26), to that of a particular idea, thought, scheme, plan or other product of thought (cf. *Iliad* 15.699–703). In what is perhaps an extension of this last sense of νόος (as the momentary state of one's mind), νόος can also refer to a particular thought, scheme, or plan. So Nestor, in speaking of a coordinated fighting style, refers to 'this νόος,' i.e., 'this plan' (*Iliad* 4.308–9).

A similar range of uses can be seen in Hesiod (e.g., *Works* 67, 483; *Shield* 5; *Theogony* 661–62). 'By the active exercise of the thought of his mind' is more natural than 'active exercise of the thought of a clever mind' or 'of a particular thought or plan.' Heitsch, Snell, and (on occasion) KRS and Guthrie opt for 'Einsicht'/'insight' (evidently following von Fritz), but it is a strained choice: divine insights could not be supposed to lead to cosmic shaking any more naturally than divine thoughts, purposes, or intelligence generally; and 'insight' fits poorly with each of the highly representative uses of νόος just listed (faculty of insight, skill in insight, insights that dart from one locale to another). The evidence assembled by von Fritz is better suited to showing that νόος in Homer and other early writers quite commonly *achieves* or *enjoys* insights rather than to showing that in all these cases 'νόος' just *means* 'insight,' 'realization,' or related sorts of discovery.

The best explanation for Xenophanes' νόου φρενί is perhaps just this: 'god shakes all things by his νόος' would credit νόος with a capacity for initiating and sustaining motion not normally regarded among its powers (cf. *Nicomachean Ethics* 1138a35: 'intellect, however, moves nothing'), but 'god shakes all things by his φρήν' would not unambiguously make reference to god's role as *thinker* (cf. fragment 24: νοεῖ). Thus, 'by the active exercise of the thought from his mind' would be the minimum description necessary to assert that the cosmos was causally linked with a divine intelligence.

COMMENTARY ON FRAGMENT 25

Line 1 The grounds for Xenophanes' assertion of a telekinetic deity are arguably as obscure as the meaning of *noou phreni*. The idea of a being who moves all things by the exercise of thought, without – as fragment 26 maintains – himself moving at all, has long been regarded as one of Xenophanes' most original and enduring ideas, and its similarities with Aristotle's Unmoved Mover (who moves simply by being an *object* of thought and desire) are unmistakable. Yet Aristotle gives us a battery of arguments for the existence of such a substance, its eternality, complete efficacy, and nature as a *nous* reflecting on itself, as is only befitting the life of a being that is by definition the best (*Metaphysics* 1072a20ff.). Here in fragment 25, by comparison, we have virtually nothing to go on: god thinks (or wills, intends, etc.) and thereby effortlessly shakes all things. We are not told why such a cosmic shaker must exist, why it shakes by thinking, or how its thinking shakes, or why and how it does so effortlessly. We are told in fragment 26 that divine movement can be dismissed as 'unfitting' or 'unseemly,' and so also (we may at least *conjecture*) would be divine labour, or lack of awareness, or cosmic irrelevance, especially for the one god designated as *megistos*. But we are explicitly told none of these things.

The existing interpretations of fragment 25 fall roughly into two groups. Some (such as Freeman and Jaeger) regard Xenophanes' account as grounded in a distinctive religious outlook: 'It ... springs from an immediate sense of awe at the sublimity of the Divine. It is a feeling of reverence that leads Xenophanes to deny all the finite short-comings and limitations' (1947, 49; cf. Freeman: 'a new concept must be substituted, purged of all human elements,' p. 96). Barnes emphasizes the systematic quality of Xenophanes' account of the divine, unpacking through a set of complex inferences a number of attributes ascribed to him or his nature; but all of these inferences may be traced back to a set of axioms (perfection, motionless, etc.) that, much as Jaeger claimed, seem to constitute the core of Xenophanes' outlook. Other commentators emphasize the degree to which Xenophanes' comments echo the details (if not always the spirit) of earlier poetic depictions of the gods, especially Zeus, the father of gods and men (cf. Heitsch, KRS, Guthrie, Snell 1953). In addition to these precedents for divine shaking, effortless existence, even for one *megistos theos*, we may add pre-eminence in wisdom or counsel (μῆτις, *Iliad* 1.508) and vastness of influence (cf. the epithets of Apollo: *hekēbolos / hekatēbolos*, 'he that smites from afar'; Zeus: *euruopa*, 'far sounding or seeing'; and Poseidon: *eurusthenēs*, 'whose might reaches far and wide').

For those in his audience familiar with Homer's famous depiction of a Zeus able to shake great Olympus with a single nod of the brow (that is, virtually everyone), Xenophanes' words here in fragment 25 would have conveyed a clear message: 'No, the really greatest god can shake *all things, without any physical effort at all.*' The allusion could hardly have been meant as a concession of a grain of truth in Homer's depiction. On the contrary, by evoking that famous scene, Xenophanes would only have heightened his audience's sense of the contrast between that crudely physical image of divine power and his own idea of an effortlessly telekinetic divine *noos*.

Fragment 26

[So also when (Xenophanes) says that it remains in the same place and does not move:]

... always he abides in the same place,[1] not moving at all,[2]
nor is it seemly for him[3] to travel[4] to different places at different
times.
[he does not mean that it remains at rest as the state of being opposite to movement, but only that it is deprived of motion and rest.]

Simplicius 23.10

NOTES

1 ἐν ταὐτῷ (en tautōi): Literally 'in the same,' but judging from
κινούμενος οὐδέν and οὐδέ ... μετέρχεσθαι (cf. infra), Xenophanes is
denying divine locomotion, hence, 'in the same place.'

2 κινούμενος (kinoumenos): Unlike the English 'move' (but like 'push,'
'budge,' 'dislocate'), κινέω has a close connection with the initial stage
of movement, and relatively less to do with continued, sustained
movements (cf. *Republic* 530ff., where Plato speaks of the movements
of the heavenly bodies as φοραί rather than as κινήσεις). Cunliffe lists
the following: (1) to move, put into motion, impart movement to; (2)
to disturb, rouse into action, irritate; (3) to move from one position
to another. Yet in Heraclitus' fragment 125 ('Even the barley-drink
separates if it is not stirred'; trans. Robinson), *kinoumenos* appears to
require the sense of *continuous* motion (stirring) in order to make its
point. On either alternative, 'move' or 'set into motion,' Xenophanes'
denial implies that god is completely stationary, hence: 'not moving
himself at all from where he is' (middle) or 'not moved at all from
where he is' (passive).

3 ἐπιπρέπει (epiprepei): In its one occurrence in Homer ἐπιπρέπει is a
matter of having a certain appearance: 'nor do you *seem like* (ἐπιπρέπει) a slave to look at your appearance and stature' (*Odyssey*
24.252–53), and the core meaning of the πρεπ-element is probably
'appear' or 'meet the eye' (cf. Indo-European *prep*: 'appear' and
πρέπω: 'to be clearly seen, conspicuous,' LSJ I, 1; and εὐπρεπέεσσιν
in Xenophanes' fragment 3: 'seemly in appearance, lovely'). Both
πρέπω and ἐπιπρέπω range across three different (but loosely related)
senses: what something seems or appears to be (or be like), what
something characteristically is (or is like), and what it is fitting or
seemly for something to be; that is, from what is empirically evident, to what is objectively the case, to what is normatively correct
(cf. the similar range of meaning for ἔοικα in fragment 35; see note
3 on fragment 35 in chapter 4 following). Although Reiche (91–96)
claimed that there must be *some* empirical content to Xenophanes'
claim οὐδέ ... ἐπιπρέπει, this would not follow from the meaning of

the various *prep*-words alone since something could easily be imagined as ἐπιπρεπές in one sense (how it appears, how it characteristically is, how it ought to be) without being ἐπιπρεπές in the others. In
particular, it might be seemly for god not to move about (as well as
characteristic of him not to move about) without it being *conspicuously
apparent* to us that he does not do so. Taken just by itself, fragment
26 may be taken in either an objective or normative sense (that is, 'it
is not like god to move about' or 'it is not seemly or fitting for god
to move about'), but in the larger context (for instance, Xenophanes'
denial of ἀθεμίστια ἔργα to the gods [fragments 11–12], his affirmation
of a greatest god [in both honour and power], and his call for certain
forms of conduct in regard for the gods [fragment 1], etc.) it is clear
that he ascribed an exalted status to the divine, hence 'unfitting to the
dignity, honour, or power of the divine' is preferable.

4 μετέρχεσθαι (*meterchesthai*): LSJ, II: 'to go to another place,' 'change
one's abode,' 'migrate,' hence 'travel' or, following Mourelatos, 'Xenophanes' god does not "budge"' (1970, 120).

COMMENTARY ON FRAGMENT 26

Fragment 26 displays the repetitive quality we have seen already in
fragments 24 and 25, and with the same effect: an impression of the
divine in complete or absolute possession of its attributes. Here god is
described as 'always,' 'abiding,' 'in the same place,' 'not moving about,'
'not coming or going here and there,' that is, as utterly immobile as he
is utterly aware and influential.

Lines 1–2 Commentators have offered differing views of the thinking
that may have led Xenophanes to this idea. Reinhardt (p. 112), sens-
ing the presence of *prior* Parmenidean thinking, explained that god's
movement was precluded by his total presence ('Allgegenwart'); cf.
von Fritz 'but he is always present everywhere' (1945, 228), but om-
nipresence provides an odd reason for a denial of divine mobility. If
god were truly already everywhere his moving about would be more
than 'unseemly,' it would be completely impossible; hence *heis* and *en
tautōi* should be given their usual meaning: a single being at a particular location. Heitsch (157) views fragment 26 in exactly the same
vein as fragments 23–25, as an *extension* of the Homeric depictions of
the gods, in so far as Homer's Zeus tended to conduct his business
from the heights of Olympus by sending his minions darting down to
carry out his wishes in the world of mortal men. But Homer's Zeus
clearly did move about from time to time (e.g., *Iliad* 1.533: Ζεύς ...

ἐὸν πρὸς δῶμα; 8.438–39: Ζεύς ... Ἴδηθεν ... Οὐλυμπόνδε δίωκε), and explaining Xenophanes' idea by reference to so minor and partial a feature of Homer's account would assign a greater importance to the Homeric provenance than Xenophanes' broad attacks on Homer and Hesiod would lead one to suppose was appropriate. It is more likely that Xenophanes is here attacking a Homeric idea than that he is following one, and so he is often understood (cf. Jaeger 1947, 45: 'criticizing the Homeric representation. In Homer the god's quickness of power is construed as a veritable token of the divine power'; KRS, 170: 'the very antithesis of a Homeric god'; see also Guthrie 1, 374). I am inclined to think that Xenophanes' account originated not from a process of reflection on Homer's depiction, but rather from his own understanding of the implications of other aspects of his new view of the nature of the divine. In particular, he holds that one god is *megistos* (fragment 23), a view which if understood in terms of power would entail instant and complete accomplishment of divine wishes and intentions across enormous expanses of space and time (just as it required the effortless impact mentioned in fragment 25). Travelling about, localized activity or effect, and a consequent delay in activity and effect elsewhere would all be alien to such a conception. As a consequence, the poets' stories about the gods' various travels, visitations, and local epiphanies would all have to be set aside as false.

Line 2 It has also been noticed that a god for whom it is 'unseemly' to move about bears a certain resemblance to the earth of Anaximander's cosmology, for which it would be 'unfitting to be borne about' (οὐθέν ... φέρεσθαι προσήκει, Aristotle *On the Heavens* 295b10). This would suggest the possibility that Xenophanes drew his idea of god from Anaximander as well as (once again) giving credence to the idea that Xenophanes' god could in some ways be identified as having a cosmic identity. But the comparison is loose and inexact: Xenophanes' god is never described as at the centre of anything, nor in *equi*poise, and Anaximander's earth does not fail to move simply because it is 'unfitting' for it to do so, but because it is already established at the centre and equally related to the extremities – a premiss without a Xenophanean counterpart.

The doxographers' accounts of Xenophanes' motionless god offer a variety of explanations for the idea, most of which can be set aside as heavily overladen with philosophical concepts and arguments that postdate Xenophanes. Simplicius (in A31) and the author of the MXG (A28), having identified god with the totality of existing things, also report that he is neither moving nor at rest (not the former since there is no one else to whose place he might move; not the latter since not-being is at rest and god/being can never share traits with not-being). Other reports (A31, A33, A36) offer the simpler and more credible view: he does not move. Hippolytus adds that Xenophanes' god was 'outside change' (ἔξω μεταβολῆς), which might explain the κινούμενος οὐδέν of fragment 26: god never moves because he never changes in any way at all (cf. *MXG* 4.16). Similarly, οὐδὲ μετέρχεσηθαι ἐπιπρέπει would then say, in effect, 'nor is he the sort of thing one could properly say moved about.' While the doxographers' identification of god with 'all things' is fraught with difficulties (see the commentary on fragment 23 above), I do not see that Hippolytus' view can be ruled out as a possible explanation of Xenophanes' thesis. Cf. also *Republic* 380d ff.: 'each of them, being the fairest and best possible, abides forever simply in his own form ... no poet then must be allowed to tell us that "the gods, in the likeness of strangers, assume many disguises as they visit the cites of mortals"' (381c8–d4).

CONCLUSION

A correct appreciation of the character of Xenophanes' thinking on this topic requires that we first recognize the diversity of topics discussed in these eleven fragments: on the true nature of the divine (fragments 23–26), mistaken conceptions of the god's nature (fragments 14, 16), mistaken ideas of divine conduct (fragments 11, 12), the causes of these mistaken conceptions and ideas (fragments 10, 15), superstitious practice (fragment 17), and a bogus claim to spiritual expertise (fragment 7). The testimonia confirm these as characteristic of Xenophanes' thinking and provide prima facie plausible reports of supplementing details (for instance, A13 on the sharp demarcation between mortal and immortal, A39 on the true nature of the Dioscuri, A52 on divination).

This diversity makes brief summary and philosophical assessment difficult, but two generalizations seem secure: in his various remarks on current religious beliefs and practices Xenophanes called for fundamental reforms; and second, the centrepiece of his reformed view was a novel and historically important concept of a single greatest god, unlike men in either body or thought, who without moving at all imparts motion to all things by the exercise of the thought of his mind. But a novel conception of the divine does not a philosopher make.

Clearly Xenophanes' teaching lacked one feature that has commonly characterized philosophical accounts of religious belief: a *defence* of theism. We can find nothing resembling an *argument* for the existence of god or a god, on the model of Aquinas' Five Ways, or an ontological argument, or even less anachronistically, arguments like those Aristotle employs in *Metaphysics* 12 to establish the existence of an eternal, non-sensible substance. So far as can be seen, Xenophanes' god was neither a necessary postulate of moral obligation and virtue, nor a necessary *first* cause of all motion and change, nor could his existence be ineluctably inferred from the order of nature or the beauty of the starry heavens.[1] In this regard Xenophanes would only be typical of the thinking of his own era, even among the most original Ionian cosmologists; prior to the emergence of an overtly atheistic position a century later, philosophers could be expected to argue about which *theoi* there really were, or what ought most properly to be called *theios*, but not about whether *theoi* existed, or whether there was a *theos*.[2] Nor is there evident anything we might count as a *defence* of religious belief or idealization, either a defence of choosing to believe in the absence of a full rational foundation, or a defence in the face of various traditional criticisms of theism (such as the existence of evil or unnecessary

1 We should not be misled by *Metaphysics* 986b21 into thinking that Xenophanes somehow came up with his idea of a greatest god by 'looking at' (ἀποβλέψας) the starry heavens (although Guthrie believed just that: 1, 380). In Aristotle ἀποβλέπειν routinely means 'with a view toward,' 'in regard to,' 'with this in mind' (*Metaphysics* 991a23, *On the Soul* 404b7, 408b1, *Categories* 5b1, etc.), hence according to Aristotle, Xenophanes said 'the one was god,' or 'the god was one,' with regard to the whole heaven. However one understands this claim it is in any case either a claim of the divinity of the one or the unity of the divine, and not a claim of the existence of god based on some observed features of the starry sky. An empirical basis for Xenophanes' theology has been claimed by H.A.T. Reiche (see fragment 25 commentary above), but I cannot subscribe either to his argument that ἐπιπρέπει in fragment 25 has an implicit empirical connotation (since that is one of the three senses of ἐπιπρέπω) or that 'When he complains that "Homer and Hesiod have attributed to the gods all manner of ἀθεμίστια ἔργα" (B11, B12), *his very wording implies, therefore* (a) that there are in fact *theoi* (B36, B34, B2), (b) *that these are empirical*, (c) and specifically, that they involve, not anthropomorphic persons, but physical processes' (93; italics mine). It seems clear that his wording implies no such thing.
2 Vlastos (1952/70, 92–129) has defended the thesis that the contrast between Presocratic philosophy and traditional Greek religious ideas is not between 'mere naturalists' on the one hand and theists on the other, but rather between 'two *types* of religious belief' (119). My point here is not that Xenophanes' outlook is not 'theistic' (it is unmistakably committed to the existence of the divine) but rather that Xenophanes' assertions about the divine cannot be plausibly construed as an attempted *defence* of theism through proofs of god's existence.

suffering). Xenophanes is beyond question a theist, but not (so far) a manifestly philosophical one.

We can see however (most recently in the account given by Jonathan Barnes)[3] how several attributes of the divine can be linked together in a systematic way, taking some as assumed and deriving others as implied qualities. There is a systematic parallel to such a view in Plato's account in *Republic* 2 which embodies the spirit of Xenophanes' conception of divine goodness as well as the consequences of this for acceptable poetic depictions of the gods (see chapter 1, preceding, especially fragments 1, 2). The ancient testimonia, moreover, supply us with a wide variety of Xenophanean 'proofs.' The most serious difficulty with these reconstructions is that there is not a single instance within Xenophanes' explicit comments on *this* subject, of that systematic, inferential, or logical point of view, even though inferential thinking (with its tell-tale inferential connectives) is evident elsewhere in the fragments. We may (and should) conjecture that Xenophanes linked together in his own mind god's absolute perfection with his moral excellence and supremacy in power, but we lack a single instance among his express remarks to confirm that Xenophanes realized that one or more of these attributes could be *used to establish* the reality of the others. In sharp contrast with the picture of an inference-sensitive Xenophanes, the Xenophanes of fragments 23–26 is all dogma and all flat assertion, even adopting the archaic poetic device of duplicative description in order to convey to his audience the impression of god's utter or absolute possession of his qualities. Either Xenophanes himself failed to develop a proof technique for his theological ascriptions or else an unkind history has deprived us of his more ratiocinative comments on the subject. But so long as we restrict our discussion to the characterizations of the divine in fragments 23–26, we ought to accept Jaeger's verdict: 'It is nothing that rests on logical proof, nor is it really philosophical at all, but springs from an immediate sense of awe at the sublimity of the Divine' (49).[4]

3 1, 84–94. Barnes himself displays a fundamental ambivalence on the extent to which his logicized reconstruction actually reflected Xenophanes' own thinking. He refers in passing to 'Xenophanes' theological reasoning' and 'the logical aspect of Xenophanes' theology' (86), but elsewhere waffles on the crucial issue: 'a simple systematic pattern can be discovered in, *or imposed upon*, his thought' (94; italics mine).

4 For a recent defence of a highly deductive Xenophanes, see Finkelberg. His account of a Xenophanes who created before Parmenides virtually the entirety of Eleatic philosophy rests crucially on the Pseudo-Plutarch *Miscellanies* (A32) as reflecting

It is only when we enlarge the focus of our attention beyond the dogmas of fragments 23–26 that a more philosophically interesting aspect of Xenophanes' thinking begins to emerge, only, that is, when we begin to consider his entire critique of human *doxa* about the gods – a critique in which his own positive theological views played only a part. Dodds recognized this larger dimension to Xenophanes when he identified him (along with Heraclitus and Hecataeus) as one of the earliest voices of the Greek enlightenment (through his attacks on Homer and Hesiod, his repudiation of divination, and his discovery of 'the relativity of religious ideas').[5] But the true extent of Xenophanes' originality as a philosopher goes even beyond this: his most remarkable accomplishment, unique among his ancient philosophical cohort, was to provide an exhaustive critique of claims to religious *knowledge*.

This may become clearer if we consider the various possible bases for our knowledge of the gods and then compare Xenophanes' position (although a full assessment of the cosmological comments must await chapter 3, and the comments on human understanding, chapter 4):

- from the gods themselves: but (fragment 26) the divine does not move about (hence no epiphanies, nocturnal visitations, etc.), nor (fragment 14) do the gods have recognizable bodies, clothing, and voices.
- from nature (through natural signs): but (fragment 32, A39) those phenomena regarded as omens, portents, or other messages from the gods have straightforward natural explanations; not from the outset did gods 'intimate' all sorts of things to mortals (see the commentary on fragment 18 in chapter 4, following).
- by the authority of the poets: but (fragments 11–12) the poets have attributed all manner of shameful qualities to perfect beings.
- from common consensus: but (fragment 10) all have learned from the poets.
- by extrapolating from our own qualities: but (fragment 23) the true divinity is not at all like men, and (fragments 15–16) the qualities

---

authentic Xenophanean ideas, but if Pseudo-Plutarch himself were influenced by Parmenides' (or subsequent Eleatic) accounts, it could not be used to establish *pre*-Parmenidean teachings. For a recent defence of a highly undeductive Xenophanes, see Classen (in Boudouris): 'his "views" appear to be conceived by contrast. They are not developed by argument or speculation but represent a static picture as it were, seen in contrast to another existing picture, supported by evidence such as examples or observation, not by reasoning' (98).

5 Dodds 1951, 180–81.

men attribute to the gods have a subjective significance – that is, men simply assign to the gods the attributes which they themselves happen to possess.

- from religious 'experts': but (fragment 7) Pythagoras claims to recognize the soul of a friend as a barking dog, and (A1) Epimenides should be rebuked.
- from 'inspiration' or 'enthusiastic' possession by the deity during ritual celebrations: but (again fragment 26), it is not fitting for the deity to move about to different places at different times.
- from seers and oracles: but (A52) *mantikē* should be dismissed and (fragment 34.3–4) even if someone were to succeed in hitting the truth in speaking of what is brought to pass (τετελεσμένον εἰπών),[6] he still would not know.

In the light of this array of critical comments, all bearing in one way or another on our prospects for gaining knowledge about the gods, we may look ahead to fragment 34.1–2 as a fitting summary conclusion: 'the certain truth no man has seen nor will there be anyone who *knows about the gods* (εἰδὼς ἀμφὶ θεῶν) as well as such things as I say about all things.' Seen in this light, a variety of otherwise unrelated observations coalesce into a striking critique of a single thesis: that men can have knowledge of divine attributes and activities. The upshot, according to fragment 34.4, is that *dokos* – 'belief,' 'opinion,' 'supposition' is 'allotted to all.'[7]

We can, moreover, attribute this overall objective to Xenophanes without risk of anachronism, either by requiring him to have interests or concerns not overtly expressed until a later period or by requiring

6 For a defence of the relevance of the repudiation of *mantikē* to the argument of fragment 34 see Lesher 1978, 1–21 (esp. 6–13); and, recently, Classen (in Boudouris).
7 The possible relevance of Xenophanes' genetic explanation of religious belief to claims of *knowledge* about the gods was recognized by Jonathan Barnes (1, 140–43). Barnes, however, understood Xenophanes' idea with respect to a single belief and a single causal chain: 'if my belief that p was caused by events having no suitable connection with the fact that p, then I do not know that p' (143). This thesis is mistaken in so far as beliefs can arise from multiple causes, some reason-related and some not, and there is no good reason to reject a claim to knowledge simply because *some* of the factors that brought it into being have no relationship with the events it concerns (for further discussion, see Lesher 1975). Xenophanes' exhaustive survey avoids this difficulty: if after reviewing the various possible causal origins of our beliefs about the gods we conclude that none provides good reasons to believe, then we may legitimately infer that 'no man knows.'

him to possess techniques of analysis and argumentation more characteristic of later philosophers. We need only presuppose a sense of annoyance with those who made extravagant claims to knowledge (cf. Cicero in A25: 'Parmenides and Xenophanes ... rebuked almost like angry men the arrogance of those who dare to say that they know when in fact nothing can be known'), and a method of analysis that amounted to a serial critique of the various possible ways of gaining knowledge of divine attributes and operations (cf. Parmenides' *elenchos* or 'critique'[8] of the various possible ways of thinking about *to eon*). In addition to Xenophanes the moralist and theological reformer we ought also to recognize Xenophanes the author of a searching critique of claims to knowledge or expertise about divine matters.[9]

8 See Lesher 1984, esp. 9–17. Perhaps the closest parallel to Xenophanes' critique of the possible sources of religious wisdom is provided by Socrates' *elenchos* of various Athenian paragons of wisdom in an attempt to vindicate the truth of the oracle's statement that there was 'no one wiser than Socrates' (*Apology* 21ff.). Socrates' conclusion is strikingly Xenophanean: 'real wisdom is the property of god ... human wisdom has little or no value' (23a); see the following commentary on fragment 34, the conclusion of chapter 4, and Lesher 1987.

9 Although a direct connection has occasionally been questioned (cf. Dodds 1951, 197n), Aeschylus' description of Zeus at *Suppliants* 85ff. is highly reminiscent of Xenophanes: everything done by the divine is free of toil; though remaining seated where he is he makes his thought become deed. Aeschylus' main thesis here is that god's intentions, while sure, lie beyond human comprehension (89–90, 95).

3

On Nature

Fragment 19

[According to some accounts (Thales) seems to have been the first to study astronomy and to foretell solar eclipses and the solstices. So Eudemus says in his history of astronomy (fragment 94 Spengel); for which reason both Xenophanes and Herodotus admire him.]

Diogenes Laertius 1.23

COMMENTARY ON FRAGMENT 19

Since it can be determined through astronomical calculation that a solar eclipse would have been visible across a large portion of Asia Minor on 28 May 585 BC, historians of early Greek thought have long employed the story of Thales' successful prediction of a solar eclipse in order to set the approximate starting date for philosophical inquiry. Thales' achievement, described by Herodotus (1.74) as 'foretelling the alteration of the day into night' is but one of many accomplishments credited to the famous scientist-philosopher from Miletus. Yet the story of Thales' prediction has also long been regarded as more fable than fact: 'The prediction may be fairly classed with the prediction of a good olive-crop or the fall of an aërolite' (Rawlinson in his 1858 translation of Herodotus). The story was rescued from total implausibility by Heath (12–18) and others who hypothesized that Thales might have had access to Babylonian records of lunar and solar eclipse cycles (of either 18 or $23\frac{1}{2}$ months' duration). But this hypothesis has itself been widely rejected as inadequate to the task: 'even three centuries after Thales no solar eclipse could have been predicted to be visible in Asia Minor –

in fact not even for Babylon ... there exists no historically manageable cycle of solar eclipses visible at a given locality' (Neugebauer 2, 604; cf. Dicks, 43; Roller, 59). One recent study (Mosshammer, 145–55) avoids the problem of explaining how Thales was able to make his remarkable prediction by denying that he made it at all; instead: 'The final version as we have it from Herodotus can best be understood as a literary assimilation of what were once entirely separate reports concerning the eclipse, the Lydo-Median war, and Thales' astronomical interests' (154).

What then should we make of Xenophanes' reported 'admiration' for Thales on the basis of something Thales may never have done? It is surely unwarranted to assume (as Heath did) that we may take the report of Xenophanes' admiration at face value as conclusive evidence (at least as conclusive as we could expect for so distant an event) that the prediction actually took place. We do not know that D.L. is 'quoting' either Xenophanes or Herodotus, and the story of Xenophanes' admiration, like other stories, may turn out to be not wholly accurate. It has in fact often been conjectured that *thaumadzei* must have had an ironic (hence critical) quality (D-K, 113; Steinmetz, 15; Bowra 1960, 113; among others), as might be guessed from the report (also from D.L., A1, 18) that Xenophanes 'held views opposed to those of Thales (ἀντιδοξάσαι).' This particular 'deflationary' explanation is not very convincing; D.L. attributes the same attitude (*thaumadzei*) to both Xenophanes and Herodotus and the latter reports the eclipse prediction without a trace of irony or scepticism (1.74). But there are no less than three good reasons not to take D.L.'s report at full face value.

First, it is entirely possible that many reports of Thales' astronomical activities exaggerated the extent of their scientific sophistication and importance. In his study of 5th-century eclipse predictions, D. O'Brien explained how a report of a *single* successful prediction could easily evolve into reports of *several* such predictions, which could in turn give rise to the idea that whoever made such predictions must have possessed a *correct understanding* of the causes of solar eclipses (115). The reports of Thales' prediction exhibit such a pattern of expansion:

(1) For Herodotus, Thales 'foretold this alteration of day into night ... setting as its limit the year [or less likely: 'the season'] in which the change actually occurred' (1.74).
(2) For Clement, Thales 'foretold the eclipse of the sun' (D-K 11 A5).
(3) For Diogenes Laertius, 'it appeared that according to some [or that Eudemus said according to some] Thales was the first to study astronomy and to foretell eclipses [in the plural]' (here at 1.23).

(4) For Theon Smyrnaeus, Thales was the 'first to discover ... the eclipse of the sun' (εὖρε πρῶτος ... ἡλίου ἔκλειψιν, D-K 11 A17).
(5) For Pliny, Thales 'investigavit primus omnium ... praedicto solis defectu' (D-K 11 A5).
(6) In the Suda, Thales was 'first to comprehend eclipses' (πρῶτος δὲ Θαλῆς ... ἐκλείψεις κατείληφεν, D-K 11 A2).
(7) For Aëtius, Thales was the first to explain the eclipse of the sun as caused by the interposition of the moon (D-K 11 A17a).

We can preserve the credibility of *some* prediction having occurred by scaling back the degree of scientific knowledge required and, of all the ancient reports, none taxes credulity less than Herodotus' account of a single prediction, successful in some measure because it could have been confirmed by any visible solar eclipse taking place during the year. Recognizing the potential for inflation in subsequent accounts of Thales' achievement does not force us to conclude that *no* prediction was made, but the discrepancies do strengthen the suspicion that Thales made only a single, broadly framed, unscientific, and very lucky guess which succeeding generations inflated into a genuine scientific discovery (a conclusion defended by Roller, 59 and Kahn 1970, 115).

Second, it is only prudent to expect some degree of misunderstanding to enter a process of historical recall that extends from Thales in the 6th century BC to Eudemus in the 4th century BC to Laertius in the 2nd and 3rd century. Consider as an example the report of Xenophanes' 'admiration.' 'Admires' is a legitimate translation of *thaumadzei*, but so also are 'wonders at,' 'marvels at,' 'is amazed,' and 'is astonished' (cf. Lysias 25.1: τῶν κατηγόρων θαυμάζω – 'I am astonished at my accusers'). As Aristotle's account (*Metaphysics* 982b) of the beginning of philosophy makes clear, one can wonder at or about what is perplexing or not fully understood as well as marvel at what is marvellous (cf. 982b17: ἀπορῶν καὶ θαυμάζων). Even if reports of Xenophanes' admiration were based on so explicit a comment as 'θαυμάζω' or 'θαῦμα ἐστί μοι' we still need to know whether the comment signified his admiration ('I admire Thales for having succeeded in predicting a solar eclipse'), wonder ('I wonder how (or whether) Thales was able to predict a solar eclipse'), or amazement ('I am [or would be] amazed if Thales should have been able to predict a solar eclipse'). Stories of the reactions of bystanders, like stories of marvellous events themselves, are eminently capable of enhancement over the course of time.

Third, both the account of Thales' activities and the range of his known philosophical interests are sufficiently broad to allow for the possibility of a misassignment of activity with admiring attitude. Fragment 19 itself is sufficiently vague to accommodate two distinct possibilities: 'the first to study astronomy and to foretell solar eclipses and the solstices ... for which reason, etc.' Perhaps Herodotus and Xenophanes admired Thales for doing all three of the items mentioned, but perhaps they really admired him specifically for *having pioneered the study of the heavens* (reading καὶ ... προειπεῖν as specifying two of the more noteworthy aspects of his inquiries: 'the first to study astronomy, even foretelling solar eclipses and the solstices, etc.'). Even admiration for activities having nothing to do with astronomy could be reassigned to Thales' most famous achievement over the course of time. Interestingly, Herodotus reports Thales' successful prediction without a word of praise but *elsewhere* (1.170) commends Thales for his 'good' or 'useful' (*chrēstē*) advice to the Ionians on a political matter. It represents no strain on normal human capacities for miscommunication for 'Thales, the famous author of an eclipse prediction, admired by Herodotus and Xenophanes' to evolve into 'Thales, the famous author of an eclipse prediction admired by Herodotus and Xenophanes.' As an advocate (fragment 18) and practitioner of Ionian science (fragments 27–33, 37; A1, A32, A33, A36, A38–48), including the study of solar eclipses (A41, A41a), Xenophanes could be assumed to have admired Thales' study of astronomy generally; and as one who had claimed recognition for the benefits his own 'good expertise' had brought to the city (fragment 2.11–14), Xenophanes would also have thought favourably of Thales' service as political adviser to the Ionians. 'Xenophanes' admiration' for Thales could have had its origins in either or both of these areas of activity having little or nothing to do with eclipse predictions.

There are in fact special problems created by the particular choice of the eclipse prediction as the motivating cause of Xenophanes' admiring attitude. The fragments reveal his special sensitivity about bogus claims to expertise and knowledge (fragment 7, 10; A25), and one specific target of Xenophanes' criticism was the supposed art of divination (*mantikē*), the ability to penetrate the obscurities of the past, present, and – quite commonly – the future (A52). Nowhere in Presocratic thought do we have so great a warrant for attributing a scepticism about the possibility of genuine knowledge of future events as we do here in Xenophanes. In fragment 34, moreover, Xenophanes appears to argue that no assertion about 'what is brought to pass' could be counted as knowledge unless confirmed as true on the basis of experience. As a consequence, assertions about 'the non-evident,' that is, about regions or events so distant in space and time as to be inaccessible to any human observer, could only be a matter of conjecture or opinion (*dokos*) rather than knowledge. Even if one were to succeed in stating the precise truth about such matters this would still amount only to a conjecture which events happened to prove true as a matter of coincidence (see note 5 on fragment 34 in chapter 4 following).

We may, therefore, accept fragment 19 as a credible account of Thales' activities, including a successful – if almost certainly unscientific – prediction of the solar eclipse of 28 May 585 BC. In view of the interests and values they shared with him we may also suppose that Herodotus and Xenophanes admired Thales – although fragment 19 is slightly vague about the basis for their admiration, and particular expressions of their esteem might easily have been misinterpreted by others. But if we are to believe that Herodotus admired Thales for the specific accomplishment of predicting the eclipse we must accept the improbable proposition that Herodotus withheld mention of his admiring attitude in his own account of the event while elsewhere choosing to commend Thales for the far less spectacular feat of offering useful advice on a political matter. And if we are to believe that Xenophanes admired Thales for the successful prediction we must assume either that he admired him for what fragment 34 would view as only a lucky guess, or else that he granted to Thales the capacity to have knowledge of the sort of truth fragment 34 argued could not be known by anyone.

Fragment 27

[Xenophanes said that everything comes forth from the earth, for this is what he says:]
... for all things[1] are from the[2] earth and to[3] the earth all things
come in the end.

Theodoretus 4.5

NOTES

1 πάντα (*panta*): Heitsch (159–60) argues in favour of Theodoretus' wording, ἐκ γῆς γὰρ τάδε πάντα over ἐκ γαίης γὰρ πάντα, which follows Sextus *Against the Professors* 10.313. τάδε πάντα, in its epic sense of 'all these (here)' (cf. *Iliad* 6.441) would make fragment 27 into something less than a universal *archē* statement, i.e., only that 'all these (here) come from earth and end up in the earth.' Since, however, τάδε πάντα

can be used to refer to the cosmos in its entirety (cf. Heraclitus, fragment 64: τάδε πάντα οἰακίζει κεραυνός), the resolution of this textual question would not in itself settle the question of interpretation (see the following commentary).

2 γαίης (gaiēs): LSJ cites this passage as an example of 'earth, as an element' (s.v. γῆ, 1.2), but recognizes 'the earth or ground' as a separate use (III). For the case for 'the earth,' see the following commentary. Untersteiner (pp. cxxxiv–clxvii) saw in Xenophanes' references to earth (γῆ) a revival of the ancient worship of Gaia and attributed to him a dual physical/theological view of all things as infused by a divine 'fluido energetico' (similarly, Reinhardt, 117). While Xenophanes does discuss various phenomena bearing the names of deities (γῆ in fragments 27–29, 33; πόντος in fragment 30; ἥλιος in fragment 31; Ἶρις in fragment 32), he never speaks of them as deities, nor does he call for them to be worshipped or held in esteem. On the contrary, he speaks of them as natural substances interacting with other natural substances through familiar physical processes (moving, warming, separating, combining, compacting, vaporizing, etc.).

3 εἰς γῆν (eis gēn): either 'into' or 'in' or 'to' earth (or the earth), but perhaps best taken here as 'to' in light of the preceding phrase ἐκ γῆς/γαίης (cf. LSJ s.v. εἰς I, 1a; Iliad 23.169: ἐς πόδας ἐκ κεφαλῆς – 'from head to foot.'

COMMENTARY ON FRAGMENT 27

For the ancient doxographer who had come to regard Xenophanes as a proponent of Eleatic orthodoxy (in so far as he appeared to advocate an eternal, motionless, spherical one), fragment 27 must have seemed a very odd comment indeed. Whatever could one make of an Eleatic who also held that everything came into being from, and returned to, earth? Theodoretus, to whom we are indebted for what is probably the fullest version of Xenophanes' utterance, suspected a lapse of memory (A36). But one need not subscribe to the view of Xenophanes as an Eleatic in order to find fragment 27 problematic. As Galen was perhaps the first to observe, if Xenophanes had opted for earth as the basic archē of all things (as Thales did for water and Anaximenes did for air), we would expect much greater confirmation of this fact than the historical record provides (for Galen this meant inclusion in Theophrastus' summary of physical opinions, but the same problem arises for us from Aristotle Metaphysics 989a5; Physics 187a12; and On the Heavens 303b9, all of which appear to deny that any of the Ionian physiologoi opted for earth as *archē*). Close parallels with an Orphic hymn to Selene and a spurious Heraclitus fragment (Stobaeus *Physical Selections* 1.120) have created additional doubts about the authenticity of fragment 27.

Line 1 There have been two main lines of thought: either (1) fragment 27 is an assertion about the causal origins of a certain group of existing things – either (1a) all plants or (1b) all living beings – or (2) fragment 27 is an assertion about the causal origins of all existing things, that is, an *archē* theory of the familiar Ionian sort.

Understood as (1a), Xenophanes' proposal (as Heitsch, 160, observed) has at least the virtue of being factually correct: 'all (vegetative growth) comes from and ends in earth,' or 'all these (forms of vegetative growth) etc. . . . ' An interest in vegetative growth could be appropriately attributed to Xenophanes in light of the botanical interests reflected in Hippolytus' testimonium (A33).

Understood as (1b), fragment 27 would parallel the claims made by fragments 29 and 33 dealing with 'everything that comes into being and grows' and 'all we who come into being.' To achieve consistency among all three claims we would need only to suppose (as Guthrie argued, 1, 386) that *gē* in fragment 27 means 'moist earth.' Hippolytus alluded also to a Xenophanean idea about the creation and destruction of all living things (A33, 6). Less formal precedents for fragment 27 (as 1b) could be found in Menelaus' curse at *Iliad* 7.99: 'may you all go to earth and water'; Hesiod's story of the creation of Pandora from earth and water (*Works* 61); and the ancient creation myth (related by Euripides in fragment 839) involving the fertilization of Gaia by the rains of Zeus. Since fragment 27 would be concerned only with the origins of life, problems relating to the fragment as a piece of *archē* theory would be avoided (for an interpretation of this sort, see Guthrie 1, 385–87).

In order to adopt any of several interpretations along the lines of (2) above, that is, to take fragment 27 as the thesis that the cosmos had its origins in earth, we must find a rejoinder to the consideration that, according to Aristotle, 'none of those who posit a unity makes earth the element' (*Metaphysics* 989a5; cf. *On the Soul* 405b8). But this line of argument rests on several debatable suppositions. In order, for example, for the *On the Soul* comments on views of the soul to have relevance for fragment 27, we must assume that the element identified as the origin of the cosmos would also serve as the *explanans* for the other items that make up the cosmos. But if anything is evident from the Xenophanes doxography it is the great variety of substances chosen to serve as *explanans* (earth, earth and water, sea, clouds, sun, and so on). We can hardly infer from the fact that Xenophanes did not (according to Aristotle) propose earth as the true nature of the soul that he could not have proposed earth as the *archē* for 'all things' generally.

We should also exercise some caution in drawing inferences from Aristotle's failure to mention an earlier theory. As Deichgräber (10–15) argued, Aristotle seems to have regarded Xenophanes as a theological rather than physical theorist, at least he speaks of him as a monist in a theological context (*Metaphysics* 986b21). He fails, moreover, to discuss Xenophanes as a two-element theorist even while willing to consider Parmenides along these lines. We must then recognize the distinct possibility that Aristotle failed to mention Xenophanes' physical views not because there were none to mention but because Aristotle regarded Xenophanes as insufficiently interested and engaged in physical theorizing to warrant discussion. We should also remember that at *On the Heavens* 303b and at *Physics* 187a Aristotle is discussing *single*-substance views (*hen legontōn*). If Xenophanes thought of two or more elements as coequal claimants to the title of *archē* (as he seems to do in fragments 29 and 33), he would not have been appropriately included in a discussion of monistic theorists. His absence from Aristotle's review need not therefore count against taking fragment 27 as an *archē* proposal. On one occasion when there is no restriction to single-substance theories (*Physics* 193a21), earth is included among the options taken.

In addition to these interpretive manoeuvres there is another, in some respects quite natural, way to assure the compatibility of fragment 27 with a rival cosmology: to read 'from ... and to earth' not as cosmology but as geophysics; that is, not as a statement about what all things *consist of*, but rather about *where* all things begin from and end up (a reading proposed by Freeman [100]: 'he was commenting on the phenomena he saw around him on the physical plane and is not suggesting that Earth is the substrate'). 'From earth' can mean not earth as such, but *the* earth – the ground beneath our feet and all about us (cf. ἐκ γαίης at *Odyssey* 10.302). It is clearly 'the earth' rather than the basic element, earth, that is described in fragment 28 as having its upper limit here at our feet, and so Theodoretus seems to have understood ἐκ γαίης in fragment 27, judging by his paraphrase: ἐκ τῆς γῆς φῦναι ἅπαντα – 'all things grow from the earth.' On this reading fragment 27 would complement the sea-based meteorology of fragment 30 (and A46) in so far as the seas occupy large regions of the earth's surface and all that goes up into the heavens in the form of mists and vapour comes back down to the earth as rain and wind. Xenophanes could easily have supposed that *panta* were *ek gaiēs* and *eis gēn* in this sense without contradicting the earth and water *archē* theory expressed in fragments 29 and 33.

Fragment 28

[Xenophanes does not think that the earth is poised in mid-air, but extends downward without limit:]
This upper limit of the earth[1] is seen here[2] at our feet,
pushing up against the air,[3] but that below[4] goes on without limit.[5]

Achilles Tatius 4.34.11

NOTES

1 γαίης (*gaiēs*): 'of the earth'; i.e., of the world of land and sea that lies all about us (see the commentary on fragment 27).

2 τόδε πεῖρας (*tode peiras*): lit. 'this limit here' (cf. GG, sec. 1008).

3 ἠέρι προσπλάζον (*ēeri prosplazon*): Mss: καὶ ρεῖ; Diels, ἠέρι; Karsten, αἰθέρι. For προσπλάζων LSJ gives 'beat or knock against, touch,' citing *Iliad* 12.285; *Odyssey* 11.583; and this passage. In Homer the verb designates the reaching of the water up to Tantalus' chin and the action of the waves warding off (ἐρύκεται) snowflakes. 'Warding off' or 'driving off' is also one common meaning of the root verb πλάζω (s.v. LSJ, I, 1). Xenophanes' point seems to be that the earth reaches up toward the air and keeps it back, but stretches downward without check or resistance. As Diels (1901) noted, the language of Parmenides' fragment 8 and his idea of a 'full-up' universe may echo Xenophanes here in fragment 28: 'what is draws near to what is' (fragment 8.25: ἐὸν γὰρ ἐόντι πελάζει ...), 'nor is there what is not which might stop it from reaching its like' (fragment 8.46: παύοι μιν ἱκνεῖσθαι).

4 τὸ κάτω (*to katō*): 'the lower' limit or portion of the earth. Since there is no lower limit to Xenophanes' earth it would be odd for τὸ κάτω to mean 'the lower limit' and for it (i.e., the limit) to 'reach without limit,' although 'this limit' in line 1 and the μὲν-δὲ structure seem to call for just such a contrast of two limits. Some doxographical summaries describe Xenophanes' theory as concerned with the earth's 'depths' (βάθη) or 'lower portion' (τὸ κάτω μέρος), and since what 'presses up' against the air must be the mass of earth (rather than

a limit in the sense of a geometrical abstraction), it is perhaps preferable to read fragment 28 as contrasting two *portions* of the earth: one which stops here at our feet and another which stretches down ἐς ἄπειρον.

5 ἐς ἄπειρον (*es apeiron*): minimally translated as 'indefinitely' or 'without limit' (cf. Plato *Laws* 910b: εἰς ἄπειρον ... αὐξάνειν), and interpreted either as of truly infinite extent or merely indefinitely large (e.g., by D-K: '*indefinitum* nicht *infinitum*,' 135; see the summary in Untersteiner, cliv–clviii). Lumpe (38) opted for the novel 'without experience,' the ἐς ἄπειρον lower depths contrasting with the *visible* earth's surface mentioned in line one. But προσπλάζων (in one direction) and ἱκνεῖται (in the other direction) both suggest strongly that we are dealing throughout with a question of the earth's *extension*. For a discussion of 'infinite' versus 'indefinite,' see the commentary following.

COMMENTARY ON FRAGMENT 28

Line 1 Xenophanes' reference to an upper limit of the earth which 'is seen here at our feet' may not seem rich in philosophical import, but it does provide a clue to his thinking about human knowledge, a much discussed but little understood aspect of his philosophy. Some ancient writers (for example, Aristocles in A49) attributed to Xenophanes the systematic scepticism about the testimony of the senses characteristic of Eleatic philosophers. At the opposite end of the interpretive spectrum, some commentators hold that 'Xenophanes characterizes as certain and exhaustive (*saphes*) only that knowledge that is empirically grounded' (Fränkel 1974, 130). We should therefore notice that Xenophanes does refer on three occasions to the faculty of sight and/or information obtained from its exercise: Iris-rainbow, which, is 'purple, red, and greenish-yellow to behold,' (ἰδέσθαι, fragment 32); 'as many things as they have made evident for mortals to look upon,' (εἰσοράασθαι, fragment 36); and here the surface of the earth, which 'is seen (ὁρᾶται) at our feet' (fragment 28.1). While other passages (fragment 38, A41a) mention features of the world that admit of misperception (or at least misinterpretation – see the commentaries on fragments 35 and 38, following), the positive reference to sense perception here in fragment 28 counts against a systematic or categorical repudiation of the testimony of the senses (cf. also those references in later reports to the evidence provided by observation, most notably the citation of fossil finds in various locations; Hippolytus in A33).

Line 2 Xenophanes' view of the earth's depths as extending *es apei-ron* or 'rooted *ep' apeiron*' provoked a stinging reply from Aristotle (*On the Heavens* 294a): ' "rooted in the infinite" as Xenophanes says, in order to avoid having to inquire into the cause.' Since only an infinite extension would obviate the need for further inquiry, we may suppose that Aristotle understood Xenophanes' phrase in that way. So also may we read Empedocles' reaction to the idea of 'unlimited depths,' since the gist of his criticism is that Xenophanes (and others who hold this view) are in no position to confirm such a claim, 'seeing little of the whole' (fragment 39). Aristotle's rejection of the theory can be accounted for by reference to his own view of natural movements and places (*On the Heavens* 273a ff., 297a–b) and denial of an actual infinite (*Physics* 205a ff.), but his disparagement of Xenophanes' intellectual seriousness is perhaps best seen as further evidence (see the commentary on fragment 27 and the introduction in part 3 following) that he regarded Xenophanes as a religious teacher rather than a student of natural science.

There is, to my knowledge, no conclusive case for 'indefinite' over 'infinite,' but I do think the scale tilts toward the former. It is demonstrable that *eis apeiron* can mean just 'indefinite' (see note 5 above), and 'infinite in size, extent, or duration' is but one of several uses of *apeiros*. We cannot assume (as, for example, Stokes does) that Xenophanes must have had 'infinite' in mind because that is how his critics understood him. The phrase *ep' apeirona* occurs in Homer, said of such non-infinite entities as a night's sleep (*Odyssey* 7.286), the earth (*Iliad* 7.445) the deep sea (*Odyssey* 4.510), and even the Hellespont (*Iliad* 14.545). In these early uses, *ep' apeirona* serves to designate large expanses lacking noticeable boundaries or borders (cf. Snell, *Lexikon*, s.v. ἄπειρον; Herodotus 1.204: 'a boundless (*apeiron*) plain stretching as far as the eye can see,' etc.).

Those who have attributed to Xenophanes the belief in a spherical universe identical with god have had special incentive to find an alternative to the reading of actual infinitude, but the one so far identified (by Guthrie, following Gilbert and Cornford), that the earth is unlimited in the sense that it is unimpeded by anything else until it hits the bottom of the sphere, is hard to believe. As Aristotle once said of a rival view (*Nicomachean Ethics* 1096a), no one would adopt such a view except to save a philosophical theory. Other aspects of Xenophanes' teaching point in the general direction of an earth of 'indefinite' or 'indeterminate' depths. If *eis apeiron* in Xenophanes always meant 'to infinity' then the sun that travels on *eis apeiron* must have gone on to infinity even though it is said to be kindled and extinguished daily (A41) and to cease when it reaches certain regions of the earth (A41a). It must also be counted anomalous that someone reluctant to commit himself to the continued existence of suns and stars when they were no longer visible (A33, A38, A41) would be willing to affirm an earth's depth of truly infinite dimensions. In general, Xenophanes speaks of familiar natural substances and processes (fragments 27, 29, 30, 33, etc.), in ways that border on the pedestrian (for example, fragment 31 on the sun's warming effect). Here, in a literally pedestrian set of circumstances (*para possin*), the affirmation of the earth's *infinite* lower extent would strike a singularly discordant note. By contrast, what Xenophanes could affirm with considerable basis in observed fact was that – for all locations – the earth below our feet stretches down indefinitely far.

This claim, it should be realized, would not be a triviality. As Reinhardt (147) noted, some doxographical accounts (A32, A33) contrast Xenophanes' account with Anaximenes' view of the earth as floating on air and, as Lebedev (1981) pointed out, Aristotle placed Xenophanes' account in contrast with that of Thales (*On the Heavens* 294a21; cf. Aëtius in A47). Seen within the context of early Ionian discussions of the shape and foundations of the earth, fragment 28 has a polemic quality: accounts of subterranean air or water lack a rational basis; what is evident below our feet is only earth and more earth.

Fragment 29

[Porphyry says that Xenophanes held that the dry and the wet were first principles, I mean (by this) earth and water, and cites a passage from him to make this clear:]
All things which come into being[1] and grow are earth and water.

Philoponus 1.5.125

Fragment 33

[According to some, Xenophanes the Colophonian appears to agree with Homer (Iliad 7.99), for he says:]
For we all come into being[1] from earth and water.

Sextus Empiricus 10.314

NOTES

1 γίνονται/ἐκγενόμεσθα (*ginontai/ekgenomestha*): Both γίγνομαι and ἐκγίγ-
νομαι can mean 'born' – especially when speaking of persons – but
both can also mean 'coming into being' (LSJ, s.v. I and I, 3 respectively). Guthrie translates fragment 29 as 'All that is born ...' and
fragment 33 as 'For we are all born ...'(cf. D-K, 'Denn wir alle wur-
den ... geboren'), but it is better to allow an Ionian thinker engaged
in natural philosophy the benefit of non-animate terminology unless
we are required by a particular context to do otherwise. The choice of
'born' in fragment 33 is less objectionable in light of the first-person
(plural) verb, but it is not mandatory (cf. KRS, 'For we all came forth
from earth and water').

The aorist ἐκγενόμεσθα may be translated by the English simple
past 'we came into being,' or by the present 'we come into being'
as a 'gnomic aorist'; i.e., an aphorism stated in the past tense with a
general application (cf. GG, sec. 1293). Thus 'we all came ...' would
mean 'we always come into being, etc.'

COMMENTARY ON FRAGMENTS 29 AND 33

Taken together, fragments 29 and 33 contain sufficient ambiguity to
spawn a large number of variant readings. We may wonder, for example, whether fragment 29 should be understood as asserting that 'all
things which become and grow' come from earth and water *combined*,
or whether some may come from earth alone while others come from
water alone. We may also wonder whether the class of *explananda* is
meant to include just those entities which *both* become and grow, or
whether it includes the much larger number of things which come into
being (without necessarily growing) as well as all things which grow.
Similarly, we may wonder whether fragment 33 asserts that 'we all'
come into being from earth and water *combined* or whether some (of
us) may come from earth alone and others from water alone. Finally,
we may wonder which (if any) of these may be consistently accepted
together with the position or positions of fragment 27 that 'all things
come from and return to earth' or 'all these come from and return to
earth.' Rather than discuss the individual merits of all (sixteen) possible interpretations of Xenophanes' earth-water doctrine, I offer an
interpretation that has at least the virtue of explanatory economy. I
assume (pace Guthrie) that Xenophanes (like his fellow Ionian *physiologoi*) would be interested not only in the origins of living beings, but
in phenomena of all sorts; that is, *panta*. I also suppose that Xenophanes
(like virtually any theorist with a novel idea) would be inclined to

apply his earth-water theory as broadly as possible; that is, to all matters that could be related to either element alone as well as to both elements combined together.

All things considered, Xenophanes is probably best regarded as a two-*archai* or 'dualist' theorist (a view defended by Lumpe, 41–43, based on the parallel status of earth and water in fragments 29 and 33 and on the fact that earth is nowhere said to have been the sum total of existing things at any time in the history of the cosmos). Philoponus in his introduction to the quotation of fragment 29 attributes this interpretation to Porphyry ('the dry and the wet' meaning 'earth and water') and characterizes them as *archas* (A29). While a two-element theorist might conceivably wish to insist on the presence of both elements in every single existing thing, to do this for Xenophanes we would have to suppose (as Aëtius supposed for Anaximenes, D-K 13 A14), that even the fires burning in the heavens contained some earthy elements. But the Xenophanes testimonia do not suggest this at all; on the contrary, Xenophanes is in this context a 'cloud proponent' (A32, A38, A40, etc.) explaining the clouds themselves by reference to the mists drawn up from the sea by the heat of the sun. Since the sea is located on the surface of the earth, there is a sense in which the clouds are *ek gaiēs* (see fragment 27, preceding) but there is no hint that the clouds still have earth in them. To be consistent with these 'earth-less' (though perhaps still earth-bound) phenomena, we should understand the two-*archai* thesis disjunctively: 'all is earth and water' means 'any existing thing is either a form of earth or a form of water or a form of earth combined with water.'

Additional evidence for the dual *archē* interpretation is provided by Xenophanes' repeated references to mixtures. The original condition of the earth is described in A33 as 'all things in mud,' also the state to which all things will some day return. A process of mingling of earth and sea is also alluded to in A32. The sea itself is recognized as containing mixtures (again, A33) and, according to Aëtius (in A46), various sorts of waters. The cryptic fragment 37, 'and indeed in certain caves water drips down,' understood as describing either the formation of rock deposits from dripping waters (D-K, 137n) or the issuing of water from rock (Deichgräber 16) is yet another reference to a mixture of elements. The prevalence of earth and water mixtures, when conjoined with the wide range of phenomena which could be linked either with earth alone, or water alone, would more than suffice as prima facie justification for designating the two elements as items of special importance in the generation, destruction, and continued existence of 'all things.'

So construed, fragments 29 and 33 represent a continuation of Milesian *archē* inquiry, seeking to explain a wide range of natural phenomena without recourse to mysterious divine forces or beings, using only the workings of familiar processes and substances. Later writers often supposed that Xenophanes identified god with 'the whole,' but this tradition rests largely on a decision made by Theophrastus to interpret Xenophanes (or perhaps to interpret just what Aristotle said about Xenophanes) in this way (see the introduction to part 3 following). In light of the contrast evident in Xenophanes' *own* language between god or gods on the one hand and *panta* on the other (cf. πάντα κραδαίνει in fragment 25, ἀμφὶ θεῶν and περὶ παντῶν in fragment 34), it is preferable to regard Xenophanes' *archē* theory as Lumpe characterized it: 'these two basic substances [earth and water] are understood not as principles of all existence, but only of the cosmos' (43); that is, they account for all things existing within the natural world, but the nature of the *divine* is another question.

Fragment 30

[Xenophanes in the *On Nature*:]
The sea is the source[1] of water and of wind,
for without the great sea < there would be no wind >[2]
nor streams of rivers nor rainwater from on high;
but the great sea is the begetter[3] of clouds, winds,
and rivers.

Scholium on *Iliad* 21.196

NOTES

1 πηγή (*pēgē*): 'running water,' 'streams,' but here 'fount,' 'source' (LSJ, s.v. πηγή, II). Deichgräber suggested (5) that πηγή here might be the equivalent of ἀρχή or φύσις, and the term πηγή is used in Empedocles' fragment 23.10 in this sense. This reading would make fragment 30 into a piece of *archē* theory, joining the theory or theories presented in fragments 29 and 33. But according to Xenophanes in Hippolytus (A33), the sea is not a simple substance but a mixture because of the 'many mixtures which flow along in it.' It could not therefore easily serve as the basic *archē* of all waters. We can more easily explain the sea as a product of the two basic *archai*, earth and water, as Xenophanes lists them in fragment 29. See, further, Cherniss 1935, 132ff.

2 < > material added by Edmonds; the text of the scholium is neither intelligible as it stands nor fully in hexameter form. For alternative supplements, see D-K, 136n, and Heitsch, 66n.

3 γενέτωρ (genetōr): 'begetter,' 'ancestor,' 'parent,' or less personally 'producer,' 'generator.' The detailed explanation of interaction between the sea and clouds, wind, and rain which Aëtius provides (A46) makes quite clear that Xenophanes had in mind thoroughly physical processes (thinning, thickening, etc.). Pace Deichgräber (7), therefore, this is not a view of thalassa as possessing 'eine lebendig-göttliche Kraft' – 'a living-divine power'; on the contrary it is Ionian natural science (see further, Lumpe, 39; Steinmetz, 62–66). We may understand γενέτωρ accordingly either as 'producer'/'generator' or (with a touch of sarcasm) as 'begetter,' 'parent.' See the commentary following on lines 5–6.

COMMENTARY ON FRAGMENT 30

Line 1 It should not surprise us that a man who spent most of his life 'tossing about' the Greek world – from Ionia to Sicily to the Italian mainland (see the commentary on fragment 8.2 above) – came to think of the 'great sea' as linked in various ways with the world's rivers, winds, and clouds (and through the last of these, with a collection of other atmospheric and celestial phenomena). As Heitsch explained (165), it would be a familiar experience for one who lived near the sea to observe mists and vapours rising from the sea's surface and to see clouds and feel winds coming onshore. It would also not have escaped Xenophanes' notice that the poets had long ago assigned a special importance to the earth-encircling rivers Oceanus and Tethys in the process of creation (Iliad 20.7–9; 21.195–97) and spoke of Pontos-Sea as the son of Gaia and begetter of other deities (Hesiod Theogony 132, 233ff.). Xenophanes' audience would have taken fragment 30 as a sign that he knew both his oceans and his epic poetry. If they had listened carefully they might also have sensed something original in Xenophanes' way of linking the sea with clouds, rivers, rains, and wind; and if they had thought about the implications of his account for the deities they had long associated with the seas and heavens they might well have been disturbed by his revolutionary idea.

Lines 2–4 Xenophanes' claim that the sea is the source of (all) winds and (all) forms of water is connected with the 'thought experiment' or hypothetical form of argument employed elsewhere in his teachings (see the conclusion of chapter 1 above; Steinmetz, 63–64; Fränkel,

331–33). But the argument reveals few details: 'for if there were no sea (ἄνευ πόντου) there would be no wind, streams of rivers, nor rainwater.' The testimonia help to explain how all these phenomena owe their existence to the sea. Diogenes Laertius explains (A1, 19) that the clouds (τὰ νέφη) are composed from 'the sun's vapour' (τῆς ἀφ' ἡλίου ἀτμίδος), a phrase that would itself be difficult to understand without the fuller account in Aëtius (A46): 'the things in the heavens happen from the heat of the sun (ἀπὸ τῆς τοῦ ἡλίου θερμότητος) as the initial cause.' Clouds are linked with the sea since 'when the moist vapour (τοῦ ὑγροῦ) is drawn up from the sea, the sweet water is separated on account of its fineness and forming mists it combines into clouds.' We are not told how the sea serves as the source of streams or rivers and fragment 30 has on occasion been identified with the theory (later attacked by Aristotle) which 'held that rivers not only flow into the sea but also out of it' (*Meteorology* 354b16–17; attributed to Xenophanes by H.D.P. Lee in his Loeb translation, 133n). But, as Cherniss explained (1935, 133), this is not likely to be Xenophanes' theory, since its authors also accept the sea's salinity as its original condition without explanation, while Xenophanes offers an explanation for its salinity in terms of the 'many mixtures which flow along in it' (A33). If, however, Xenophanes were aware (as it is hard to imagine he would not be) that rains swell streams which feed rivers which in turn empty into the sea (cf. *Iliad* 16.385–92), his linkage of the sea with the formation of clouds and the 'trickling down of rain through compacting' (again, A46) would suffice to link all streams and rivers with the sea.

But it is much less clear how Xenophanes understood the sea to be the source of wind. Neither differential atmospheric pressures nor the differential rates of heating of land and sea water (the specific cause of onshore breezes) were known to him or any of his contemporaries. He might well have believed that the winds were somehow created from within the clouds themselves (cf. the mss: ἐν νέφεσιν). It has been thought (Zeller 1920, 671n, Heitsch, 167, and Gilbert, 518) that we should regard Xenophanes' view as simply a continuation of Anaximenes' idea of wind as 'compacted air' (D-K 13 A7.3). But Aëtius' phrasing (καὶ καταστάζειν ὄμβρους ὑπὸ πιλήσεως καὶ διατμίζειν τὰ πνεύματα) places 'compaction' (ὑπὸ πιλήσεως) with rain and not specifically in connection with the process of 'vaporizing' (διατμίζειν). Aristotle explained rain along just the lines Xenophanes described (*Meteorology* 354b), but resorted to a completely unrelated 'dry vapour' in order to explain the wind (*Meteorology* 360b). Since Xenophanes' objective in fragment 30 was to trace all winds, rain, and clouds back to the sea as their *genetōr*, an independent, second vapour would have been completely at odds with his account (pace Gilbert, 518n). Nevertheless, in an argument elsewhere against the separation theories of Empedocles and Democritus, Aristotle employs the verb διατμίζειν in a way that might shed some light on Xenophanes' view: 'But when air is formed from water, it does occupy more space, for the finer body takes up more room. This is evident in the very process of change. For when the moisture vaporizes and turns into air (διατιμιζομένου γὰρ καὶ πνευματουμένου τοῦ ὑγροῦ) the vessels containing the substances burst for lack of room' (*On the Heavens* 305b13–17). It is possible that the 'vaporizing' process Aëtius mentions here has the same dynamic force, hence the blowing of wind would be just the 'blowing out' of a cloud whose moisture had been heated by the sun until it turned into steam. Anaximander may already have linked the wind with the sun's 'melting' effect (D-K 12 A24) and Aristophanes' crude restatement of Ionian wind theory uses an analogy from the kitchen to explain the bursting effect (*Clouds* 404; there related to a 'rising dry wind' which bursts the overheated cloud sacks). The sea serves as 'source of wind,' therefore, either because its sweet waters are drawn up into the heavens and *squeezed* in some way, or *expanded* into winds by the heat of the sun, or changed into wind by some force which Xenophanes neither understood nor attempted to explain.

Lines 5–6 The impact of Xenophanes' account is augmented by its brevity: the *genetōr* of all these is just 'great sea.' Without explicitly announcing their banishment, Xenophanes has dispatched an array of traditional sea, river, cloud, wind, and rain deities (hence Zeus himself) to the explanatory sidelines. Like ἠέλιος ὑπεριέμενος in fragment 31 and Ἶρις in fragment 32, μέγας πόντος here at 30.5 has a polemic quality to it: the poets say that Pontos was the begetter of fifty goddesses, but for Xenophanes, *pontos* 'begets' only clouds, wind, and water. Cf. Fränkel 1974, 120; Vlastos 1975, 62ff. Empedocles' fragment 50 (Ἶρις δ' ἐκ πελάγους, etc.) appears to follow Xenophanes' account here in fragment 30.

Fragment 31

[The sun must be thought of as Hyperion, 'the one who always goes over the earth,' as I think Xenophanes the Colophonian says:]
... the sun both passing over[1] the earth and spreading warmth
over its surface[2] ...

Heraclitus 44.5

NOTES

1 ὑπεριέμονος (hyperiemenos): 'going or passing over or above' (ὑπέρ plus
  ἱέμενος); Edmonds: 'the Sun that goeth over ...'
  Heitsch (1986, 431) takes ὑπεριέμενος to mean 'steigend' – 'going
  up,' 'rising,' and regards fragment 31 as an application of Xenophanes' 'cloud theory': the sun is created by the rising vapours from
  the sea. But this seems improbable. ὑπερίων should be distinguished
  from ἀνίων ('going up or upward') and means not 'rising'/'steigend'
  but 'moving while on high or above' (cf. Cunliffe, s.v. Hyperiōn: 'He
  that is on high, that bestrides the heavens'; and Heraclitus' intro-
  ductory comment: ὑπεριέμενον ἀεὶ τῆς γῆς). For ὑπέρ as 'over' see Iliad
  15.382; 12.424; etc.
2 ἐπιθάλπων (epithalpōn): The ἐπί-element indicates that the warming
  (θάλπων) is being directed over the surface (of the earth); cf. LSJ, s.v.
  ἐπιθάλπω and ἐπί, G, 3.

COMMENTARY ON FRAGMENT 31

Line 1 Xenophanes' ideas about the nature and movement of the sun
appear to alternate between the painfully obvious and the truly bizarre.
Here he refers to the obvious fact that the sun warms the earth as it
passes over it. (For a discussion of his more unusual ideas about the
sun see the conclusion of this chapter.) It is probably a mistake to insist
on a deeper meaning embedded within this brief comment, either to
suppose as Heitsch did that fragment 31 is really a disguised statement
of Xenophanes' cloud/vapour theory (see the comments on the translation of hyperiemenos above) or that it implicitly asserts a causal linkage
between the two processes, that is, warming by moving. Xenophanes
does elsewhere try to explain the flashing or shining of heavenly bodies by reference to movement (A39 – the Dioscuri; A44 – shooting stars,
comets, meteors; A45 – lightning), and we know that Aristotle resorted
to the generation of heat from friction ('the chafing of the air') in order
to explain how our air becomes heated by the sun (On the Heavens 289a,
Meteorology 341a20). But the correspondence is inexact; Xenophanes,
unlike Aristotle, holds that the sun and other fiery celestial and atmospheric phenomena are just made out of fire or burning clouds; and
instead of attempting (as Aristotle does) to explain the sun's heating
effect, he seems content to use it in order to explain other natural phenomena (A46).

What does emerge from the testimonia is a thoroughly natural, literally 'down to earth' conception of the sun: it comes into being each

day from the gathering of small fires (A33), is quenched at sunset and created anew for the next rising (A41), and it is described as 'useful' (*chrēsimon*) to the world and its inhabitants. As Diels (1897b, 533) noted, this would contrast sharply with the older idea of an 'all-seeing, all-hearing sun-god.' The correspondence of *hyperiemenos* with the sun's poetic epithet 'Hyperion' (*Odyssey* 1.24), 'Ēelios Hyperion' (*Iliad* 8.480) can hardly be accidental. Xenophanes seems to be saying that the sun does not act like a god who kindly bestows heat and light on us (or who can threaten to take his sunshine elsewhere – *Odyssey* 12.383); instead, the sun simply goes through the sky and warms the earth's surface. Perhaps the revolutionary quality of this comment is not obvious to us because the Ionian revolution of which it was a part has become our orthodoxy.

Fragment 32

['snakes ... like rainbows' in curve or colour, for Xenophanes says:]
And she whom they call Iris,[1] this too[2] is by nature[3] a cloud, purple, red and greenish-yellow[4] to behold.[5]

Scholium on *Iliad* 11.27

NOTES

1 Ἴριν καλέουσι (*Irin kaleousi*): 'Iris-messenger' as mentioned by both Homer (e.g., *Iliad* 2.686) and Hesiod (*Theogony* 780). While she occasionally assumes the form of mortals, she is often identified with the rainbow (cf. the epithets 'storm-footed' [*Iliad* 24.77] and 'golden-winged' [*Iliad* 8.398; *Hymn to Demeter* 314] and regarded as a sign or portent (τέρας) sent by Zeus to men (*Iliad* 11.28; 17.548). In an unpublished paper Mourelatos has suggested that the Greek ἴρις might have referred to a whole set of rainbow-like phenomena: what we call 'halos,' 'coronae,' and 'cloud iridescence' – and points out that Homer's characterization of *iris* as a portent of changes in weather such as a 'chilling storm' (*Iliad* 17.548) makes better sense for solar or lunar halos than for rainbows appearing at the end of a storm (cf. Aristotle on *iris* as the lunar halo at *Meteorology* 375a18). In any event, fragment 32 offers a naturalistic account of a phenomenon commonly regarded either as a deity or a sign sent by a deity (see KRS, 174; Guthrie 1, 393; Steinmetz, 67; and Lumpe, 31–32; against Deichgräber, 17–18).

Deichgräber was right, however, to maintain that Xenophanes' phrase 'whom they call' (rainbow) does not *necessarily* have a negative or pejorative overtone (i.e., equal to 'the so-called rainbow'). Anaxagoras' similar account of the rainbow is put in the first person – 'we call (καλέομεν) the reflection of the sun in the clouds a rainbow (ἷριν)' (fragment 19) – and Xenophanes uses the same 'they call' (καλέουσιν) phrase in fragment 2 without a negative overtone ('the contest which they call the pankration'). Nevertheless it is hard not to sense *some* negative force in the fragment taken as a whole (see the following commentary on line 2).

2 καὶ (*kai*): Alternatively 'also,' 'even,' or 'actually.' I understand καὶ τοῦτο to mean that rainbows – *just as other celestial phenomena* – can be explained by reference to his 'cloud-theory' (a feature noted by D-K, 136n; KRS, 174; Deichgräber, 17; Edmonds, 210), as we can tell by the testimonia relating to such matters (A1, A32, A33, A38–46). Mourelatos (1989) gives καὶ τοῦτο a more pointed meaning in connection with Anaximenes' prior explanation of rainbows as light reflected by thick clouds (A18, Aëtius); Xenophanes' fragment 32 would be the reply 'No, there are not two things – the rainbow and the cloud – but only one thing; the rainbow itself is also a cloud.' I suspect, however, that the opponent in fragment 32 was not Anaximenes but 'them' (see the commentary following).

3 πέφυκε (*pephuke*): LSJ, s.v. φύω: 'produce, grow, spring up, become or be by nature, or naturally be'; Marinone: 'essere per propria natura,' 65. Although the noun φύσις appears nowhere in the fragments of Xenophanes, the φύσις of things – both of individuals and of πάντα – is the subject of many of his accounts, as the φύσις of the rainbow is here.

4 χλωρὸν (*chlōron*): Cunliffe: 'an adjective of colour of somewhat indeterminate sense' ranging in use from green, greenish-yellow to yellow, or more generally 'pallid' and 'pale.' Although χλωρόν when coupled with honey (μέλι, as in Xenophanes fragment 38) would mean 'yellow' or 'golden,' here the context points toward 'greenish-yellow' as the logical choice. Not only are green and yellow adjacent colours in the spectrum, but after Xenophanes has mentioned πορφύρεος (purple) and φοινίκεος (red), the colours on the inside and outside of the rainbow, only the yellow-green band in the middle would remain as a perceptively distinct element warranting mention.

5 ἰδέσθαι (*idesthai*): While εἴδω has a large number of special uses and senses (Cunliffe lists ten different meanings of εἴδω in the Homeric epics – in just the active voice), here the conjunction of ἰδέσθαι with colour terminology points toward the basic meaning of the term: 'see, behold with one's eyes, look at.'

COMMENTARY ON FRAGMENT 32

Line 1 While the limitations of Xenophanes' 'cloud theory' – as a scientific explanation – are obvious, they should not lead us to overlook its several virtues. Here, at least, his account is factually correct as far as it goes, although he does not mention – as do Anaximenes (D-K 13 A18) and later Anaxagoras (D-K 59 B19) – the essential role played by sunlight in generating the appearance of the rainbow. While his cloud theory fares poorly in dealing with celestial phenomena, it is nevertheless easy to see its explanatory attractiveness: clouds are not only midway in their perceptible form between air and water, they are also close enough to the earth's surface to be tied to ground mists and vapours and far enough above the earth to be linked with 'the things above' – sun, moon, stars, and so forth.

The relative simplicity of Xenophanes' 'science' has occasioned the suspicion that his remarks were really aimed at a popular audience (Reinhardt, 150) or reflected his interest in popularizing Ionian science rather than in furthering its development (Jaeger 1945, 170). Guthrie also comments: 'The impression is irresistible that in these physical matters Xenophanes was not bothering his head very much. Anaximenes could certainly have taught him a more sophisticated explanation of the rainbow' (1, 393n; cf. Reinhardt, 146, and Zeller 1920, 1, 664). But Guthrie's criticism confuses sophistication with explanatory detail; the full measure of Xenophanes' sophistication cannot be gained within the orbit of meteorological theory but in the larger context of early Greek thought about the world of nature and the conduct of life generally. Dodds (1951, 196n) was one of the few to have noticed that Xenophanes gave 'naturalistic explanations of the rainbow (Fr. 32) and of St Elmo's fire (A 39), both of which are traditional portents,' and he adds with reference to the reports of Cicero and Aëtius (in A52): 'If this [reported denial of divination] is true, it means that, almost alone among classical Greek thinkers, he swept aside not only the pseudo-science of reading omens but the whole deep-seated complex of ideas about inspiration [i.e., of prophets, oracles, and other forms of "divine madness"]' (181). We know from many of the questions asked of the oracles that there was hardly any detail of ordinary life too small to bring to the oracle for interpretation and illumination (see Bouché-Leclercq; Lesher 1978, 21n). We know also from the Greek historians (most famously from Thucydides' account at 7.50 of Nicias' decision to postpone his departure from Syracuse 'until they had remained twenty-seven days, as the soothsayers prescribed,' resulting in the destruction of the Athenian army) that there was hardly any matter of military or political importance that would not have called for consultation with the seers and oracles. Seen in the setting of his own time and place, Xenophanes' assertion that what men call Iris and regard as a divine portent is actually a cloud would have been regarded not as a 'popularizing' of Ionian science but as an attack on the whole enterprise of divination through natural signs (cf. ὑποδείκνυμι in fragment 18, chapter 4 following).

Line 2 It is not clear what purpose Xenophanes intended to be served by his description of the rainbow as 'purple, red, and greenish-yellow to behold.' Diels (1897b, 533) regarded the mention of the colours as a sign of Xenophanes' sceptical attitude toward the senses. Like the reference to the sun's true path (A41a), it would serve to remind his audience of the 'optical illusions' that can occur in the heavens and perhaps elsewhere. Obviously it is possible to regard the show of colours which is the rainbow phenomenon as a transient optical effect, one that results in the appearance of colours unrelated to the true qualities of the air and clouds (that is, those qualities they possess both before and after the rainbow effect occurs). Mourelatos (1965, 350) made the similar suggestion that fragment 32 was intended to serve not as an account of the *nature* of rainbows but merely as a 'hard-headed empiricist' account of *appearances,* that is, of what is, strictly speaking, there to be seen (a view modified to some extent in his recent discussion of Xenophanes' cloud theory; 1989). I suspect, however, that Xenophanes intended neither to indict appearances nor to distinguish them from the true natures of things, but rather to call attention to the specific nature of rainbows and to suggest, in a polite way, how we ought to go about gaining a correct understanding of rainbows and other natural wonders.

One clue to the intended message of fragment 32, specifically of 32.2, is provided by the structure of the couplet. Xenophanes divides his statement into three main parts: (1) 'and she whom they call Iris,' (2) 'this too is a cloud,' and (3) 'purple, red, and greenish-yellow to behold.' Each element in part (1) is matched by a corresponding element in part (2): she/this, and/too, they call/it is, Iris/cloud. The first line thus divides symmetrically into two parts, with *nephos* (cloud) occupying centre stage between *Irin* and *touto.* The arrangement has the effect of enhancing the contrast created by what his words say: the focus of attention is on *nephos,* in both form and content. Line 2 contributes to that focusing effort by linking up grammatically with *nephos*, the noun taking the infinitive as a limiting accusative: 'a cloud purple, red, and greenish-yellow to behold' (cf. GG, sec. 1534). Each of the three adjectives with its neuter form points back to *nephos* (rather than to the feminine *Irin*). Line 2 as a whole serves to call attention to *nephos* and to specify the features which serve to distinguish it (cf. GG, secs. 1056, 1057). As a consequence, the fragment embodies a three-stage movement from an initial state of awareness to proper identification to proper definition and understanding. Part (1) expresses the conventional view of the rainbow's identity, part (2) identifies its true nature, and part (3) specifies the sort of cloud it is – that is, 'a visibly purple, red, and greenish-yellow cloud.' Rather amazingly, Xenophanes has managed to encapsulate within his brief comment the view of scientific discovery later proposed by Aristotle (*Posterior Analytics* 2.8–10). The testimonia confirm that Xenophanes thought of the clouds as being of different sorts and show how he made use of their different types in order to explain the real nature of various celestial bodies (cf. A1, A32, A33, A38–40, A43, A44). These considerations suggest that Xenophanes' comments on the colours of the rainbow served neither to impugn the credibility of appearances nor to isolate them from the realities, but rather to explain how the apparent qualities of objects can be utilized in order to gain a correct understanding of the marvels of nature.

It is probably significant that Xenophanes concludes his comment by speaking of the rainbow as (νέφος) χλωρὸν ἰδέσθαι. For his audience, the rainbow was obviously a 'marvel' (*thauma*), perhaps the quintessential marvel (Hesiod describes Iris as the daughter of Thaumas at *Theogony* 99). The phrase θαῦμα ἰδέσθαι occurs frequently in Homer, always in line-final position (*Iliad* 5.725; 10.439; 18.83, 377; *Odyssey* 6.306; 7.45; 8.366; 13.108). On two occasions (*Odyssey* 6.306; 13.108) he speaks of a marvellous woven item as 'purple, a marvel to behold.' The term *thauma* refers to objects or persons possessing an extraordinary appearance, usually a god or an object belonging to a god (for instance, the shield of Hephaestus, *Iliad* 18.549). When, therefore, Xenophanes speaks of the rainbow as a νέφος ... χλωρὸν ἰδέσθαι, his audience – raised on the songs of Homer and Hesiod – would hear both what he said and what he did not say the rainbow was.

For a modern audience accustomed to think of rainbows as insubstantial displays of colour caused by the refraction and reflection of light through droplets of water vapour, Xenophanes' mention of colours in fragment 32.2 would naturally suggest a view of the appearances of things as distinct from their real properties. Heard in its original setting, however, fragment 32 would have sounded a different note, challenging the old idea of the rainbow as the goddess 'Iris Thaumantias' by redefining its nature in terms of qualities easily perceived by all. In fragment 32 Xenophanes advocated both a revolutionary view of the nature of the rainbow and a new way of gaining an understanding of nature, an approach that led to results the 'fictions of old' could never achieve.

Fragment 37

[And Xenophanes says:]
... and indeed in certain caves water drips down ...

Herodian 30

COMMENTARY ON FRAGMENT 37

Line 1 The full significance of this odd phrase may well lie beyond re- covery. The explanation most often proposed – that it relates to Xeno- phanes' theory of a constant interchange between earth and water (A32, A33) – in so far as some caves contain stalactite formations (D-K, 137n) – places greatest interpretive weight on just that portion of the text (τεοῖς) which is least secure. But, perhaps for want of a better expla- nation, this water-into-earth account has been generally accepted (see Heitsch, 189–92; Guthrie 1, 388n; KRS, 178; Deichgräber, 16).

It may be useful to note that at least one other Ionian *physiologos* (Anaxagoras), and probably others, expressed an opinion on subter- ranean moisture (D-K 59 A42; Hippolytus *Refutation of All Heresies* 1.8; trans. KRS): 'Rivers owe their origin partly to rain, partly to the waters in the earth (ἐξ ὑδάτων τῶν ἐν τῇ γῇ); for the earth is hollow and in its hollows contains waters (ἔχειν ὕδωρ ἐν τοῖς κοιλώμασιν).' Even if Xeno- phanes did not subscribe to the view (attributed to some Presocratics by Aristotle at *Meteorology* 349bff.) of the rivers of the earth as arising from an underground reservoir, this brief reference to the presence of water in caves might well relate to such a view.

We can say in general that an 'inquiry into the things below the earth' (to use the language of the indictment later drawn up for Socrates) would have been entirely characteristic of an Ionian *physiologos*, and fragment 28 already establishes Xenophanes' interest in the extent of the earth's depths. In A47 Aëtius attributes to Xenophanes the view that the earth below is 'compounded of air and fire'; since fire is elsewhere accounted for by reference to moist vapours (A40), the existence of underground moisture would be implied by the conjunction of these two views. Alternatively, fragment 37 might reflect nothing more than typical Ionian fact-finding, or speculation about unusual conditions which would not be peculiar to the Ionian philosophers (cf. Plato *Phaedo* 109b; Lucretius *On the Nature of Things* 1.348).

Even if we cannot be certain of the precise point of Xenophanes' words here in fragment 37, we may still see in them (as we have seen in fragments 30–32) his evident interest in phenomena and regions long associated with supernatural beings; here in those mysterious underground caverns, fabled entrances to the underworld, the habitat of magical beings (e.g., Calypso at *Odyssey* 1.15) and fearsome powers (cf. *Odyssey* 12.84–85, 93; Hesiod *Theogony* 297, etc.).

CONCLUSION

The fragments relating to Xenophanes' views on nature are philosophical only in that archaic use of the term 'natural philosophy,' that is, (with some qualifications)[1] 'natural science.' Several features of his account of atmospheric phenomena show the influence of his predecessor Anaximenes (see the commentary on fragments 29 and 33 above), and his comments on earth and water (fragments 29, 33) confirm (contra Aristotle) the seriousness of his interest in the Ionian dispute concerning the *archē* or *archai* of things. But the particular objects of his inquiries suggest that he practised Ionian science in order to displace an existing, predominantly religious outlook on the natural world. As Fränkel explained: 'He strips visible celestial phenomena of all divine aspects; he even denies these phenomena their dignity and permanence, as well as their celestial origin, just as, on the other hand, he refuses to recognize all possible comparisons of his God with earthly bodies ... he made the chasm between the here and the beyond unbridgeable' (in Mourelatos 1974, 130). Xenophanes' utilization of Ionian *historiē* for this purpose has given rise to the suspicion that he had little intrinsic interest in scientific explanation, merely using science as a convenient weapon against popular religion (Heidel, 269, 272), or 'for

1 Like the Presocratic philosophers generally, Xenophanes seems not to have either understood or practised 'the experimental method' (see Cornford), but, as Vlastos (1955/70) explained, it is an even more basic failing that their theories were often stated in such general and unquantified terms that neither experimental confirmation nor disconfirmation would have been possible.

theological and moral reform' (Guthrie 1, 383; cf. Burnet, 122). When one adds to this the bizarre character of many of Xenophanes' views about natural phenomena – a new sun every day, suns in various regions of the earth, an 'infinite' number of suns and moons, eclipses that occur when the sun enters uninhabited regions (as though the eclipse were caused by a lack of observers), the moon as condensed cloud – what Guthrie called Xenophanes' 'cosmological aberrations' (1, 395) – it is not obvious that Xenophanes deserves high marks for his 'natural philosophy.'

But both criticisms are unwarranted. Xenophanes' ideas, while certainly original in many respects, were not bizarre. The stranger doctrines credited to him can be shown to be either misunderstandings of what he had in mind or otherwise plausibly connected with observation or with other theories themselves grounded in observation. His understanding of the daily (or monthly) rekindling of various celestial bodies, while incorrect, was at least based on his awareness of other recurring fires in the heavens (lightning, St Elmo's fire, comets, meteors, and so on) and constituted an appropriate extension of a theory to less accessible and less well understood cases. For those who believe that even two suns are one too many, we should remember that the ancients had long believed in at least two sources of heat in the heavens, both the sun and Sirius, the 'Dog Star' (whose very name means 'scorcher'), the cause of the excessive heat of late July and August (our 'dog days of summer'), long linked with the flooding of the Nile, sickness, sexual promiscuity, and other fevers.[2] Like the accounts of the moon's nature,[3] this idea of multiple suns is therefore not without *some* basis in observation. The other 'aberrations' almost certainly involve some degree of misunderstanding, either by insisting that we read *apeiron* as 'infinite' rather than merely as 'indefinitely large' or by overlooking other aspects of Xenophanes' theories which would remove their sense of oddity.[4] It is, moreover, a philosophical error to measure the quality of a scientific theory by reference to a sense of the bizarre –

2 Cf. Archilochus, fragment 61 (Edmonds): 'I hope the Dog-Star (*Seirios*) will wither up many with his keen rays'; see also *Iliad* 22.26–31; Hesiod *Works* 587; *Shield* 153, 397; Alcaeus, fragment 347a (Campbell); and for the widespread belief in these effects, see van der Waerden, 244–46.

3 P.J. Bicknell (1967a) suggests that the idea could have been based on perceptual similarities between the clouds and moon when the latter is still visible during the daytime.

4 For a refutation of the view that Xenophanes' sun ceased to shine whenever it had no one to be useful to (cf. Freeman, 102), see Bicknell, 1967b, 73–77, summarized

from either a historical or contemporary perspective. Nothing would have struck the Ionians as more bizarre than the real nature of the cosmos as we now understand it, and there are no Ionian ideas as bizarre as the paradoxes of modern quantum theory.

There are in fact several indications that Xenophanes' accounts stemmed not from a desire for a convenient weapon with which to attack religious belief, but from a desire for an accurate and comprehensive understanding. Heitsch, for example, has pointed out (170) that Xenophanes' explanations exhibit a principled approach in two distinct respects: his accounts are couched in terms of natural, observable causes; and he adopts as a governing principle that similar effects must be assigned to similar causes (cf. the similar accounts given of various forms of celestial lights and fires in A38–41a, A43–45). To these two guidelines we may add a third: Xenophanes' cosmology fully coheres with his earth science. The earth, identified in fragment 27 as the origin and destination of all processes, provides the two key elements (earth and water) in terms of which all other things must be explained. The earth's surface is also the location of the sea, identified in fragment 30 as the source of all other forms of water and in A46 as the source of clouds. Clouds in turn serve to explain a whole cluster of celestial bodies and changes.[5] Since the sea contains mixtures and is involved in a long-term cycle of destruction and recreation of dry land (A32, A33) it is also a prime embodiment of the two basic elements. The whole complex of explanations displays not only logical consistency but an evident interest in explanatory coherence, an orderliness of theory to parallel that of the cosmos. These qualities of consistency, coherence, and convergence in explanation would be hard to explain on the assumption that Xenophanes pursued *historiē* merely to obtain an expedient weapon to use against the fabrications of poets, seers, or other self-styled experts. They point instead to his having a desire for both a correct and a coherent explanation of all things, one that could account for a wide variety of phenomena without inconsistency, ad hoc adjustment, or reference to occult powers and supernatural beings. It is true that fragment 34.1–2 disavows *knowledge* with regard to 'such things as I say about all things,' and in its line 4 allots only 'opinion to all,' but a proper understanding of those remarks (see the

---

in part 3 following under A41a. For the meaning of *apeiron* see the notes and commentary on fragment 28 above.

5 For a discussion of the systematic character of Xenophanes' cloud theory, see Mourelatos 1989, 280–90).

commentaries on fragments 34 and 35 following) leaves Xenophanes fully committed to the truth of the accounts we have considered here.

Yet in several related respects, Xenophanes' scientific ideas would have been faulted (perhaps were faulted) by his contemporaries and immediate successors. He seems not to have focused on the *periodic* character of many natural changes[6] and fails to utilize the governing cosmic principle of equality and justice widely adopted by the Presocratics.[7] He also fails to think of nature as striving toward what is good or best, and seems not to have distinguished between the levels of excellence or perfection achievable in the sub- and super-lunar regions. Circular motion, for example, the only sort of motion appropriate to the perfect bodies of the heavens (according to *Metaphysics* 1072b), is mentioned only once in all the fragments and testimonia, and there (A41a) only to say that the sun only seems to follow a circular path. Not only do the celestial bodies of Xenophanes' world not go on forever in their courses, but the moon is recreated every month and the sun and stars are quenched and rekindled every day and night (A38, A41). By 5th- and 4th-century standards these would all have to be repudiated as incorrect, even scandalous views.[8] We, however, are free to regard Xenophanes' value-free conception of nature, his rejection of circular heavenly motions, and his assumption of the presence of common causes for earthly and celestial phenomena as just a few of his many progressive ideas.

6 This has, however, been denied by Reiche, 88–110. The only cycles mentioned by Xenophanes or his doxographers were those of successive wet and dry eras (Hippolytus in A33) and the sea-rain-rivers-sea cycle (suggested by fragment 30 and Aëtius in A46). These are mentioned (or at least alluded to) without a suggestion of equal periods of dominance or overarching 'measures' of any sort. In sum, Xenophanes does not appear to have subscribed to a Heraclitean conception of the cosmos as ruled by justice and ordered through perpetual alternation among the opposites. It may have been precisely this difference between the two philosophers that 'earned' Xenophanes his place on the list of all those who proved that 'much learning does not teach understanding' (fragment 40).

7 For a detailed account, see Vlastos 1947/70, 56–91.

8 Cf. Plato's severe punishments for practitioners of Ionian science (*Laws* 10.886ff.). The minimum punishment for espousing the 'dreadful theory' (886) that the heavenly bodies are not gods (or are not inhabited by souls bent on doing only what is best; 899b) would be five years of solitary confinement, with the death penalty for a second offence (909a).

4

On Human Understanding

Fragment 18

[Concerning the true nature of time, both its parts and of how much it is a cause: Xenophanes:]
Indeed not from the beginning did gods intimate[1] all things[2] to
mortals,
but as they search[3] in time[4] they discover[5] better.[6]

Stobaeus 1.8.2

NOTES

1 ὑπέδειξαν (*hupedeixan*) as in Stobaeus *Anthology* 19.41, rather than the
   παρέδειξαν of Stobaeus' text at *Physical Selections* 1.8.2. As Heitsch
   (135) explains, the latter means 'to display side by side, compare,
   indicate' or 'assign,' 'deliver,' and is characteristic of later writers
   (Xenophon, Isocrates, Plato). ὑποδείκνυμι is used by Herodotus (1.32)
   in the sense of 'show,' 'give a glimpse of': 'for there are many to
   whom god has given a glimpse of happiness (ὑποδέξας ὄλβον) and
   then utterly ruined.' The basic meaning of δείκνυμι is 'show,' 'point
   out,' here combined with the prefix ὑπο-, 'under,' indicating showing
   in an 'underhanded,' secret, or indirect manner (LSJ, s.v. ὑπό, F, III),
   hence 'intimate' (cf. also Xenophon *Memorabilia* 4.13).
2 πάντα (*panta*): 'all things' or, perhaps, 'all sorts of things' (cf. LSJ, s.v.
   πᾶς, D, II; Xenophanes' fragment 11.1).
3 ζητοῦντες (*dzētountes*): Taken as a circumstantial participle indicating
   either the condition under which or the means by which discovery
   takes place (cf. Aristophanes *Birds* 1390: σὺ δὲ κλύων εἴσει τάχα – 'but

you will soon know if you listen'), and translated as a finite verb 'as they search' (GG, sec. 1567).

4 χρόνῳ (chronōi): LSJ: 'in process of time' (s.v. χρόνος, 3c), but it is not clear whether it is the searching that involves the passage of time, or the discovering, or whether some time must have passed (since the beginning) before mortals discover by searching. Although Stobaeus assigns a positive causal role to time itself (πόσων εἴη αἴτιος) this is not implied by Xenophanes' language.

5 ἐφευρίσκουσιν (epheuriskousin): In Homer, the verb typically designates a discovery made in a moment of encounter (cf. Odyssey 5.439: a sloping beach; Odyssey 10.452: one's comrades while feasting; Odyssey 24.145: Penelope while weaving; etc.). Heitsch translates: 'vorfinden,' 'antreffen' ('find,' 'hit upon').

6 ἄμεινον (ameinon): The comparative of ἀγαθός, usually understood as 'better than before,' i.e., 'improvement' (in the conditions of life generally). D. Babut (1977) argued that ἄμεινον here in fragment 18 must be given a relative or 'provisional character': we never discover, strictly speaking, that which is good, but only that which is, relatively speaking, better than before. But Xenophanes' earlier emphatic statement of his own worth to the city (fragment 2) makes this an unlikely claim: his 'expertise' is better than (ἄμεινον) the strength of men and horses, and it is a good expertise (τῆς ἀγαθῆς σοφίης) because it (and not athletic prowess) benefits the city. Since the neuter accusative singular of the comparative form of an adjective serves also as the comparative of the adverb (GG, sec. 421), ἄμεινον is ambiguous between 'find a better (thing)' and 'find out better.'

COMMENTARY ON FRAGMENT 18

Xenophanes' comments here on divine revelation and mortal discovery have commonly been read as an early expression – perhaps the very first expression – of a 'faith in human progress' (as usually explained, a conviction that mankind has made and will continue to make improvements in the arts and in the conditions of life across a broad front). Nevertheless, the fragment remains problematic in many respects. Xenophanes did not actually speak of an advance by mankind as a whole, but only of the success open to individual 'seekers' (zētountes); and he spoke only in broad terms of 'discovering better,' making no references to the arts or to social institutions. There is no obvious reason, moreover, why Xenophanes should have embraced so optimistic an outlook, especially at so early a period. The usual supporting arguments for the 'faith in progress' view, the mention of the Lydians' invention of coinage in fragment 4 and Xenophanes' 'admiration' for Thales' eclipse prediction in fragment 19 (as evidence of Xenophanes' awareness of current progress), provide exceedingly slight support. The latter may fairly be regarded as an uncertain third-hand report of Xenophanes' attitude concerning what was almost certainly an inflated and quite possibly wholly fictitious account of Thales' astronomical activities (see the preceding commentary on fragment 19). The former may well have occurred in the context of Xenophanes' *attack* on Lydian values, thus tending to prove just the opposite thesis – that men have a propensity to put the survival of their cities at risk through an incessant pursuit of pleasure (see the preceding commentary on fragment 4).

Given the brevity, ambiguity, and lack of a surrounding context for fragment 18, it is probably impossible to identify any of the large number of alternative possible readings as the message Xenophanes intended to convey. It has been argued, by a kind of interpretation by triangulation, that earlier poets had spoken of the gods as the 'givers of all good things' (e.g., at *Odyssey* 8.325; Hesiod *Theogony* 664, etc.) and of an original 'golden race' or paradise (Hesiod *Works* 109ff.) and that later poets discarded this view, telling instead of mankind's gradual rise from a original, brutish form of life (cf. the 'hymn to man' of Sophocles' *Antigone* 332ff.). Hence, situated in time midway between these two points of view, fragment 18 begins to sound like one of the earliest steps along this path toward the later point of view; for this 'hymn to progress' reading see the accounts by Barnes, Cherniss (1957), Dodds (1973), Edelstein, Fränkel (1925), Guthrie, Havelock, Heidel (1943), Heitsch, Kleingünther, Lumpe, Steinmetz, and Zeller (1920), among others.

But other fragments sit uncomfortably with the idea that Xenophanes had a faith in social and intellectual progress. In fragments 1–3 he complains about socially destructive practices, and in fragment 3 he comments specifically on the wisdom – or the lack of it – embodied in the arts of perfume-making, gold ornamentation, and purple garments. In A1 he alludes to his own experience of the demise of a city, and elsewhere notes the reliance of the populus on misguided poets and self-styled religious experts (cf. fragments 7 [on Pythagoras], 10, 11, 12 [on Hesiod and Homer], and A1 [on Epimenides]). Nowhere in these remarks can one sense the pride in the works of human intelligence that pervades the later hymns to 'fearfully clever man.' The possibility of a Xenophanean 'hymn to progress' cannot, for all this, be completely discounted, but it is clear that optimism on this topic would have been out of character with his generally dour view of the species. (M. O'Brien and Woodbury [1970] have, moreover, recently argued that there is no warrant for dating either the use of the term *thēriōdēs* ('brutish') or interest in a state of 'primeval brutishness' earlier than the middle of the fifth century.)

A convincing account of the meaning of the fragment is made especially difficult by the absence of any information about its original context (a history of human social institutions, a discussion of prospects for scientific knowledge, or comments on the role of the gods in human affairs?), as well as a number of ambiguities in the text. If indeed the gods did not reveal *all* things, are we to imagine that they might have revealed a few? If indeed the gods did not reveal all things *at the outset*, are we to understand that they might have revealed some things later on? Are we to infer from Xenophanes' words that mortals will in time discover something that is better (than what existed up until then), or will continue to discover better and better things (in the future) or discover something better than what the gods were assumed to have revealed to them, or discover in a better way, or do better at discovering? Finally, are we to understand Xenophanes to be proposing 'search' or 'inquiry' as a means by which mortals discover *on their own*, or proposing instead that human inquiry works in tandem with divine agency (cf. the reference to the role played by the gods in fragments 36 and 38), so that what mankind achieves by search is just what the gods provide? Virtually all of these interpretive options are represented in the scholarly literature on fragment 18 (for representative examples, see the studies by Barnes, Untersteiner (1956), Gomperz, Kleingünther, Loenen, Lumpe, Shorey, and Verdenius (1955).

One plausible (though hardly definitive) version of Xenophanes' intended message would restrict its intended scope to matters of scientific thinking or inquiry, thus avoiding the complication that Xenophanes did not appear to be at all sanguine about the prospects for continuing *social or cultural* progress. Here at least a positive outlook would square with Xenophanes' own willingness to offer novel accounts of various natural phenomena (fragments 27–32) and to learn first-hand about distant lands and peoples (cf. A1, 18, and A33, on his fossil finds, and fragment 16 and A13, on differing conceptions of the gods). It is not clear, however, why Xenophanes would have wished to reject the idea of divine revelations to mortals while simultaneously embracing a similarly speculative thesis of perpetual scientific progress.

I believe that a more compelling version of the 'scientific' reading of fragment 18 would regard the 'discover better' of 18.2 not as a reference to future scientific progress but as a reference to a superior approach to discovery – superior, in other words, to any previous or current alternative. In fragment 3 Xenophanes speaks of his own 'expertise' as better (*ameinōn*) in just this sense: superior to the strength of men and horses so lavishly (and thoughtlessly) honoured by his fellow citizens. A parallel claim that his way of searching into truth would lead in time to the 'discovery of something better' or constitute a 'better way of discovering' is what one would expect from a philosopher prone to remind his fellow citizens of the excellence of his philosophical insights. Identifying one approach or plan of action as 'better than' another previously or currently available would be an entirely natural use of the adjective (as the Greeks before Troy often proposed 'plans' or 'counsel' better than – *ameinon* – the one currently in effect: *Iliad* 7.358; 9.104, 423; 14.107; 15.508; etc.).

To get a sense of the contrast between the two approaches, and of why Xenophanes might have held the second to have been superior to the first, we need to consider briefly the nature of the divine *hupodeixis* to mortals rejected in line 1. As noted earlier, the Greek verb ὑποδείκνυμι meant not 'endow' or 'give,' but rather 'reveal' or 'show,' especially 'show in a partial, indirect or secretive manner' (cf. the scholium on Lycophron, 344: 'Sinon having secretly shown [ὑποδείξας] a signal light to the Hellenes,' etc.). What Xenophanes rejects is not divine aid to mortals in all its various forms, but rather divine *communication* with them, especially through the medium of signals or cryptic signs. He does not, moreover, rule this out only for some original period in the past (as is often supposed: 'at the outset' or 'in the beginning') but rather 'from the very beginning forward' (see LSJ, s.v. ἀπό, II, 'from,' 'after'), as if to rule out the possibility that his comment might be read as signalling a recent change in the divine disposition toward mortals. The idea that the gods communicated with mortals through a variety of signs or signals was virtually ubiquitous in antiquity, as is clear from Greek authors from Homer (e.g., *Iliad* 13.243–45; *Odyssey* 3.174–75), Hesiod (*Works* 448–51, 825–28), the Homeric Hymns (*to Selene* 13; *the Dioscuri* 14–16; *Hermes* 525ff., etc.), and Pindar (fragments 116, 131; *Paean* 9) to Herodotus (1.209; 7.37), Thucydides (7.50), and Xenophon (*Memorabilia* 4.13). In each of these passages, the operative verb for divine communication with mortals is either δείκνυμι or one of its compounds (e.g., with ὑπο- or προ-). Fragment 18, therefore, specifically contrasts the idea that from the outset gods secretly communicated or 'intimated' all sorts of things to mortals with (what is apparently) Xenophanes' own view that mortals in time 'find out better' by seeking.

There are clear and compelling Xenophanean grounds for such a thesis. He offers thoroughly natural explanations for various phenomena long supposed to be deities themselves (see the preceding commentaries on fragments 27–33) and he was reported to have explained a whole family of traditional omens or portents as in reality only the ignition and quenching of burning clouds in the heavens (cf. A39, A41, A41a, A43, A44, and the report on *mantikē* in A52). Nowhere does the contrast with the older outlook emerge more clearly than in his comment on 'she whom they call Iris' (fragment 32), a couplet contrasting the conventional (theistic) view of a natural marvel (the paradigmatic 'messenger' phenomenon – cf. *Iliad* 11.28; 17.548) with Xenophanes' view of how its real nature is to be discovered and defined ('this also is by nature a cloud ... to be looked at').

If, as I believe, the contrast embedded in fragment 18 lay not between two rival views of the development of human civilization but rather between two competing conceptions of how mortals ought to attempt to understand the significance of the marvels of nature (either as divine intimations to mortals or – Xenophanes' own approach – as physical realities to be described and understood in terms of observable properties and familiar natural forces), then we can employ what is known about Xenophanes' own inquiries into natural phenomena in order to shed light on the meaning of the 'finding out better' in line 2.

Among early writers ζητέω bears the rather prosaic meaning of 'searching about for' (as, for example, a lost possession or a particular location – cf. *Iliad* 14.258; Hesiod *Works* 400), and is often coupled with forms of ἐφευρίσκω to describe a process of searching about ('throughout the land,' 'throughout the house') in search of persons or things in hopes of coming upon them (*Iliad* 4.88; 5.168; 13.760; etc.). Xenophanes' audience would therefore have heard 'by searching they find out better' and understood him to be recommending not simply 'inquiry' (i.e., 'armchair reflection'), but inquiry involving travel to different locations and discovery through encountering new persons, places, and things. Inquiry in the form of travel to different parts of the world for the purpose of direct observation and record making is of course just the *historiē* first practised by the Milesian philosopher-scientists (with some degree of legendary fame, Thales, but more assuredly by Anaximander; cf. D-K 12 A1, A3), and by the Ionian geographer Hecataeus and his successor, the historian Herodotus.

That Xenophanes would have counted himself among the practitioners of *historiē* seems likely in light of his interest in differing conceptions of the divine among different peoples (cf. fragment 16, A13), and in natural phenomena in distant locations (fragments 37, 21a, A41, A41a, A48), and his evident use of the information gained from observation as a basis for his theories: that all things that come into being and grow are earth and water (fragments 29, 33), that various phenomena in the heavens can be reduced to the workings of clouds (A32–45), that all the phenomena of the heavens can be traced back to the sea (fragment 30, A46), and that the whole of nature is perpetually destroyed and regenerated (A32, A33).

For this last theory we are fortunate to have the remarkably detailed testimonium from Hippolytus reporting Xenophanes' citation of the presence far inland of various forms of marine life as evidence in support of a theory of cyclical cosmic destruction and regeneration. Twice in one sentence Hippolytus speaks of what 'is found' or 'was found,' in the latter case reporting that Xenophanes 'says that in quarries in Syracuse imprints of a fish and seals were found (λέγει εὑρῆσθαι).' We need not suppose that Xenophanes himself had used the verb *heuriskō* in describing these fossil-finds in order to see in Hippolytus' report a clear example of Xenophanean search and discovery, of the travel and observation that could lead to discovery of the larger forces at work in nature. Xenophanes' success as an inquirer, I would argue, is what motivated his claim that χρόνῳ ζητοῦντες ἐφευρίσκουσιν ἄμεινον. Fragment 18, therefore, may not have been the exercise in a priori sociology (of either the 5th-century BC or the 19th-century variety) it has often been taken for, but rather the rejection of an older, inadequate approach to the understanding of natural marvels through myth, legend, or simple superstition – and a call, in so many words, to natural science (for further discussion see Lesher, 1991).

Fragment 34

[Xenophanes, according to those who interpret him differently, when he says:]
... and of course[1] the clear and certain truth[2] no man has seen[3]
nor will there be anyone who knows about the gods and what I
                                        say about all things.
For even if, in the best case, one happened to speak[4] just of what
                                        has been brought to pass,[5]
still he himself would not know. But opinion[6] is allotted[7] to all.[8]

[appears not to abolish all apprehension, but that which is scientific and infallible ...]

Sextus Empiricus 7.49.110

NOTES

1 μὲν οὖν (*men oun*): The message of fragment 34 is framed within a contrast between lines 1 and 4: no knowledge of τὸ σαφές ... but there is δόκος. Denniston (473) cites this passage as an example of οὖν emphasizing a prospective μέν (cf. LSJ, s.v. μέν, II, 2). A partial complementary statement of the same contrast is provided by fragment 35: 'of course these are to be accepted as like the realities ...'

2 τὸ σαφές (*to saphes*): Variously translated as 'the truth' (KRS), 'the certain truth' (Guthrie), 'the clear truth' (Barnes), 'the distinct truth' (Nahm), 'the exact truth' ('das Genaue': D-K, Fränkel, Heitsch). While each of these is an appropriate choice, I would argue that 'the certain truth' or 'the clear and certain truth' is the best choice here in fragment 34. Heitsch, for example, concludes his discussion by citing passages he regards as establishing that σάφα knowing (the form σαφές does not occur in Homer) is a matter of knowing the *precise facts* or the *exact truth* (e.g., *Odyssey* 3.89: 'But for Odysseus the son of Cronos has made even his death to be beyond learning [ἀπευθέα], for no man can say σάφα where he has died'). But here, either 'not knowing exactly' or 'not knowing for certain' would fit the context, and other passages Heitsch cites cannot easily be construed as a matter of precision or exactitude (e.g., *Iliad* 5.183: 'I do not know σάφα if he is a god'; *Iliad* 2.252: 'nor do we know σάφα how these will turn out, whether for good or for ill'). Here, as occasionally elsewhere in Homer (*Iliad* 2.192: 'the mind of Atreus'; *Iliad* 7.226: 'face to face what our leaders are like'; *Iliad* 15.632 'how to fight a wild beast'; etc.), not knowing σάφα is lacking sure or reliable information or understanding, resulting from a lack of direct access, exposure, or experience. It would be more accurate, therefore, to say that Homer can use σάφα οἶδε to mean *either* 'he knows exactly, precisely' *or* 'he knows clearly, hence reliably that,' and this second use is probably closer to the original meaning of σαφές (cf. Chantraine, s.v. σάφα, 991). It is probably in this second sense that Anchises is οὐ σάφα εἰδώς when he lies with Aphrodite (*Hymn to Aphrodite* 167): not clearly realizing the consequence of sleeping with a goddess. Quite frequently in Herodotus σαφές or σαφέως knowing is a 'reliable, certain knowledge' based upon direct observation or testimony: 'wishing to σαφές τι εἰδέναι ... I took ship to Tyre in Phoenicia where I heard there was a temple

... There I saw it ... therefore what I have discovered plainly shows (τὰ ἰστορημένα δηλοῖ σαφέως; 2.44); 'Because you have now learned σαφέως of our thoughts and are sure we will never betray Hellas ...' (9.7); cf. 3.122; 7.228; (The similarity in outlook of fragment 34 with Herodotus' expressions of esteem for direct, first-hand observation was noted by Fränkel 1974, 125.) The element of direct awareness is implied in Alcmaeon's contrast (fragment 1) between god who has σαφήνεια and mere mortals who 'infer from signs' (τεκμαίρεσθαι), and a clear, unmistakable signal (σαφές ... τέκμαρ, Nemean 11.43–47) is what Pindar laments that men never receive from the gods (cf. Euripides Hippolytus 925–26: τεκμήριον σαφές). A connection between a σαφές account and the availability of eyewitnesses is evident also in Thucydides (e.g., at 1.22.4). The narrow limits of human experience are the subjects of at least two other fragments (see the commentaries on fragments 36 and 38 following). The σαφήνεια relevant to fragment 34 is therefore a direct, clear, hence reliable, awareness of things and τὸ σαφὲς οὔτις ἀνὴρ ἴδεν means 'the clear and certain truth (about the gods and such as I say about all things) no man has seen.'

Although he does not use the term σαφές (or σάφα, σαφέως, etc.), Parmenides' account of truth attempts to provide an answer to Xenophanes' pessimism concerning σαφήνεια (see the conclusion of this chapter). Like Xenophanes, Socrates appears to have allowed for *some* knowledge, but believed that σαφήνεια about the most basic truths exceeded human capacities (*Phaedo* 69d, 85c; for a discussion of this aspect of Socratic 'scepticism' see Lesher 1987, 275–88). Aristotle's jibe at Xenophanes, 'he made nothing clear' (A30, *Metaphysics* 986b: οὐδὲν διεσαφήνισεν) may be a play on Xenophanes' use of σαφές here in fragment 34, but it is also an important term for Aristotle in so far as the course of development for all knowledge begins from things 'clearer (σαφέστερον) to us' – i.e., apparent through sense perception – and ends in things 'clearer in themselves' – i.e., the highest principles of explanation (cf. *Physics* 184a; *On the Soul* 413a). Compare, at a far greater remove, Descartes' insistence in the *Meditations* that only what is seen 'clearly and distinctly' to be true has the power to convince him completely.

3 ἴδεν (*iden*): Recent editors have accepted Snell's (1924) recommendation of Sextus' ἴδεν over the γένετ' of Plutarch's text (for reasons having to do with a genuine archaic style of exposition). Fränkel (in Mourelatos 1974) argued that Xenophanes' use of the perceptual verb ἰδεῖν – 'to see' in line 1 would require that we understand εἰδώς in line 2 not generally as 'knowing,' but in its original, literal sense of 'having seen.' As a consequence, Fränkel regarded fragment 34

as concerned not with all knowledge (as the sceptics believed) but 'only a knowing rooted in vision, or at least in experience' (123). But this semantic thesis not only drastically reduces the impact of Xenophanes' argument (see the commentary following), it also does not reflect the fact that already in Homer ἰδεῖν can mean something other than 'seeing with one's eyes' (cf. LSJ, s.v. εἴδω, I, 3; e.g., *Odyssey* 19.567: 'seeing a dream' – ὄνειρον ἴδηται – or *Iliad* 21.61: 'seeing in one's mind' – ἰδέσθαι ἐν φρεσίν). Thus, even if ἴδεν meant 'saw' or 'has seen' and εἰδώς meant 'having seen,' there is no reason to suppose that such 'seeing' must have been a form of *sense* perception. For further discussion of Fränkel's interpretation see Heitsch 1983, 174, and 1966, 108–16; Barnes 1, 138; and the commentary following.

4 τὰ μάλιστα τύχοι ... εἰπών (*ta malista tuchoi ... eipōn*): In support of the thesis of line 1, Xenophanes offers a 'thought experiment' (see the conclusion of chapter 1) in the form of a 'best case scenario': even if one happened to speak the truth, still one would not know. τὰ μάλιστα has been understood as an adverb modifying τύχοι (Fränkel: 'he hits the mark most closely, he hits it better than others'; cf. D-K: 'höchsten Maße gelänge'; Wright: 'by the greatest chance to speak the truth'), but also independently as a statement of the best thing that could happen: 'even if, at best, one were to succeed' (Verdenius 1953). The 'best case' use of τὰ μάλιστα (cf. LSJ, s.v. μάλα, III, 2) matches the logic of the argument: one might speak the truth, without knowing it to be true in a clear and certain way. τυγχάνω when conjoined with the participle conveys a suggestion of coincidence (LSJ, s.v. τυγχάνω II; Heitsch, 181), hence 'say just what is brought to pass,' 'happen to describe exactly what has occurred.'

5 τετελεσμένον εἰπών (*tetelesmenon eipōn*): Variously translated as 'saying something that is the case' (Barnes), 'saying the complete truth' (KRS), 'saying what is true' (Guthrie), 'declaring what is actually present' (Fränkel: 'das wirklich Vorhandene auszusprechen'), 'declaring an accomplished thing' (D-K: 'ein Vollendetes auszusprechen'), etc. The term τετελεσμένος occurs often in Homer and means 'what has been brought to completion or fulfilment' (lit. 'brought to a τέλος,' from τελέω). τετελεσμένον εἰπών is, accordingly, describing, predicting, or speaking in some way about that which has been brought to pass.

Parmenides also refers to what exists as τετελεσμένον (fragment 8.42), with the same meaning in mind, but in connection with a different point of view. On his view, what exists is always fully completed, perfected, actualized, etc.' since generation and destruction have been repudiated, 'driven far away' (fragment 8.27–28).

6 δόκος (dokos): opinion, conjecture, supposition; cf. fragment 14: 'men suppose' (οἱ βροτοὶ δοκέουσι); fragment 35: 'these must be accepted' (ταῦτα δεδοξάσθω). In light of the inferior status of mortal δόξα in Parmenides' account (and subsequently in Plato's) one might imagine that δόκος here in Xenophanes must have contained an implicit element of error or falsity. But this does not appear to be the case. Fragment 35 recommends that 'these' be accepted in so far as they are 'like the realities' without an implication of inferiority in *truthfulness* (see the commentary on fragment 35 following). δόκος, therefore, like δοκέω, involves what one 'takes' to be the case, what one 'opines' (cf. Callimachus, fragment 224 [Pfeiffer]: τῷ γ᾽ ἐμῷ δόκῳ – 'at least in my opinion'), without an inherent suggestion that what one opines is false.

7 τέτυκται (tetuktai): perfect passive of τεύχω – 'make' or 'fashion,' and in the passive 'made ready,' 'brought about,' 'happen,' often used in Homer in speaking of what Zeus or other gods have fashioned for mortals (*Iliad* 4.84; 10.6; etc.), hence also 'appointed,' 'allotted,' etc. In light of references elsewhere to what 'they' or 'god' made (ἔφυσε) or 'made evident' (πεφήνασι) to mortals (fragments 36, 38), it is reasonable to take Xenophanes to be saying here that δόκος is the state of awareness men possess in virtue of their existence as mortal beings (cf. *Odyssey* 18.130–37; Archilochus, fragment 70, etc.; and the commentary on fragment 38 following). τετύκται echoes the τύχοι of line 3 (cf. LSJ, s.v. τεύχω), as if to say 'one might *happen* to speak the truth, but opinion is what *happens* for all.'

8 ἐπὶ πᾶσι (epi pasi): either as the masculine 'to all men' or the neuter 'to all things.' Since δόκος is said to be 'fashioned' or 'allotted' (suggesting 'by god' or 'by the gods') and Xenophanes elsewhere discusses what the gods have done for mortals (θνητοῖσι), 'to all men' would be a natural reading (Burnet, 121n; cf. Dodds' interpretation, 'though we can all have our opinions,' 1951, 181). Nevertheless the πᾶσι of line 4 echoes the πάντων of line 2 and can be read as 'to all things' (Heitsch, 183; Fränkel 1974, 128). Since Xenophanes has been concerned from the outset to deny the possibility of an exceptional individual knower (cf. οὔτις ἀνήρ, οὐδέ τις, εἰ ... τύχοι, αὐτός), 'to all men' would be the most consistent conclusion for him to draw.

COMMENTARY ON FRAGMENT 34

Xenophanes' fragment 34, like Heraclitus' fragment 1 and Parmenides' fragment 7, is something of a 'master fragment' (I owe the expression to M.M. Mackenzie): while it discusses human knowledge generally it also makes reference to the philosopher's other teachings (here: ἄσσα λέγω περὶ πάντων) and provides guidance on how these must be regarded in order to achieve whatever insight is available to 'mortal men.' It is clear therefore that fragment 34 looks back upon the results of Xenophanes' inquiries and reflection and assumes a body of teaching of some magnitude. While we can only speculate about the actual course of Xenophanes' personal philosophical development (see for example Gigon, 154–59; discussed by Lumpe, 21–22), it is impossible to wrestle with so dense a pronouncement as fragment 34 and not feel that one is in contact with a mature philosophical intelligence.

In spite of repeated efforts to do justice to the details of terminology and contemporaneous usage, the social and literary context, and the internal structure of Xenophanes' argument there is as yet no 'received' or 'standard' view of fragment 34. Perhaps the best known and most frequently discussed interpretation, Fränkel's account of fragment 34 as the avowal of a 'robust empiricism,' is almost certainly not correct as it stands (see note 3 above and section 2 following), and many other existing accounts have both virtues and limitations. The most promising accounts, in my opinion, see fragment 34 in the light of a traditional 'poetic pessimism' voiced frequently in epic and archaic Greek poetry, place a significant weight on the sharply limited direct experience available to 'mortal men' over the course of their lifetimes (in contrast to the *noos* possessed by the divine), and connect these traditional ideas with the special sort of inquiry Xenophanes and his fellow Ionian philosophers practised, perhaps even invented. Interpretations including some of these elements have been offered in recent years by Barnes (1, 138–47) and Heitsch (173–84), but disagreement remains concerning which unstated but necessary background assumptions about the nature, conditions, or distinguishing marks of knowledge should be ascribed to Xenophanes. The relevance of other Fragments (especially fragments 18, 35, 36, and 38) also remains a matter of debate. *To saphes* about fragment 34, in short, no one has yet seen.

The existing accounts can be summarized under six main headings: Xenophanes as (1) Sceptic, (2) Empiricist, (3) Rationalist, (4) Fallibilist, (5) Critical Philosopher, and (6) Natural Epistemologist. Before defending what I regard as the most plausible interpretation (a variant of 6, just mentioned), I offer a summary of each of these approaches (but not an exhaustive survey; see further Lumpe, 31–36; Untersteiner, ccxiii–ccxxxvi; Steinmetz, 31–40; Schwabl, 201–8; and Wiesner 1972, 10–14).

1 *Xenophanes as Sceptic*

Several ancient authorities tell us that Xenophanes either embraced a total scepticism concerning human knowledge (Sotion as reported in A1, 20, Cicero in A25, Pseudo-Plutarch in A32, Hippolytus in A33, and Sextus Empiricus in *Against the Professors* 7.49), occasionally succumbed to such a view (Pseudo-Galen and Timon in A35), or else adopted a modified but still universal sceptical doctrine (Sextus at 7.110). It is not difficult to understand how a number of Xenophanes' remarks could acquire a sceptical cast when seen in the light of later sceptical debates. Like the counterposing sceptical tropes, fragments 15 and 16 would serve to undermine confident belief by pointing out inconsistencies among different groups of believers; fragments 32 and 38 would serve to undermine complete confidence in the testimony of the senses (as would the view about the misleading appearance of the sun's path attributed to Xenophanes in A41a); in attacking the leading poets and religious figures of the time, fragments 10–12 appear to be rejecting the idea of an authoritative opinion; in speaking of only 'happening to speak the truth,' fragment 34.3 seems to be pointing up the need for a criterion of truth that would enable us to tell when we had done so; and in attributing *dokos* to all, fragment 34.4 seems to be consigning human thought either to sheer deception or, at best, sheer guesswork. In such a setting, οὔτις ἀνὴρ ἴδεν τὸ σαφές would sound very much like the universal, abject scepticism of a later period.

Yet neither Diogenes Laertius (A1, 20: 'Sotion ... is misled') nor Sextus (in 7.110) found this interpretation compelling, and it has found few adherents since. Later sceptics aimed for indifference and a suspension of judgment as the best route to human happiness; Xenophanes was anything but indifferent about the true nature of the gods or the proper measures of moral and civic excellence, and his own theological tenets were affirmed without reservations. In order to identify Xenophanes as even the 'probabilistic sceptic' Sextus suggested he might have been, we must overlook other incongruities: neither the precise phrasing of fragment 34 nor the discussions of Xenophanes' contemporaries suggest that the issue was quite as universal as Sextus makes it out to be. Fragment 34.2 speaks of the scope of the knowledge denied as *to saphes* concerning both 'the gods and such as I say about all things' (not simply 'all things'); the focus of 6th-century comments on human knowledge was not on what men could know *simpliciter* but rather on what they could know of the gods and the world at large beyond the narrow circle of their own adventitious experience (see the commentary on fragment 38 following). Sextus concedes as much in his paraphrase by recognizing that Xenophanes' thesis may have been aimed at inquiries into 'non-evident' matters (D-K, 137n). Xenophanes was in all probability not the first sceptical sage, nor was fragment 34 a discourse on the conditions of knowledge per se.

2 Xenophanes as Empiricist

It seemed highly improbable to Fränkel that Xenophanes the 'investigator and portrayer of reality who took delight in the gathering and contemplation of facts' could also have been a 'tired doubter or a deft dialectician.' Far more credible would be a Xenophanean theory of knowledge that fully respected the information about the world gained through perception; that is, an empiricist theory. Fränkel found evidence of such an outlook in early poetic lamentations on the narrow limits of human knowledge and within the key epistemic terms present in fragment 34. Not surprisingly, Fränkel's detailed study has gained wide acceptance (see, for example, its prominent role in the accounts by Guthrie, Rivier, Snell, Untersteiner, and von Fritz 1945/74).

Nevertheless, there are serious difficulties in the empiricist view as Fränkel proposed it. The semantic thesis concerning *idein* and *eidenai* exaggerated the perceptual orientation of these two terms (see note 3 above). Moreover, in narrowing the scope of the meaning of these key terms, Fränkel's interpretation severely weakened the force of Xenophanes' claim; fragment 34 now asserted only that a direct, perceptual knowledge of the certain truth about such non-evident matters as the nature of the gods was impossible for men. So modest a proposal would hardly require argument; nor could it serve as sufficient preparation for the very strong conclusion regarding *dokos* affirmed in line 4.

Elsewhere Fränkel presented his thesis in a more promising, less semantic form: Xenophanes believed that only what can be directly perceived could *qualify as* or *be rightly regarded as* certain knowledge (1974, 127), and also that whatever 'appears' or 'comes into mortal view' is something that can be reliably known (1974, 128). Here 'seeing' and 'perception' are not regarded as part of the very meaning of 'know' or 'certain,' but instead as the only avenues open to mortals for gaining knowledge (that is, 'knowledge,' broadly construed). Sense perception, in short, is being urged by Xenophanes as both necessary and sufficient for reliable knowledge. But even here Fränkel's thesis is still too strong; Xenophanes speaks on occasion as though sense perception were not completely reliable for men: misleading appearances, mistaken identification, even misinterpretation of what is perceived are not altogether unknown (see the commentary on fragment 36 following). The sufficiency portion of this non-semantic version of Fränkel's interpretation would therefore still be untenable.

3 Xenophanes as Rationalist

Among ancient authorities only Aristocles and Aëtius (in A49) said that Xenophanes harboured 'rationalist' sentiments (in the narrower 'epistemological' sense of 'rationalist,' as opposed to an empiricist account of knowledge): 'attacking perceptions and impressions and trusting only in reason.' Among modern commentators, this idea has been adopted by Gigon (19) who suspected that Xenophanes had been influenced by the Pythagoreans to regard cosmological theory as conjecture but theology as the certain truth, by Deichgräber (29–31), and recently by A. Finkelberg. The 'rationalist' proponents sense in Xenophanes' theological comments sufficient evidence of a sensitivity to conceptual truths or relationships to justify attributing to him some sense of a distinction between apodeictic and contingent truths. On this view, fragment 34 would be understood to be concerned simply with conventional religious conceptions and physical inquiries, directing its verdict of *dokos* just toward these two areas where uncertain results are only to be expected.

This understanding of *theōn* in line 2 (= 'their gods,' or 'the gods of conventional religious belief') must however be regarded, to use KRS' terms, as 'most unlikely' (180). Not only does Xenophanes show some indifference on the question of the number of *his* gods (fragment 36, 'they'; fragment 38, 'god'; fragment 23, 'one god greatest among gods'), but when he voices a fervent call for homage and regard to the divine (fragment 1), his own reference to the gods is in the plural (θεῶν δὲ προμηθείην). Here in fragment 34, therefore, it is extremely difficult to take *theōn* as referring only to *their* gods. Furthermore, while it is easy to view *later* explications of Xenophanes' theology (for instance, the MXG account) as highly apodeictic in character, it is, I think, impossible to find evidence of a deductivist approach within the statements by Xenophanes himself; on the contrary, in his theological pronouncements, Xenophanes is all assertion and no proof (see the conclusion of chapter 2, above). Xenophanes displayed his capacity for logical exposition when he argued in support of his claim to civic importance superior to that of the victorious athlete (fragment 2), but, significantly, the logical connectives he used there (γάρ ... τοὔνεκεν) are completely absent from the theological fragments. In general, the fragments show much more regard for information gained from sense perception than any self-respecting epistemological rationalist would allow (cf. ὁρᾶται in fragment 28, ἰδέσθαι in fragment 32, εἰσοράασθαι in fragment 36). There are, therefore, difficulties in both elements in the rationalist view: Xenophanes does not show sufficient (that is, *systematic*) contempt for information gained through the senses, nor do his theological remarks have so clear a deductive structure that we could comfortably ascribe to him a sense of special character of apodeictic truth. It would consequently be unwarranted to read fragment 34 as a repudiation only of knowledge within those areas where apodeictic certainty would be unattainable.

4 Xenophanes as Fallibilist

According to another commonly adopted interpretation, Xenophanes regarded his own inquiries as well as those undertaken by others as capable of modest, fallible results; men may gain a partial insight into the truth, or adopt what is probably the truth, but never enjoy an infallible grasp of the whole truth – that is reserved for the divine (accounts of this sort have been given by Diels, Dodds, Guthrie, Jaeger, KRS, Popper, Steinmetz, and Zeller). Xenophanes is thought to have arrived at this conclusion not through abstract reflection on the nature of knowledge but rather through his own personal experience as an inquirer (Zeller) or, alternatively, through a confrontation with the superior power and wisdom of the divine (Steinmetz), or under the influence of a traditional poetic contrast between divine wisdom and human ignorance (Guthrie, KRS). The 'fallibilist' view seems plausible enough (especially when compared with its sceptical, empiricist, and rationalist rivals), but it does not supply a clear and satisfactory explanation of the *argument* Xenophanes actually presents. For example, while a contextual contrast of divine and mortal awareness seems secure (cf. Arius Didymus in A24 and Varro in Augustine *City of God* 7.17: 'hominis est enim haec opinari, Dei scire'), it is not obvious how or where the ideas of fallibility and a perpetual possibility of error are to be found in fragment 34. 'Fallible,' 'probable,' 'possibility of error' go well beyond anything found within Xenophanes' text. (Popper's view of fragment 34 as an anticipation of his own theory of knowledge as proceeding from 'conjectures and refutations' rests on several dubious interpretations: of *dedoxasthō* in fragment 35 as 'we conjecture,' of *tetelesmenon* as 'the final truth,' and of *dokos* as 'web of guesses'; see further Lesher 1978.) The argument of lines 3 and 4 (εἰ γάρ . . . οὐκ οἶδε) is devoid of any suggestion of fallibilism: 'even if he were to happen to speak the truth' and 'still he would not know,' just at the point when one would have expected 'still for all that he could be mistaken' or 'still he is not infallibly correct.' If Xenophanes' conclusion really had resulted from a deep conviction of human fallibility (or corrigibility), one would expect to see *some* suggestion of this sentiment here in the heart of his argument. But there is none. It is hardly surprising that other accounts have sought to delve more deeply into Xenophanes' argument in order to identify the single condition or set of conditions which might explain why one would not know even if he were to speak the truth.

5 Xenophanes as Critical Philosopher

Three studies of fragment 34 explain Xenophanes' pessimism as a consequence of his recognition of 'the critical problem,' that is, that the human mind must always be separated to some extent from things as they are in themselves. For Untersteiner (ccxiv–ccxix) and Heitsch (1966, 222ff.) the fatal schism lies within language as a medium capable of both representing and misrepresenting the truth. After Hesiod (in *Theogony* 27) succeeded in articulating the distinction between truths and falsehoods that merely resemble the truth, it could no longer be assumed that language could be relied upon as a means for achieving knowledge (hence even if one spoke the truth, one would still not have reliable knowledge). Similarly, Lumpe found sufficient reason to attribute to Xenophanes a Kantian 'critical realism,' that is, the view that a genuine knowledge of the realities in themselves was not possible for men; what men may know are 'things as they appear' (fragment 36), which may or may not turn out to be 'like the realities themselves' (ἐοικότα τοῖς ἐτύμοισι, fragment 35). Hence men can never know *to saphes* – 'the exact truth' about the realities themselves. Yet the correspondence between Hesiod's ἐτύμοισιν ὁμοῖα and Xenophanes' ἐοικότα τοῖς ἐτύμοισι is only partial; Hesiod refers to 'falsehoods which appear like truths,' while Xenophanes (I would argue) had in mind *truths* which ought to be believed since they are 'like the realities' (see the commentary on fragment 35 following). A Kantian distinction between appearances and things in themselves would, moreover, require us to assign a 'subjectivist' meaning to *phainesthai* and a super-phenomenal meaning to *etumos* that are hard to imagine before the time of Descartes' *Meditations* and Locke's *Essay*. The 'critical problem' of escaping from the world of the mind's own contents to knowing what things are like independently of how they may appear to us is almost certainly not the crux of fragment 34.

6 Xenophanes as Natural Epistemologist

Finally, two recent discussions of fragment 34 locate the problem at the heart of Xenophanes' teaching, not within the veil of appearance or language that separates knowing minds from the external world, but rather in the sizeable distance between the conditions in nature which causally determine human beliefs and the natural states of affairs which render those beliefs either true or false. Barnes, for example, sees fragment 34 as a reminder of how often our beliefs are generated by extraneous or irrelevant causal circumstances. What men believe (for instance, about the sweetness of figs or the nature of the gods) is all too often only a consequence of where they have happened to have lived and what little they may have seen, heard, tasted, and so on. But if my belief that p has no causal nexus with the facts of the matter (that is, if *my* believing that p is not tied through some causal chain to the state of affairs which renders my belief true), then my belief does not qualify as knowledge (1, 140–43). Fragment 34, therefore, implicitly asserts that 'men's beliefs do not amount to knowledge because they have unsatisfactory causes' (1, 143). Heitsch's account of fragment 34 focuses on the natural limitations imposed on human knowledge by the small circle of human experience: men are fated to encounter only a small portion of the natural world during the course of their brief lifetimes; lacking as they do a reliable means for telling when they have really spoken the truth, men must rest content with unconfirmable inferences beyond what is directly observed, inferences which must remain only *dokos* or conjecture. I am inclined to believe that a 'naturalist' interpretation along the lines proposed by Heitsch is probably the best approach to take to fragment 34. Contrary to Barnes' proposal, Xenophanes in fragment 38 seems to complain that our beliefs are too determined by external circumstances rather than that they are causally isolated from them (see the commentary on fragment 38 following).

Line 1 Xenophanes' assertion has sometimes been thought to require some qualification: 'no man' that is other than Xenophanes himself. The idea is not without foundation: Xenophanes' statement in fragment 14 about what 'mortals believe' about their gods cannot be understood as including himself; fragments 2, 3, and 8 convey an impression of Xenophanes the individualist, critic of the beliefs and values of the common run of man; and the fervour of his attacks on mistaken conceptions of the gods would be hard to understand if he regarded his own theological credo as itself mere conjecture. Yet I suspect that Xenophanes intended to subject himself and his accounts to the same constraints and restrictions he found imposed on others, for a variety of reasons. As Heitsch (175) noted, Xenophanes' statement is as much a promise (cf. *Odyssey* 16.437) as it is a description, a promise he would have been in no position whatever to make if he had known that one such knowing man already existed. What fragment 34 denies to men is not so much the truth (that, as line 3 concedes, they might succeed in saying), and not even a passionate conviction that they have said the truth, but rather *saphēneia*, a clear and therefore reliable vision of the truth. To lack *saphēneia* is therefore not to feel uncertain or doubtful, but rather not to have achieved incorrigible or unerring belief. That a philosopher could have strongly affirmed and believed a whole set of propositions about goodness, the gods, the soul, and the nature of wisdom itself without claiming either to know or to have achieved *saphēneia* is obvious from the portrait Plato provides of Socrates (e.g., *Gorgias* 509; *Phaedo* 69d; and elsewhere). Furthermore, Xenophanes' distinction between *eidenai to saphes* and *dokos* was almost certainly connected with a contrast between gods and men (cf. Arius Didymus in A24, Varro in Augustine *City of God* 7.17; Alcmaeon, fragment 1), especially between the single greatest god of fragments 23–25 and normal mortal consciousness. In order to claim an epistemic exemption for himself Xenophanes would have had to raise himself above the level of other mortal men and regard himself as enjoying a vision of the truth characteristic of the divine. Since he spoke on several occasions against others (such as Epimenides in A1, 18, and Pythagoras in fragment 7) who claimed superhuman powers and elsewhere (A13) refuses to muddy the distinction between mortals and the gods, so exalted a status on epistemic grounds would have been sharply out of character. '*Outis anēr*,' therefore, includes Xenophanes.

Line 2 Understood broadly as 'about the gods and what I say about everything,' ἀμφὶ θεῶν τε καὶ ἄσσα λέγω περὶ πάντων is doubly peculiar: the gods *are* among the matters discussed by Xenophanes, hence already included in 'everything.' Moreover, so broad a thesis would imply that Xenophanes thought men had never known and would never know the certain truth about *anything*, no matter how minor, ordinary, or obvious a matter it might be (how, for example, Homer and Hesiod have depicted the gods – fragments 1, 11; how athletes are treated royally by their home cities – fragment 2; how the Colophonians used to behave back before the tyranny – fragment 3, etc.). But Xenophanes speaks as though these were matters of common knowledge among the members of his audience. On the one occasion (fragment 8) when he actually expresses doubt ('if I know how to speak truly concerning these things'), the subject-matter (his exact age) shows that his doubt is natural rather than 'philosophic.' For this reason, and in order to serve as a coordinate expression with θεῶν, ἄσσα λέγω περὶ πάντων must mean something less comprehensive than 'what I say about everything' or 'everything that I say' (as in Heitsch's 'alles, was ich sage'). Based on the close parallels between the language of fragment 34 and both Alcmaeon's fragment 1 and *On Ancient Medicine* 1, Barnes proposed that 'Xenophanes means to say that knowledge about things divine and knowledge about natural science lie beyond our human grasp' (1, 139; similarly Jaeger: 'about the highest questions there must always be some doubt,' 1947, 43). That this is the correct gloss on ἀμφὶ θεῶν ... περὶ πάντων is made more credible by the fact that Xenophanes states his accounts of nature in two fragments (fragments 27 and 29) in the form of generalizations about *panta*. Two later accounts (Sextus in *Against the Professors* 7.49 – quoted in D-K, 137; and Epiphanius in *Against Heresies* 3.2.9 – quoted in Diels 1879, 590) mention that Xenophanes' thesis was directed 'at least' (Sextus: *ge*) or 'especially' (Epiphanius: *malista*) toward things in the 'non-evident' realm (*ta adēla*), a phrase applicable both to the realm of the divine and to the regions in the heavens and below the earth explored by natural science. The thesis presented in lines 1 and 2 is, therefore, best taken to mean that *statements concerning the non-evident realm of the divine as well as the far-reaching generalizations of natural sciences* cannot be known as *to saphes*; that is, they cannot be directly observed or confirmed as true, hence they cannot be reliably known or known with certainty (see note 2 above on *to saphes*).

Lines 3–4 The logic of the 'for even if ...' argument is difficult to make out, in part because the referent of *tetelesmenon* is unspecified. Understood as referring to *an individual event* which has been brought to pass, the argument attacks the idea that anyone can achieve knowledge, arguing that even those whose predictions are proved true by subsequent events (typically seers, oracles, diviners, and so forth – see Lesher 1978) still do not themselves know. If these paragons of human wisdom are only guessing even when they are right (cf. Euripides *Helen* 744: 'the good prophet is one skilled in conjecture') then no man can hope to gain knowledge of the gods and all things. Understanding *tetelesmenon* as referring to *what exists as a whole*, 'speaking of what has been brought to pass' would be the sort of *archē* theorizing typical of the Ionian scientists. Xenophanes' argument would be that even if these accounts of the cosmos were correct, they could not be *known* by their proponents to be true. The underlying reason, on either understanding of the argument, would stem from the requirements for *saphēneia*, that is, for a clear and certain apprehension of the truth. As Sextus (*Against the Professors* 7.49; 8.324ff.) explains, in dealing with matters lying beyond our immediate experience, we are like men searching for treasures in a dark chamber; even if we were to put our hands right on one, we would have no way of telling that we had done so (cf. Plato *Meno* 80c–d, 99c). One may *say* the truth without oneself (*autos*) having any clear or evident basis for doing so, either about particular events or about reality as a whole.

Line 4 The conclusion of the argument (lines 3 and 4) echoes the negative opening generalization (of line 1): *dokos* – 'opinion' or 'conjecture' – is all that is available or 'allotted' to men. Such *dokos* is neither inherently erroneous (see note 6 above) nor fated to be only approximately correct (see the commentary on fragment 35 following), but it is the best anyone can do 'about the gods and what I say about all things,' since the direct observation necessary for a clear and certain knowledge of the truth about such matters is not possible. On this score, at least, the 'empiricist' interpretation (of Fränkel, Rivier, et al.) was correct: Xenophanes must have regarded the testimony of the senses as *necessary* for certain (sure) knowledge (even though it was not sufficient for it, and even though 'know' did not simply *mean* 'know through sense perception'). The problem which fragment 34 identified, that the scope of what mortals wanted most to know was vastly greater than what they were able to experience directly, would become a recurring issue in early Greek philosophy (see the conclusion of this chapter).

Fragment 35

[Ammonius here quoted, as was his custom, the words of Xenophanes:]
Let these be accepted,[1] certainly,[2] as like[3] the realities[4] (but ...)

Plutarch 9.7.746b

NOTES

1 δεδοξάσθω (*dedoxasthō*): Edmonds reads δεδοξάσθω for Plutarch's δε-
δοξάσθαι, following Wilamowitz who cited the somewhat distant parallel of Theognis 681: ταῦτα μοι ἠνίχθω κεκρυμμένα τοῖς ἀγαθοῖσιν – 'Let
these be my riddling oracles for the good.' Since δοξάζω embodies
some element of choice (see note 1 on δοκέω in fragment 14 in chapter
2 above), a recommendation to 'opine,' 'suppose,' 'accept,' 'assume,'
or 'think of as true' would be a natural form of expression (δεδοξάσθω
– 3rd singular perfect passive imperative). Heitsch retains the infinitive form and translates – 'of course these are to be accepted as valid
conjecture.' In conjunction with μέν (see note 2 following), a positive
recommendation could be conveyed by either form (cf. GG, secs. 1276
and 1541).

2 μέν (*men*): Denniston comments (359): 'The primary function of μέν,
as of μήν, is emphatic, strongly affirming an idea or concentrating
the attention upon it. But ... μέν acquires a concessive or antithetical sense, and serves to prepare the mind for a contrast of greater or
lesser sharpness'; cf. D-K, Heitsch: 'zwar' – 'of course ... but.' The
μέν-δέ contrast of fragment 34 (no knowledge of the clear and certain truth, but opinion is allotted to all) and the correspondence of
δεδοξάσθω with the noun form δόκος (34.4), invite the conjecture for
the missing answering statement to fragment 35: 'but they cannot be
known with certainty' (Barnes 1, 140; Heitsch, 184). It has also been
held that fragment 35 contrasts an account which merely resembles
the truth with one which states it exactly (but see the commentary
following).

3 ἐοικότα (*eoikota*): LSJ gives 'to be like,' 'seem,' and 'beseem' as the
main meanings of ἔοικα and 'seeming like,' 'fitting,' and 'likely, probable' for the participial forms. Although the last of these is commonly
adopted for ἐοικότα here in fragment 35 (cf. Fränkel, 336; Guthrie 1,
396), the dative form of ἐτύμοισι makes 'like,' 'seem like,' and 'befitting' more natural choices than 'being probable or plausible to the
true ones' (cf. GG, sec. 1176). A probable or merely plausible account
might nevertheless have been the implicit referent of ταῦτα (reading
ἔτυμος as 'true account') since an account recommended for acceptance as 'like a true account' could only be one which was probable,
plausible, or approximately true. The choice of the best translation for
ἐοικότα depends on the particular meaning assigned to ἐτύμοισι and
the force given to δεδοξάσθω (see note 4 following and the following
commentary).

4 τοῖς ἐτύμοισι (tois etumoisi): 'the true or real ones or things.' Like its
cognates ἐτεός and ἐτήτυμος, ἔτυμος can mean either 'true' = veridical
(said of words, stories, dreams, predications, etc.) or 'true' = real,
actual, genuine (said of things, events, persons, qualities). Xenophanes employs the adverbial form ἐτύμως in the former sense in
fragment 8.4: 'if I know how to speak truly concerning these things.'
'Saying things like the truth' is an activity known both to Homer
(Odyssey 19.203: λέγων ἐτύμοισιν ὁμοῖα) and to Hesiod (Theogony 27:
λέγειν ἐτύμοισιν ὁμοῖα). Homer also speaks of τὰ ἔτυμα in the second
sense (real things, happenings) when at Odyssey 19.565ff. he contrasts
dreams that remain unfulfilled (ἀκράαντα) with those having 'true
issues' (ἔτυμα κραίνουσι), i.e., dreams followed by the events they foretold. Parmenides employs the reduplicated form ἐτήτυμος in characterizing the true = genuine way of thinking (fragment 8.18), and both
Pindar Olympian 10.53–55) and Theocritus (12.35–37) use ἐτήτυμον to
refer to that which testing proves to be genuine. The first option was
accepted by D-K ('gleichend dem Wahren' – 'being like the true'),
the second by Heitsch ('gleichend dem Wirklichen' – 'being like the
real'); 'true ones' or 'true things' would be the most literal translation
of ἐτύμοισι, but the 'true ones' should be understood as 'the realities'
(see the commentary following).

COMMENTARY ON FRAGMENT 35

Quoted by a speaker in Plutarch to encourage a bashful companion
to state his opinions, fragment 35 is fraught with ambiguity and uncertainty. Since we lack any information about its original context and
intended purpose we are forced to speculate about the real meaning
of Xenophanes' comment, constructing interpretations on the basis of
small and incidental features, no one of which decisively determines
its meaning.

There are four main areas of uncertainty: (1) Assuming that Xenophanes' words represent some sort of recommendation, what were the
'these' (tauta) he urged his audience to accept, believe, or suppose to
be true? Were 'these' the explanations he gave of various natural phenomena; or the 'appearances' of things which were 'like' or 'merely resembling' the realities; or were they fictions offered in the same spirit
as the poems of Homer and Hesiod, that is, as stories merely resembling the truth? (2) What was the force of Xenophanes' phrase 'to accept
these' (tauta dedoxasthō/thai)? Was it meant as a positive recommendation of a satisfactory situation ('accept these, certainly, as ...') or was

it a caution or admission of an inadequate state of comprehension (that is, 'accept these anyway, or nevertheless, or in any case as mere opinion'), or was it merely a *reference* to accepting opinions rather than a *recommendation*? (3) Did Xenophanes mean by *eoikota tois etumoisi* that 'these' were 'like the true ones' in some parallel or corresponding respects, or did he mean that they 'merely resembled the true ones' in some approximate or inexact manner? (4) Were 'the true ones' the realities themselves or were they true accounts of how things really are?

In attempting to remove some of these uncertainties previous accounts have drawn upon other similar statements made both before and well after Xenophanes' time. For Heitsch (1966, 232–33), the key to the meaning of fragment 35 was provided by the similarity between Xenophanes' phrase *eoikota tois etumoisi* and Hesiod's *etumoisin homoia* (*Theogony* 27): 'Shepherds of the wilderness, wretched things of shame, mere bellies, we know how to speak many false things as though they were true [ἴδμεν ψεύδεα πολλὰ λέγειν ἐτύμοισιν ὁμοῖα]; but we know, when we will, to utter true things' (trans. Evelyn-White). The poet's power to create enchanting accounts of things that seem real (though never were) laid the foundation for the philosopher's recognition of the critical problem of truth: we may conjecture, but never say exactly, how things really are.

Alternatively, we may view fragment 35 in retrospect from the viewpoint of 5th-century expressions of scepticism with regard to the senses: what we know clearly are just the *phainomena*, 'the appearances' of things; what things themselves really are must forever remain a matter of conjecture (cf. Anaxagoras, fragments 21, 21a; Democritus, fragment 6: 'none of these appears according to the truth but only according to opinion,' fragments 7–11, etc.). We may also retrospectively detect in fragment 35 something of the negative attitude evident in Parmenides' account in accordance with mortal opinion as a 'whole likely ordering' (διακόσμον ἐοικότα πάντα, fragment 8.60; also termed a 'deceitful ordering' – κόσμον ... ἀπατηλόν at 8.52), as well as in Plato's characterization of his account of the physical world as only a 'likely story' (εἰκότα μῦθον at *Timaeus* 29d, 49c, and elsewhere). Seen in the light of these later developments, fragment 35 acquires a prophetic but negative cast, expressing Xenophanes' willingness to settle for mere probabilities or mere conjectures (cf. Popper's 'merely similar,' p. 11) based on the superficial appearances of things.

This 'likely story' about the real import of fragment 35 does not, in my opinion, do justice to various features of Xenophanes' remarks. Apart from the general improbability that Xenophanes took his cues to philosophical truth from anything Hesiod had to say (except, perhaps, to assume on principle that an opposing point of view would be correct), there is a fundamental difference between the two references to things 'like the truth': Hesiod has in mind *falsehoods* which have been dressed up to look like truths; Xenophanes, since he is urging his audience to accept them, must have in mind *truths* that are like the *etuma* (a point noted by Guthrie 1, 396n). The ability of the gifted (or divinely inspired) poet to achieve fictional verisimilitude may create a problem, but it is not the issue here. Further, while there are clearly correspondences between Xenophanes' philosophy and later sceptical accounts (see the concluding essay of this chapter) there are also significant differences between them. Xenophanes' 'scepticism' is best understood as based on the disparity between the limited extent of individual perceptual experience and the scope of what must be known (see the commentary on fragment 34 above); the scepticism concerning sense perception voiced by Plato and Parmenides was based on their conviction that the world encountered in sense experience was inherently contradictory and inconstant, a world of shadows and illusion. These metaphysical views have no parallel in Xenophanes' robust naturalism.

One might argue, nevertheless, that Xenophanes must have glimpsed *some* distinction between the 'appearances' of things and the realities themselves. Fragment 38 implies that our view of the relative sweetness of figs and honey would be altered by different circumstances; fragment 32 implies that what men think they see in the rainbow is not really there; A41a reports Xenophanes' view that the real path of the sun is not what it appears to be; and any proponent of a theory about the *archē* or single basic principle of all things must have realized that the manifold appearances of things do not represent their true reality. When, therefore, Xenophanes refers (in fragment 36) to 'however many as have appeared,' we may not unreasonably conclude that he has in mind both there and here in fragment 35 the realm of appearance as such. Seen in this light, his recommendation to think of 'these' as merely resembling the realities themselves would represent the onset of philosophical reflection on the distinction between appearance and reality.

While this account is perfectly reasonable, it is not entirely persuasive. The 'perceptual errors' cited in fragments 32, 38, and A41a are in part errors in interpretation or assessment and even a realist account can accept the occasional occurrence of perceptual distortion or illusion. Xenophanes' *archē* theory (that is, the earth and water theory of fragments 29 and 33) is *not*, as Mourelatos explained (1965, 346–65), the 5th-century thesis that we *never* perceive things as they really are (Mourelatos' Stage III), but only the thesis that certain entities among all those we experience have a privileged status as the basic reality or *phusis* of things (Stage II). One can imagine how a decision to privilege one sort of entity as *phusis* could have led, over time, to the more radical view that this basic substance can itself be further explained by reference to some non-sensible reality (such as Democritus' atoms; see Mourelatos 1965, 353–57), but the two views can be distinguished. Fragment 36, moreover, cannot be understood as referring to *phaino-mena* or 'appearances' without strain: *things* may 'have appeared to mortals,' but 'appearances which have appeared' is difficult, and while mortals may 'look upon' or 'look at' *things*, it is not clear that they can 'look upon or at appearances.' Thus fragment 36 is most easily construed in the terms of the realist metaphysics reflected generally in Xenophanes' poems: what there is for mortals to look at and inquire into is the natural realm of physical objects and persons existing in space and time. All of these have perceptible physical qualities, but these are not the superficial 'appearances' of the true, non-sensible realities themselves. Perceptual error and misinterpretation notwithstanding, Xenophanes' remarks do not warrant the attribution of a concept of 'appearances' which resemble, or are like, or are similar to, the realities themselves.

While we cannot expect to remove every uncertainty inherent in Xenophanes' brief comment, I would argue that we should accept the following conclusions as warranted by particular features of his comment and by other fragments.

(1) Xenophanes' statement, ταῦτα δεδοξάσθω μὲν, is plausibly regarded as an emphatic (cf. Denniston, 359) and decisive imperative (cf. GG, sec. 1276): 'Let these be accepted, certainly ...' His comment could well have served as a concluding or summary remark, urging his audience to agree with what he had previously said or to accept as sufficient the account he had provided. Herodotus often concluded his discussions of particular topics with similarly phrased imperatives (cf. 2.33: 'This is enough to say concerning the story told by Etearchus' – ὁ μὲν δή ... δεδηλώσθω; cf. also 1.140; 2.28, 35; 4.15, 36, 45; 6.55), as did Aristotle (*Nicomachean Ethics* 1097a14–15: 'Let what has been said on this subject be final' – περὶ μέν τούτων ἐπὶ τοσοῦτον εἰρήσθω; cf. also 1095a12, 1096a10, etc.). Since an author would not normally urge his audience to accept his account while simultaneously demeaning it by describing it as inadequate or inferior, it is difficult to take

Xenophanes' comment to mean 'Let these be accepted, certainly, they are merely conjectures only resembling how things really are.'

(2) If, as (1) maintains, fragment 35 was intended to serve as a positive injunction to Xenophanes' audience, we should expect what accompanies the injunction to square with it and perhaps to bolster the recommendation by explaining why it should be accepted. That 'being like the realities' would serve naturally in this capacity we may infer from Hecataeus' opening statement to his history: 'I write these things as they seem to me to be true' (τάδε ... δοκεῖ ἀληθέα). While a likeness represented by the term *eoikōs* can on occasion be only rough or approximate (for example, *Iliad* 3.449, where Achilles is likened to a 'wild animal'), it can also be quite close (for instance, *Iliad* 2.337, where Nestor complains that the Achaeans are acting 'just like foolish children' – παισὶν ἐοικότες ... / νηπιάχοις. The phrase ἐοικότα τοῖς ἐτύμοισι can be taken either as 'merely resembling the realities' or as 'like the realities,' but the latter explains – as the former does not – why Xenophanes' accounts should be accepted as true by his audience.

(3) Since a speaker would not expect to succeed in encouraging his companion to express his opinions by quoting an admission of perpetual inexactitude or an unavoidably inferior state of awareness, it would appear that Plutarch understood fragment 35 in a positive vein: since, as Xenophanes put it, we ought to accept these opinions as like the realities, please tell us your opinions.

(4) Since *dedoxasthō* (from *doxadzō*) and *dokos* are cognate expressions describing the forming or having of an opinion, we may assume some degree of correspondence between the doctrines of fragments 34 and 35. Consequently, the 'these' being recommended for acceptance in fragment 35 may be reasonably supposed to be the subject-matters under discussion in fragment 34, that is, 'about the gods and what I say about all things.' Thus, fragment 35 recommends, perhaps as a concluding summary statement (Barnes 1, 140), the acceptance of Xenophanes' teachings on these topics.

(5) While the *men* of fragment 35 may well have served as the first half of a *men-de* contrast, the particular contrast of 'resembling the truth but not the exact truth' would be inconsistent with the admission at fragment 34.3 that someone might succeed *ta malista* in speaking of what is brought to pass, that is, describe exactly what happens.

(6) The correspondence between *dedoxasthō* and *dokos* would also suggest that fragment 35 formed a part of a larger antithetical statement, paralleling the *men-de* structure of fragment 34: 'Let these be accepted, certainly, as like the realities, but they cannot be known as

the clear and certain truth.' On this reading *dedoxasthō men* would remain a positive recommendation (of Xenophanes' accounts of the gods and all things), but it would need to be paired with a reminder of the limitations under which all such inquiries must be conducted in order for it to tell the full story.

So understood, both fragment 35 and fragment 34 would count as pioneering reflections on the nature, limits, and varieties of human understanding. They jointly articulate a distinction between genuine knowledge (apprehension of the truth based upon clear and reliable indications) and opinion (acceptance of what is potentially correct but unconfirmable) which became a commonplace in succeeding philosophical reflections on human knowledge (cf. Plato *Meno* 97–98; Aristotle *Posterior Analytics* 1.33). In fragment 34 Xenophanes had stated the distinction as a primarily negative thesis: 'no man has known or will ever know ... but men may have their opinions.' Here in fragment 35 he issues a positive injunction to his audience to accept his accounts 'about the gods and what I say about all things' in so far as they are like the realities – they correspond with how things really are – even if no one can know the clear and certain truth about such matters.

Fragment 36

[And again:]
... however many[1] they have made evident[2] for mortals to look
upon.

Herodian 296.9 (following fragment 10)

NOTES

1 ὁππόσα δὴ (*hopposa dē*): Literally 'how many soever' (LSJ, s.v. ὁπόσος, I, 3; GG, sec. 410b); cf. Herodotus 5.20: 'to have intercourse with them all or with however many (ὁκόσῃσι ὧν αὐτέων) you might like.' Diels (followed by Burnet, 121n) suggested – without any discernible grounds – that Xenophanes was referring here to the stars which appear to men. For the reasons given in the commentary on fragment 35 above, I understand ὁππόσα as referring not to 'appearances' but to the objects, persons, and places which populate the natural world.

2 πεφήνασιν (*pephēnasin*): φαίνω in the active voice commonly means 'cause to appear,' 'bring to light' or more broadly 'make evident,' 'reveal,' and in this sense 'the gods' would be a natural understood

subject (who else could make things evident to mortals except immortals?). LSJ also notes an intransitive use of the second perfect (s.v. φαίνω, A, III, 2), hence 'appear' (Edmonds) and 'are evident' (Guthrie) are acceptable. For φαίνω as divine disclosure, cf. *Odyssey* 3.173.

COMMENTARY ON FRAGMENT 36

Line 1 If Herodian had been only half as interested in philosophy as in the length of syllables he would surely have preserved more of Xenophanes' words than this tantalizing brief snippet. 'Appearance,' 'perception,' 'make evident,' 'mortals and immortals' – all of these are matters of importance in other fragments. Yet what Xenophanes was actually asserting (before, after, and during fragment 36) about these topics is difficult, perhaps impossible, to tell.

Fränkel regarded fragment 36 as integral to the generally 'empiricist' outlook he detected in fragments 34 and 35 as well as in the thoroughgoing naturalism of Xenophanes' scientific accounts: '[Xenophanes] distinguished between the percepts of the senses (cf. Fr. 36: 'All things which show themselves visibly to mortal eyes'), which he takes unquestioningly as certain, and that which is merely inferred or surmised. The last can at best be merely probable' (336). So understood, fragment 36 might conceivably have served as prelude to conclusions such as 'are things which men can know with certainty' or 'are all that can be known with certainty.' The 'percepts of the senses,' as Fränkel interpreted Xenophanes' theory of knowledge, would be both sufficient and necessary for certain knowledge.

Yet it has seemed equally obvious to others that this robust empiricism would be sharply at odds with other aspects of Xenophanes' teachings (see Guthrie 1, 397; Heitsch, 186-87). Not only does fragment 38 suggest that our judgments about a thing's sensible qualities (for instance, the sweet taste of figs) might be corrected in the light of subsequent experience, but Aëtius (in A41a) attributed to Xenophanes the view that our belief in the sun's circular orbit was in error and resulted from the misleading appearance of its curved path across the heavens – or perhaps from its nightly disappearance (see note 3 on A41a). We ought also to acknowledge the frequently unintuitive nature of Xenophanes' scientific accounts (for instance, that the sun and stars are really clouds, are unlimited in number, and are quenched and rekindled daily). If, therefore, we regarded fragment 36 as an expression of his belief that sense perception was both sufficient and necessary for knowledge we would reduce Xenophanes' overall philosophy to hopeless inconsistency.

As an alternative to the unacceptable 'empiricist' theory proposed by Fränkel, Heitsch has conjectured that fragment 36 is concerned not with *knowledge*, but with *belief* or *judgment*, and that it reflects the same critical attitude toward human belief (as subjective, adventitious, and constrained by personal circumstances) that Xenophanes displays in fragment 38 (on figs and honey) and fragments 15–16 (on the relativity of religious conceptions). In defence of this interpretation Heitsch notes that neither *eisoran* nor *phainesthai* should be construed simply as *perceptual* seeing and appearing, citing such examples as Herodotus 1.190.2, 'seeing (ὀρέοντες) that he attacked all nations alike,' and *Iliad* 2.5, 'this advice seemed (φαίνετο) to be the best.' Xenophanes, then, must be understood as having subscribed to a widely assumed assimilation of seeing with judgment. Since we know from elsewhere (fragments 15–16, 38, etc.) that he regarded mortal beliefs or judgments as largely the result of adventitious personal experience, we may regard fragment 36 in this light, as a statement that what men judge or believe is a function of whatever the gods may have made visible to them to look upon and consider.

The conclusion of this argument is almost certainly more credible than its premisses. Even if Greek perception verbs sometimes possess a broader judgmental meaning, it remains true that often they do not (for instance, fragment 32, 'purple, red, and yellowish-green to behold with one's eyes [ἰδέσθαι].' Nor do judgmental uses of perception verbs imply a *conception* or *theory* of perception as judgment. There is, therefore, no good reason to suppose that Xenophanes' references to 'what appear' and 'what we look upon' were really just references to forms of judgment or belief. Nevertheless, that Xenophanes, along with other early writers, held that seeing, hearing, and other forms of sense perception were of great importance for our general understanding of the world seems highly likely. As we have seen (above) in our discussion of fragment 34, Xenophanes echoes the ancient lament about the narrow limits of human experience (speaking truly, at best, of what is *tetelesmenos* – 'what has come to pass,' in contrast to 'the certain truth both about the gods and what I say about all things'). By contrast with the gods who are present everywhere and know all things, 'men hear only a report and know nothing' (*Iliad* 2.485ff.). Empedocles similarly describes Xenophanes, perhaps quoting his own words against him, as 'seeing little of the whole' (fragment 39.3). In short, for Xenophanes and for many others of his time, what is 'made evident for mortals to look upon' – the total body of their perceptual experience – constitutes their *primary source* of information about the world, the single greatest influence on what they think about and believe; and its narrow limits provide a cardinal index of the limitations of human understanding. *If* fragment 36 stood in some relation to this traditional 'sceptical' (or better 'pessimistic') view, its message would be clear enough: 'however many things the gods have made evident for mortals to look upon ... men will still only think of things in the manner in which they have perceived them, unable as they are to go beyond the limits of their own experience.'

Further, in so far as fragment 36 would be highlighting the limits of human understanding in quantitative terms (that is, however *many* ...), Xenophanes would be speaking about human knowledge in just the terms adopted by both Heraclitus (fragment 17: ὁκόσοι [Diels' reading] ἐγκυρέουσιν – 'as many as they encounter'; fragment 1: λανθάνει ὁκόσα ἐγερθέντες – 'they forget as many things as they do while awake') and Parmenides (fragment 7: ἔθος πολύπειρον – 'custom born of much experience'; etc.). We can in short tell a plausible story about fragment 36 as a full-fledged participant in this traditional indictment of human ignorance.

But it is not by any means a definitive account. It remains entirely possible that fragment 36 served not as an ingredient in a negative statement but instead as part of a larger, positive remark. *Hoposos*, for example, occurs in fragment 1 in a positive setting: 'it is not wrong to drink as much (πίνειν ὁπόσον) as allows any but an aged man to reach his home without a servant's aid,' and Empedocles' fragment 3 shows that a philosopher may speak of 'whatever' without intending to cast aspersions: 'by whatever way (ὁπόσῃ πόρος) there is a channel to understanding ... grasp each thing in the way it is clear.' The structure of fragment 36, 'as many as ... to look upon,' partially parallels that of fragment 32, 'a cloud ... to behold,' suggesting that just as the cloud is a natural phenomenon 'mortal men' may observe and come to understand, so there might be other phenomena they could study – as many, in fact, as the gods have made evident for them to look upon.

The upshot is that plausible interpretations for fragment 36 may be constructed along both positive and negative lines. In light of its brevity and the dual nature of Xenophanes' philosophical outlook – encouraging inquiry resulting in discoveries while denying the possibility of achieving certain knowledge – it is entirely possible that our understanding of fragment 36 will remain suspended in a philosophical state of limbo between these two points of view.

Fragment 38

[The form, *glussōn*, used by Xenophanes, is peculiar:]
If god had not made yellow honey, they would think[1]
that figs were much sweeter.[2]

Herodian 41.5

NOTES

1 ἔφασκον (*ephaskon*): D-K translates 'würde man meinen' – 'one would
think'; Heitsch: 'würden sie meinen' – 'they would think.' The implied subject is almost certainly 'men' or 'mortals' – in contrast to
the θεός who made the honey (cf. fragment 14: οἱ βροτοὶ δοκέουσι;
fragment 36: θνητοῖσι πεφήνασι); hence 'men would consider, etc.'
(Barnes, Guthrie, KRS) is equally appropriate. Edmonds translates
'they had said,' but for φάσκω as 'think,' 'consider,' 'deem,' cf. *Odyssey*
22.35: 'you thought (ἐφάσκεσθε) that I would never return home from
Troy' (LSJ, s.v. φάσκω, 2). For a discussion of the close association of
thoughts with words see Onians, 66–72.

2 γλύσσονα (*glussona*): Comparative of γλυκύς (as in Xenophanes fragment 1.8) – 'sweet to the taste or smell' (LSJ). D-K adds '(als sie uns
jetzt erscheinen)' – '(than they now seem to us).' The point of Xenophanes' comment seems to be that *now* men think of figs as only
moderately sweet (as compared with honey). Without that comparison case of exceptional sweetness available to them, men would have
had a different view of the sweetness of figs. The alternative reading,
'sweeter than honey,' while grammatically possible, makes no sense;
if honey had never existed, men would be unable to compare figs (or
anything else) with honey.

COMMENTARY ON FRAGMENT 38

Lines 1–2 Xenophanes elsewhere (fragments 15–16) maintains that
what men 'say' (that is, think or believe) is to some extent a function of
the physical and social circumstances in which they find themselves:
some of the qualities believers ascribe to their gods are reflections of
their own physical traits. Here in fragment 38 he observes similarly that
the judgments men make about the qualities of physical substances are
to some extent a function of the perceptual experiences they have had.
As Heitsch (193) notes, what Xenophanes says here about sweetness
can be generalized to apply to many other qualities; thus, the observation may well have been intended to serve as a caution concerning

the relativity and variability of human judgment generally. So understood, fragment 38 would have provided support for the reservations Xenophanes voiced in fragments 34, 35, and (perhaps) fragment 36 about our prospects for achieving certain knowledge. Pace Barnes (1, 142–43), fragment 38 should not be read as asserting that our beliefs are insufficiently grounded in the realities to qualify as knowledge. On the contrary, fragment 38 laments the fact that men's beliefs are grounded in (hence limited by) what they experience. What men believe about the sweetness of figs and honey is a causal consequence of their experience of both. A causal nexus with both could not be the *solution* to the problem Xenophanes is here identifying; on the contrary, it is the experience of both that has given rise to the problem.

Xenophanes' comment can be placed within a broader poetic tradition of lamenting the narrow limits of human understanding and the 'heteronomy of *noos*' – the extent to which mortal *noos* is simply a consequence of 'whatever the gods have made evident for mortals to look upon.'

... for such is the *noos* of earthly man, like the day that the father of gods and men brings to them. (*Odyssey* 18.137)

there is no *noos* in men, we live each day as it comes, like grazing cattle, not knowing how god shall end it ... from evil fortune nothing is exempt: defeat and death and many thousand unexpected woes and griefs crowd in on mankind. (Semonides, fragment 1)

... such is the *noos* in men ... for he thinks such things as he meets with. (Archilochus, fragment 70)

As we have seen already in fragment 34, there is no suggestion that Xenophanes considered himself exempt from these limitations; while the one greatest god could be conceived of as enjoying a complete seeing, hearing, and *noēsis* (fragment 24), Xenophanes speaks throughout from a strictly mortal point of view (fragments 1, 2, 7, 10, 17, 18) about how men should behave and the extent of his own *sophiē*. 'We are all,' he evidently believes, 'created of earth and water' (fragment 33). Fragment 38 is thus cautionary rather than nihilistic; it serves to remind men that they 'see little of the whole' and that their opinions are shaped by what little they have experienced. Democritus will, however, cite the 'customary' character of our perceptual judgments – including sweetness (νόμῳ γλυκύ) – in connection with his broad statement of scepticism (fragment 9).

Fragment 38 might also have been intended to convey a moral message: 'men would think that figs were far sweeter if they had never tasted honey'; that is, men would have found a life of moderate pleasure perfectly satisfactory if they had not been exposed to more intense pleasures. As Xenophanes explains (or at least hints) in fragments 1, 3, and 22, the best life for man is not a life devoted to the pursuit of wealth and useless luxuries but a life of moderation in desire and pleasure (as Plato will later characterize it in *Republic* 2.372, 'banquets of figs and chick-peas'; see the commentaries on fragments 1, 5, and 22 in chapter 1 above).

CONCLUSION

While it is clear that Xenophanes' comments on the prospects for human understanding are of considerable intrinsic interest, one might well wonder whether they were regarded as important by his contemporaries and immediate successors. A close correspondence in thought and terminology has led some scholars to identify Alcmaeon fragment 1 and the Hippocratic treatise *On Ancient Medicine* (I) as early and favourable exegeses of fragment 34.[1] Other possible points of contact have been mentioned but not explored.[2] Certainly none of Xenophanes' successors report in any surviving remark that his critical comments awoke them from their dogmatic slumbers or otherwise provoked a philosophical response. And yet there is considerable evidence that the challenge which Xenophanes raised in fragment 34 (and perhaps on many other occasions) was both heard and taken seriously by Greek philosophers, at least until the time of Aristotle.

The crux of the problem identified in fragment 34 (and the related fragments 35 and 38) lay in the disparity between the resources for

1 Fränkel 1974, 129. Barnes also credits Alcmaeon with coming up with a solution to Xenophanes' problem, the genetic account of knowledge built up from perception, memory, and experience provided by Plato at *Phaedo* 96b; although he concedes that others have denied that the *Phaedo* theory can be confidently attributed to Alcmaeon (cf. Vlastos 1955/70 47n). The question does not admit of a clear answer, but it may be noted that if Alcmaeon had taken himself to have solved Xenophanes' problem, he could no longer have subscribed to the thesis of his own fragment 1 – since *saphēneia*, and not merely inference from signs, would be possible for men.

2 Fränkel (1974, 129) also mentions Heraclitus, fragment 1, and Empedocles, fragments 2 and 4. Dodds (1951, 196n) mentions Heraclitus, fragment 28; Gorgias *Helen* 13; Euripides, fragment 795.

knowledge available to men and the requirements for the sort of knowledge they most wanted to have: what they were in a position to know (that is, accept with confidence on the basis of clear evidence) was the world of persons, things, and events with which they were in direct contact; but what they now sought to know (the nature of the gods and the truth about all of nature) were matters lying far beyond the limits of that personal world. So basic and far-reaching a challenge as Xenophanes' would be difficult to ignore, especially by those claiming to have penetrated just such obscure matters as these. Any philosophers claiming *eidenai to saphes* here should expect to be asked how they had overcome the impediments to knowledge identified by Xenophanes or else, failing that, to concede that all such accounts – including their own – amounted to no more than conjecture, *saphēneia* on such matters being reserved for the gods. How often during the next several centuries did the philosophers fit the terms of this description, either claiming to have risen above the circumstances of ordinary men or else succumbing to the negative conclusion of Xenophanes' argument?

In focusing on similarities between Xenophanes' greatest god and Parmenides' motionless and uniform being, little notice has been given to the close correspondence between the 'sceptical' conclusion of fragment 34 and the attack on mortal *doxa* from which Parmenides begins his own account. Parmenides' goddess characterizes the current condition of human understanding as 'knowing nothing ... believing that being and not-being are both the same and not the same, and that the path of all things is backward turning' (fragment 6.8–9); that is, a nest of inconsistent beliefs about what exists.[3] In the account of mortal *doxa* that follows the goddess' account of the one true way of thought, various philosophical or scientific views of reality are also diagnosed as infected with error: in speaking of divisions, opposites, mixtures, changes, and so on, they all readmit not-being into their scheme of things, that is, they all speak of what does not exist as though it existed.[4] The current state of human understanding, both common and expert, is a morass of conflicting and internally inconsistent opinions about what exists, a situation aptly described by Diels as a 'multi-lateral dispute' among mortal *doxai*.[5]

---

3 G.E.L. Owen explained: 'Ordinary men want to keep *both einai* and *ouk einai* in use: horses exist, mermaids do not; there is sandy soil here but not there; there are dodos at one time, not at another' (in Furley and Allen 2, 56).

4 I adopt the explanation of the significance of the *doxa* section provided by A.A. Long (1963/75), 90–107.

5 H. Diels, (1897a, 62–63): 'Die vielstimmige Weltanschauung der Menschen erfordert eine vielseitige Prüfung und Widerlegung ...'

Distancing himself from this benighted condition, Parmenides describes what really exists as though he had received a divine warrant for knowledge. He speaks of a goddess who bears a youth along the pathway which 'carries straight ahead the man who knows' (fragment 1.3) and his education in the truth is said to be in accordance with 'right and justice' (fragment 1.28). The way of thinking about *to eon* – 'being' – which she imparts is 'far indeed from the beaten track of men' (fragment 1.27), resulting in a completely trustworthy account (cf. πίστιος ἰσχύς at fragment 8.13) of what assuredly, certifiably exists (the δοκίμως εἶναι promised at fragment 1.33). Divine assurances notwithstanding, Parmenides grounds his account of *to eon* not on blind faith in revelation but on a series of arguments against the possibility of generation, destruction, movement, change, discontinuity, and incompleteness[6] – all organized within an orderly, serial review of all the possible ways of thinking about what exists. Each of these ways is put to the *elenchos* and only one survives: thinking only and always 'it exists.'[7] In short, Parmenides begins his account of the truth about reality from just the circumstances described by Xenophanes at fragment 34.4: pervasive human *dokos/doxa*. Distancing himself from the habitual reliance on sense perception that dominates ordinary consciousness he sets out an alternate path to discovery, 'deciding through the *logos*' (κρῖναι δὲ λόγῳ) the 'strife-rich' *elenchos* he has set out. Along this extraordinary path of thinking, but only here, it is possible to acquire trustworthy true belief, hence knowledge, about what can and must exist. In sketching out this alternative path to knowledge Parmenides effectively undermined the correlation of knowledge with sense experience that had formed the theoretical basis for Xenophanes' negative conclusion.

These same features, a distancing of the philosopher from the unenlightened state of the common run of men, a rejection of current expert opinion, and a claim to a special avenue to the discovery of the truth about the nature of all things, are clearly visible in the teachings of Heraclitus[8] and Empedocles.[9] Conversely, when Democritus

6 A thesis defended by Vlastos (1955/70, 49).
7 For a defence of this summary statement see Lesher 1984, 1–30.
8 For the ignorance of ordinary men: fragments 1, 17, 19, 34, 71–73, 104; for the ignorance of the experts: A23, fragments 40, 42, 56, 81, 104, 129; for a claim to a special insight into truth: fragments 1, 40, 101, 108. For an account of the nature of the special insight Heraclitus claimed for himself and denied to all others, see C. Kahn 1979, 96–110; Lesher 1983, 155–70.
9 For the ignorance of ordinary men: fragment 2, 'Narrow are the powers that are spread through the body, and many are the miseries that burst in, blunting thought.'

denies that men know how things really are, he reaffirms the essential role played by sense perception[10] and cites the usual impediments to human knowledge.[11] Socrates' famous 'disavowal of knowledge' bears some resemblance to Xenophanes' denial of knowledge of *to saphes*,[12]

Men behold in their span but a little part of life ... who, then, boasts that he has found the whole? Not so are these things to be seen or heard by men, or grasped by the understanding' (trans. KRS). For Empedocles' claim to a special wisdom: fragments 17, 23, 111–12, 115. In fragment 39 (Aristotle *On the Heavens* 294a26–27), Empedocles attacks those who hold that the depths of the earth are *apeirona*, almost certainly referring to Xenophanes (perhaps among others). These, Empedocles says, are foolish words for those 'seeing little of the whole' (ὀλίγου τοῦ παντὸς ἰδόντων). The phrase is applicable to men in general (cf. fragment 2 above), but it has a special piquancy when used in criticism of Xenophanes: in effect, 'you who hold that men never know *to saphes*, etc., how would *you* (of all people) be in any position to say what the earth's depths were like?'

10 Fragment 125: 'wretched mind, do you take your assurances from us and then overthrow us [sc. the senses]? Our overthrow is your downfall' (trans. KRS).

11 Fragment 11: 'But in actuality we grasp nothing for certain, but what shifts in accordance with the condition of the body and of the things which enter it and press upon it.' Fragment 7: 'This argument too shows that in reality we know nothing (*ouden ismen*) about anything; but belief (*doxis*) is an influx (*epirusmiē*) in each of us.' The 'materialist' tradition in Presocratic views of the mind has been recently summarized by M. Wright (1990, 207–25). Wright notes (212) that fragment 34 is part of this traditional denunciation of the limits and unreliability of human experience and argues that the Presocratics generally set themselves apart from this benighted state as 'men of reason.' This seems correct for Parmenides, Heraclitus, and Empedocles, but not for Xenophanes and Democritus.

12 Perhaps most closely at *Phaedo* 69d4–6: 'Whether I was right in this ambition [to philosophize] and whether we have achieved anything, we shall know for certain (τὸ σαφὲς εἰσόμεθα) if God wishes it, when we reach the other world'; and Xenophon, *Memorabilia* 1.1.7–8: 'For the craft of the carpenter, smith, farmer, or ruler, and the theory of such crafts, and arithmetic and economics and generalship might be learned and mastered by the application of human powers, but the deepest secrets of these matters the gods reserved to themselves; they were dark to men.' Socrates disavowed having much to do with Ionian *historiē* (*Apology* 19c; *Phaedo* 96b; Xenophon *Memorabilia* 4.7), but his conception of god is very Xenophanean (*Memorabilia* 1.4.17ff.: god sees everything at once, takes thought of all things at once, can see and hear everything, be present everywhere, at the same time, etc.), as are his attack on pretensions to wisdom, his encouragement to inquire (*Meno* 81d), and his disavowal of knowledge about non-evident matters such as the afterlife (*Apology* 42a), and, consequently, about the ultimate rewards of acting justly (*Gorgias* 509). Some later writers attributed a restricted sort of scepticism to Socrates (cf. the description by Pseudo-Galen [Diels, 597]: 'he regarded secure cognition of non-evident things as utterly difficult'), but, like Xenophanes, he was also transformed into a complete sceptic, perhaps in the first instance by Arcesilaus (cf. Cicero *On the Orator* 3.67). For a detailed account of the process, see A.A. Long 1988, 150–71.

and both Plato and Aristotle devised accounts of knowledge which respond to the challenge posed by fragment 34, the former (perhaps following Parmenides) minimizing the role played by sense perception and opting for an *elenchos* of competing conceptual hypotheses,[13] the latter offering a novel account of how we may proceed from an awareness of individuals in perception to a secure grasp of the most universal and 'clearest' principles of explanation.[14] While neither Xenophanes nor fragment 34 was explicitly mentioned in any of these later accounts, it is nevertheless clear that they all dealt with the issue he there raised: how is it possible, given the narrow limits of what men can directly experience for themselves, for anyone to achieve sure knowledge either of the divine or of how 'all things' are?

---

13 For Platonic dialectic as *elenchos/elenchein*, see *Republic* 534; *Theaetetus* 161; *Philebus* 52d.

14 Cf. the famous account at *Posterior Analytics* 2.19: from *aisthēsis* of individuals to *nous* of first principles by induction (*epagōgē*). For the nature of Aristotelian *saphēneia*, see *Physics* 1.184a ff.

PART 3
ANCIENT TESTIMONIA AND IMITATIONS

INTRODUCTION

A detailed accounting of the origins and reliability of all the Xeno-phanes testimonia would call for another volume longer than this one. Nevertheless, some comments are in order by way of introduction to this complex and controversial body of material. Many testimonia have already been alluded to in earlier chapters in connection with particu-lar fragments; additional explanatory notes accompany fourteen of the selections which follow; and additional information is provided in the following section, Sources and Authorities. The doxographical tradi-tion for Xenophanes is the subject of recent discussions by Finkelberg, Lebedev, Mansfeld, and Wiesner (see the Select Bibliography).

For the purposes of this introduction, the testimonia may be di-vided into six main groups: (1) the criticism of Xenophanes by Hera-clitus and Empedocles; (2) the imitations of and borrowings from Xeno-phanes' teachings contained in the writings of Plato, Euripides, and Aristotle; (3) Theophrastus' *Opinions of the Inquirers into Nature* and the many later accounts deriving from it (that is, those by Cicero, Aëtius, Pseudo-Plutarch, Galen, Hippolytus, Eusebius, Theodoretus, Stobaeus, Pseudo-Galen, and Simplicius); (4) the philosophical critique and (also derivative) summary of Xenophanes' account of god and/or 'the one' in the anonymously written treatise *On Melissus, Xenophanes, Gorgias*; (5) the accounts by Timon and later writers of Xenophanes as 'sceptic'; and (6) the doctrinal summary and biography by Diogenes Laertius.

(1) The Xenophanes mentioned by name in Heraclitus' fragment 40 and referred to in Empedocles' fragment 39 appears to be an Ionian *physiologos*. Heraclitus pairs him with the Ionian historian Hecataeus (αὐτίς τε Ξενοφάνεά τε καὶ Ἑκαταῖον) and suggests that their fact-finding has not brought them true understanding (*noos*). Empedocles groups Xenophanes with others who have spoken about the shape and posi-tion of the earth and ridicules them for not being fact-finding enough ('seeing little of the whole'). While one might wish to defend Xeno-phanes against both criticisms, the general conception of his interests presented by Heraclitus and Empedocles is well supported by various fragments dealing with natural phenomena, especially fragment 28 on the 'unlimited' extent of the earth's depths.

(2) Plato mentions Xenophanes only once in the dialogues, referring (at *Sophist* 242d) to 'the Eleatic tribe beginning from Xenophanes and even earlier.' Elsewhere (*Republic* 2), Plato appears to follow Xeno-phanes' ideas about the goodness of the divine, and about the impor-tance of pious depictions of the gods for the education of the young

and for the order of society, and (in *Republic* 5) his view of political statesmen as more deserving of honours from their cities than the victors at Olympia. These views, like the imitations in Euripides' *Heracles* and *Autolycus* (D-K C1 and C2), can be traced back to the call for pious stories in Xenophanes' fragment 1, the attack on excessive honouring of athletic victors in fragment 2, and the attacks on Homer and Hesiod in fragments 11 and 12. We may also conjecture that the distinction between knowledge and true opinion that Plato draws at *Meno* 98a owes something to the *eidenai/dokos* distinction of Xenophanes' fragment 34 (or a fuller version of fragment 35), and some details of Plato's morality of moderate desire (*Republic* 372ff.) may echo the moderation of Xenophanes' attack on Lydian luxuries in fragment 3, directions for wine mixing in fragment 5, and instructions for symposia in fragments 1 and 22.

It is, however, not easy to determine why, or even whether, Plato spoke of Xenophanes as an Eleatic monist. What Plato says is that the Eleatic tribe 'begins from Xenophanes and even earlier' and that the tribe 'relates its stories on the assumption that what are called "all things" are really one.' Must Xenophanes have adopted the same assumption in order for the tribe to have 'begun from him' (among others), or might a related but different doctrine (for example, that there is one greatest god) have been sufficient to have earned him this status? If Plato could call Homer the 'captain of the Heracliteans' (*Theaetetus* 153a) merely because Homer spoke of the flowing river Oceanus as the source of all gods, Xenophanes could just as easily be characterized as one of those from whom Eleatic philosophy began simply because he believed in 'one greatest being.'

Precisely the same question of Xenophanes' relation to Eleatic monism is raised by Aristotle's characterization of Xenophanes as 'the first of those to have been a partisan of the One for (γὰρ) Parmenides is said to have been his pupil' (*Metaphysics* 986b). Aristotle immediately renders a negative judgment on the extent of Xenophanes' contribution to our understanding of 'the principles of all things' or 'reality' (the topic under discussion since 983b): 'he made nothing clear nor does he appear to have touched on the nature of these' (causes identified by Parmenides and Melissus). By contrast ('but' – ἀλλὰ), 'with regard to the physical universe he said the one was god' (986b25; for *apoblepein* as not 'with his sight on the whole of the world' [Finkelberg], but the more modest 'with regard to,' see note 1 in the conclusion of chapter 2 in part 2). We may well wonder about the basis for Aristotle's description of Xenophanes as a 'partisan of the One' in light of his negative view of the relevance of Xenophanes' ideas for the inquiry into the principles of reality. It is scarcely credible that Aristotle would have explained his classification on the basis of a reported (*legetai*) affiliation between Parmenides and Xenophanes if he had known of any Xenophanean comment on *cosmic* unity. I conclude that Aristotle's comment amounted to no more than the dual assertion that Xenophanes affirmed 'one' (something – namely god) *and* was said to be Parmenides' teacher (which is probably just what Plato supposed as well). In light of Aristotle's respectful comments about Xenophanes' religious opinions (*Rhetoric* 1399b5, 1400b5; *Poetics* 1460b35), his dismissive remark on Xenophanes' opinion on the earth's depths (*On the Heavens* 294a), and his silence on Xenophanes' earth or earth and water theory, Deichgräber's thesis becomes quite compelling: Aristotle regarded Xenophanes as a religious or theological thinker, not a serious student of nature and its principles. We should therefore understand 'with regard to the physical universe, he said the one was god' in just this way; that is, on the subject of the principles of 'all things' Xenophanes had nothing helpful to say, talking instead about the oneness or unity of god.

(3) Although we know the nature of Theophrastus' account of Xenophanes' doctrines only partially and indirectly by way of extrapolation from later derivative accounts, it is quite likely that his *Opinions of the Inquirers into Nature* either equated or closely linked Xenophanes' theology with a monistic metaphysics. Simplicius writes (A31): 'Theophrastus says that Xenophanes of Colophon, the teacher of Parmenides, supposes that the first principle is one, or that what exists and the whole universe are one – and it is neither limited nor unlimited nor moving nor at rest – admitting that the citing of this man's opinion belongs more to another inquiry than to an inquiry concerning nature. For this is what god is: one and the whole universe, and he shows him to be one from his being the strongest of all things.' Setting aside for the moment the thesis that god must be 'one' in so far as he is the strongest, as well as the two pairs of predicates limited and unlimited, moving and at rest (see the discussion of the *MXG* in section 4, following), we may identify three Aristotelian features in this presentation: (a) Xenophanes was the teacher of Parmenides; (b) Xenophanes' god is (the) one; (c) Xenophanes' account does not really belong in a discussion of the principles of nature.

What is importantly new is the Xenophanean view of the '*archē* as one' or of 'what exists and the whole universe as one.' Simplicius attributes the view to Xenophanes and credits the information to Theophrastus (but we do not know the basis for that attribution; see Finkelberg,

148ff.). The idea becomes a leitmotif in other accounts deriving directly or indirectly from Theophrastus: the *MXG* (A28) alternates between 'god,' 'what is,' and 'the one'; for Cicero (A34), 'all things are one ... unchanging and (this) is god'; for Hippolytus (A33), 'the whole is one'; for Theodoretus (A36), 'the whole is one, spherical'; for Pseudo-Galen (A35), 'all things were one and that this was god.'

The actual basis for Theophrastus' characterization of Xenophanes remains a matter of conjecture. Perhaps other fragments relating either to god or the cosmos were known to him (for instance, fragment 24 on the *oulos* which sees, thinks, hears, etc.), which made the attribution of an Eleatic metaphysical monism irresistible. Alternatively, Theophrastus' view might have stemmed only from Xenophanes' comment on the oneness of the divine, a historic association with Elea, and the two loose identifications of Xenophanes made by Plato and Aristotle as, in some sense, a partisan of the One. In any case, Xenophanes the metaphysical monist becomes an orthodoxy – varying from one account to the next only in so far as the One is limited or unlimited, unmoving or neither moving nor at rest, spherical, all-alike, and either perceptive or rational.

(4) The 'Xenophanes' section of the treatise *On Melissus, Xenophanes, Gorgias* (A28, 977a14–979a9) purports to be a summary (ch. 3) and critical commentary (ch. 4) on Xenophanes' teachings on 'the One' or 'what exists' or 'god.' The credibility of its version of Xenophanes' philosophy has often been challenged, but it must be granted that *some* kernels of the doctrines expressed in the fragments appear during the author's exposition in chapter 3: (a) god does not come into being (cf. fragment 14); (b) god is eternal (cf. fragment 14 and A12); (c) god is the strongest of all things (cf. fragments 25 and 26 and A1, note 7); (d) god is one (cf. fragment 23); (e) he is alike in every way, perceptive in every part (cf. fragment 24). To these arguably Xenophanean elements the author (or perhaps the author of an earlier reconstruction he might have been following) adds sphericity. In support of this attribution one might cite the homogeneity of (e); the existence of 'sphere resemblance' in Parmenides' fragment 8.43 and of Empedocles' 'rounded sphere' in fragments 27.4, 28.2, and 29.3; as well as Xenophanes' status as the originator of all subsequent Eleatic ideas. Next comes 'neither limited nor unlimited' and 'neither moving nor at rest,' attributes generated (so Zeller 1963, Guthrie, KRS, and others have suggested) by a misunderstanding of a statement by Theophrastus to the effect that Xenophanes had nothing to say on these topics (namely, 'he says neither that it is limited nor unlimited, moving nor at rest'), an inference which

Theophrastus might have drawn from Aristotle's comment (at *Metaphysics* 986b20) that Xenophanes did not make it clear whether what exists is limited (as Parmenides thought) or unlimited (as Melissus thought). To establish the presence of these attributes the author deploys a number of arguments drawn from a running Eleatic debate (cf. the hypotheses of the second half of Plato's *Parmenides*, especially 137c–139a, 145a–b). The whole exercise is predicated on the highly questionable assumption that Xenophanes' comments about god can be taken equally well as statements about 'one' and 'being' or 'what exists' (for instance, 977b8–9: τὸ δὴ τοιοῦτον ἕν, ὂν τὸν θεὸν εἶναι λέγει). The 'Xenophanes' of the *MXG* is therefore something of a composite: a Colophonian-Eleatic-Peripatetic mélange.

A Peripatetic provenance for the *MXG* was suggested by Diels (1900), who set the date of composition in the third-century BC, later moving this back to the first century AD. Others have found evidence of Megarian ideas (Untersteiner, Reale) and sceptical tropes (Gercke, Mansfeld). None of these accounts has yet won general acceptance (the most recent proposal, Mansfeld, 1988 – that 'Anonymous' shows his Pyrrhonian colours by not taking sides on 'Xenophanes'' claim that god is neither limited nor unlimited – is not consistent with the line of argument at 978a16ff.). The following generalizations are warranted: (a) the author is au courant with the terms of the Eleatic debates of the second half of Plato's *Parmenides*; (b) the author deploys one argument against 'Xenophanes' based on a distinction between 'un-x' and 'not-x,' a contrast drawn as early as Plato's *Sophist* (257); (c) the author deploys another argument against 'Xenophanes' based on the principle that in some cases we may neither affirm nor deny a particular predicate, a point made as early as Aristotle *Categories* 12; (d) the author raises one objection to 'Xenophanes' on the ground that his idea of god is 'unconventional,' and is not acquired from what 'is agreed.' These comments, when linked with an earlier allusion to the opinions of the wise (975a17) and appeals to what 'seems' or 'appears' (977b28 and 978b34) and what 'we say or think' (977b29–30, 978a28, 978a36, and 978b32), mark the *MXG* author as a practitioner of Aristotelian analysis, examining views in light of previous and current opinions, either of 'the many' or 'the wise' (cf. *Nicomachean Ethics* 1098b9ff.; *Metaphysics* 933a30; etc.); and (e) the quality of the argumentation suggests that we are not dealing with a philosophical critic of the first rank. Diels' conjecture, therefore, remains credible: the author of the *MXG* was a minor Peripatetic thinker conversant with Eleatic debates who lived and wrote sometime after the third century BC (or at least far enough removed in place and time from Theophrastus to allow for uncorrected errors to enter into his account of Xenophanes' philosophical views).

(5) Some two centuries after his death Xenophanes reappears in fictional form as Timon's guide to the philosophical spirits of the past. In fragment 60 Timon awards him the qualified praise (so D.L. construes it: ἐπαίνεται ... φησι γοῦν), of being 'partly free of conceit' (ὑπάτυφος), that is, avoiding to some degree the state of confusion, dogmatism, vanity, and thirst for fame, pleasure, and luxury characteristic of the common run of men, total *atuphia* being the truly independent and blessed state of the sceptic sage (that is, Pyrrho). We may conjecture that the basis for Timon's praise was provided by the renunciation of knowledge of *to saphes* in fragment 34, various attacks on popular paragons of wisdom (Homer, Hesiod, Epimenides, Pythagoras), and the criticism of the Colophonians for their attachment to Lydian luxuries (fragment 3). Timon's reservations may have stemmed from Xenophanes' dogmatic sounding theological fragments (fragments 23–26; cf. Sextus' comment, *edogmatidze*) as well as from the high level of self-esteem Xenophanes displays in fragment 2: 'not being as worthy as I.'

Timon's comments on Xenophanes' philosophy display some ambivalence on the relationship between god and the universe. In fragment 59, Xenophanes is depicted as a recidivist monist, unable to adhere to full sceptical indifference, reverting instead to a belief in a 'single, uniform, stationary nature.' Yet in fragment 60 Xenophanes is credited with having fashioned a god who is 'equal in every way, <unshaken>, unscathed, and either thought or great in thought.' Timon does not say in either comment how the reduction of 'all that ever was' to a single nature can be squared with a god existing separately from men (although Sextus does not hesitate to blend them together: 'the whole is one, god is bound up with all things,' etc.). In assessing the credibility of Timon's portrayal of both Xenophanes' 'scepticism' as well as his metaphysics it is worth remembering that Timon was writing satire, not a history of philosophy. In much the same way that Aristophanes capitalized on Socrates' sometime involvement with Ionian science and his occasional moral scepticism in order to create a target for an attack on sophistry, Timon's portrait of Xenophanes may have a basis in isolated features of Xenophanes' teachings without being intended as an accurate and balanced summary of his doctrines.

Later versions of the 'sceptical' Xenophanes draw upon several different aspects of his teaching (as well as upon one another) to create something of a sceptical medley. For Sotion (whom we know to have written about Timon's *Silloi*), Xenophanes 'was the first to maintain that all things are incomprehensible' (ἀκατάληπτα εἶναι τὰ πάντα in D.L. A1, 20). Hippolytus makes the same claim in similar language (πρῶτος ἀκαταληψίαν in A33), and although Sextus rejects this interpretation (*Against the Professors* 7), he is aware of it. Both Sextus and Hippolytus quote portions of fragment 34 and we may at least suspect that Xenophanes' language there (e.g., τὸ σαφὲς οὔτις ἀνὴρ ἴδεν ... περὶ πάντων and δόκος ... ἐπὶ πᾶσι) inspired the *panta akatalēpta* interpretation in Sotion as well. By contrast, Cicero (in A25) speaks of Xenophanes and Parmenides as focusing their hostility upon false claimants to knowledge, 'those who dare to say they know when nothing can be known,' an inference which Cicero may have drawn from the *silloi* against Hesiod, Homer, and Pythagoras (fragments 7, 11, 12). Aristocles and Aëtius follow a third route, ascribing to Xenophanes a scepticism with regard to the senses, speaking in very general terms and grouping Xenophanes with an unusual collection of 'fellow sceptics' (Aristocles in A49: 'for Xenophanes, Parmenides, Zeno, and Melissus said something of this sort'; Aëtius in A49: 'Pythagoras, Empedocles, and Xenophanes [say that] sense perceptions are deceptive'). In Pseudo-Plutarch (A32), Xenophanes repudiates not only the senses, but (inspired by Democritus' fragment 125?) 'he rejects reason along with them.' Three centuries later, Pseudo-Galen provides what might be termed the logical extension of these inconsistent earlier views (A35): Xenophanes 'having doubted all things, believed firmly only that all things were one and that this was god, limited, rational, and changeless.'

(6) Perhaps nowhere is the term 'medley' more apposite than in connection with the account written by Diogenes Laertius early in the third century AD. Diels (1879, 140–41) compares Laertius' version of Xenophanes with those of Aëtius, Hippolytus, Plutarch, and (ultimately) Theophrastus. The closest correspondence on points of doctrine is with Hippolytus (Sotion on incomprehensibility, unlimited worlds, the sun's role in the formation of clouds, a spherical and eternal god, and the perishability of all things). Apart from his direct quotations from Timon and Xenophanes, Laertius' main contributions are his reports of a disagreement between Thales and Xenophanes (perhaps drawn from Aëtius' statement, in A47, of their differing opinions about the earth's shape), Xenophanes' disagreement with Pythagoras (based on fragment 7?), his repudiation of Epimenides (perhaps in some *sillos* which did not survive?), a non-breathing god (see note 1 on fragment 24 in chapter 2 above), a cryptic comment on *noos* (see note 8 on A1 following), and (in book I) a questionable report of Xenophanes' 'admiration' for Thales' ability to predict eclipses and the solstices (see the

commentary on fragment 19 in chapter 3 above). While no one would describe the *Lives of the Philosophers* as cautious, principled, intellectual history, it must be conceded that the two most popular constructions of the ancient testimonia, Xenophanes as Eleatic monist and Xenophanes as complete sceptic, were absent from Laertius' account.

Except where noted to the contrary, the following are translations of the ancient Xenophanes testimonia contained in D-K. Square brackets, [ ], and pointed brackets, < >, when they occur within translated texts, indicate material deleted from or added in D-K. Parentheses, ( ), mark off material supplied to facilitate translation or assure clarity. Asterisks, ***, mark portions of the translation where the Greek text is either unknown or highly uncertain. References included within brackets are limited to material contained elsewhere in D-K. References to these passages follow the format in D-K; e.g., '1.86.18' would mean 'volume one, page 86, line 18.' References to Diels are to his *Doxographi Graeci* 3rd ed. (Berlin 1879).

LIFE AND TEACHING

A1

Diogenes Laertius *Lives of the Philosophers* 9.18ff. (18) Xenophanes, son of Dexius, or – according to Apollodorus – Orthomenes, from Colophon, is praised by Timon; at least he says [fragment 60 Diels, cf. 21 A35]:

Xenophanes (*Xeinophanē*), partly free of conceit,[1] perverter of Homer,[2] satirist.

When he was driven out of his homeland he spent time in Zancle in Sicily <and having joined the colony sent to Elea, also taught there>. He also spent some time in Catana. According to some he was no man's pupil, but according to others he was a pupil of Boton of Athens, or, as some say, of Archelaus.[3] Also, as Sotion says, he lived about the time of Anaximander. He wrote in both elegiac and iambic verse against Hesiod and Homer, criticizing the things they say about the gods. But he also recited his own works. He is said to have held views opposed

1 ὑπάτυφον: see note 2 on Timon, fragment 60 (A35).
2 D-K: ὁμηραπάτην, although some mss read ὁμηροπάτην – 'one who tramples on Homer' (from πατέω), and Sextus at 1.224 (A35) shows by his explanation that he understands Timon to be characterizing Xenophanes as a critic of the deception (*apatē*) there was in Homer.
3 D-K (p. 113n) suggests that this improbable claim resulted from a confusion of Xenophanes with Xenophon.

to those of Thales [fragment 19] and Pythagoras [fragment 7], and he also rebuked Epimenides [fragment 20]. He lived to a very great age, as indeed he himself says: 'already ... truly' [fragment 8].

(19) He says that there are four elements of existing things, an unlimited number of worlds, but not overlapping one another.[4] The clouds are formed by the sun's vapour[5] raising and lifting them up to the surrounding (air). The being of god is spherical, having no similarity to man. Whole it sees and whole it hears, but it does not breathe, being wholly mind and thought and eternal.[6] He was the first to declare that everything that comes to be is perishable and that the soul is breath. He said also that the multitude of things cannot compete with mind[7] and that he encountered tyrants as seldom or as pleasantly as possible.

(20) When Empedocles said to him that a wise man goes undiscovered he said 'Naturally, since it takes a wise man to recognize a wise

4 οὐ παραλλακτοὺς δέ: LSJ gives 'liable to change' (for παραλλακτός), which results in the difficult 'unlimited worlds, but not liable to change.' παράλλαξις can, however, mean 'alternation,' 'overlapping,' as in the overlapping of broken bones (Hippocrates *Concerning Fractures* 15; cf. *On the Art* 16), and so construed here, Xenophanes' assertion would mean that 'there are an unlimited number of worlds, but they do not overlap with one another,' i.e., over vast stretches of time there would be many worlds or 'world arrangements' (cf. πᾶσι τοῖς κόσμοις in Hippolytus, A33), but there would be only one such world existing at any time. The 'overlapping' metaphor by itself might suggest the possibility of the later conception of multiple worlds existing during the same period of time (and οὐ παραλλακτός would mean only that these worlds were spatially isolated from one another), but Hippolytus' account points toward understanding the plurality of worlds as existing *successively*. See further, Gilbert, 98n.

5 τῆς ἀφ' ἡλίου ἀτμίδος – 'the sun's vapour' or 'the vapour from the sun.' The phrase has been thought problematic (Guthrie 1, 391n; Heidel 1913, 693), but Xenophanes' explanation of the waters that rise from the sea through the heat from the sun (Aëtius in A46) provides a clue to its meaning. The vapour that forms itself into clouds is the 'sun's vapour' since it is produced by the sun's heating of the surface of the sea (cf. LSJ, s.v. ἀπό, III, 3).

6 For an account of the meaning of this assertion see the note on οὖλος and the commentary on fragment 24 in chapter 2 above.

7 τὰ πολλὰ ἥσσω νοῦ εἶναι: alternatively 'the mass of things falls short of thought' (Hicks). The only mention of νόος in Xenophanes' fragments relates to the divine νόος which shakes all things by the active exercise of its thought (fragment 25). Since god can achieve this effect on 'all things' (πάντα) in a completely effortless manner, this might explain why 'the many' (τὰ πολλά) 'give way' (ἥσσω, cf. LSJ, s.v. ἥσσων, IIc) to νόος/νοῦς. Cf. Simonides, fragment 31 (Edmonds): ἅπαντα γάρ ἐστι θεῶν ἥσσω – 'all these give way to the gods.' It is also possible that the remark refers to potency of normal human intelligence, i.e., 'most problems give way to intelligence,' as in Xenophanes' fragment 18 (ζητοῦντες ἐφευρίσκουσιν ἄμεινον, etc.). Finally, the comment might be a statement of the general *inferiority* of most things to intelligence (cf. LSJ, s.v. ἥσσων, I, and Aristotle *Nicomachean Ethics* 1178a1–2).

man [cf. 31 A20]. Sotion says he was the first to say that all things are incomprehensible [cf. fragment 34], but he is misled.

He created poems about both the founding of Colophon and the settlement of a colony at Elea in Italy, two thousand verses. And he flourished during the sixtieth Olympiad[8] [cf. fragment 8.4]. Demetrius of Phalerum says in *Concerning Old Age,* and Panaetius the Stoic says in *Concerning Cheerfulness,* that he buried his sons with his own hands, just as Anaxagoras did. It is thought that he was sold into slavery, <*and released from it> by the Pythagoreans Parmeniscus and Orestades, so Favorinus says in the first book of his *Memorabilia.* There was also another Xenophanes, an iambic poet from Lesbos.

A2

Diogenes Laertius 9.21. Parmenides, son of Pyres, from Elea, was a pupil of Xenophanes. Theophrastus in his *Epitome* [fragment 6a; Diels, 482] says he[9] was a pupil of Anaximander. Cf. 28 A1.

A3

Heraclitus, fragment 40 [22 B40]. The learning of many things[10] does not teach one to have understanding,[11] or else it would have taught Hesiod and Pythagoras, and again[12] Xenophanes and Hecataeus.

A4

Cicero *Prior Academics* 2.118 (D-K: from Theophrastus). Xenophanes (who was) a little earlier (D-K: than Anaxagoras) (said that) all things were one.

---

8 I.e., 540–537 BC; see the note on A8.
9 Diels argues (103–04) that the statement about Theophrastus is an editor's marginal note referring to Xenophanes.
10 The emphasis should be placed on the idea of plurality, in contrast to true wisdom, which is to know *one* basic truth (ἐν τὸ σοφόν· ἐπίστασθαι γνώμην, etc. fragment 41).
11 ἔχειν νόον: Here νόος appears to be an acquired state rather than a natural endowment (i.e., 'mind'), hence parallel to the meaning of νόος and φρήν in Heraclitus' fragment 104 and of φρενί in Xenophanes' fragment 25.
12 The grouping of Xenophanes with the Ionian historian Hecataeus (rather than with the two claimants to special religious information, Hesiod and Pythagoras) suggests that Heraclitus regarded Xenophanes as a man of some learning, but deaf to the deep principle of unity that governs the kosmos, i.e., lacking in ξύνεσις (see the concluding essay in chapter 3 above).

A5

Diogenes Laertius 8.56 [see 31 A1]. (According to) Hermippus, he (D-K: Empedocles) was an admirer not of Parmenides but of Xenophanes with whom he lived for a time and whose poetry he imitated [cf. A1].

A6

Pseudo-Lucian *Long Lives* 20. Xenophanes, the son of Dexinos, a pupil of the natural philosopher Archelaus, lived ninety-one years.

A7

Censorinus 15.3. Xenophanes of Colophon lived more than a hundred years.

A8

Clement *Miscellanies* 1.64 (2.40.20). Of the Eleatic school of philosophy, the founder is Xenophanes, who Timaeus says [fragment 92, *Fragmenta historicorum Graecorum* 1.215] lived in the time of Hieron, tyrant of Sicily,[13] and Epicharmus, the poet; Apollodorus (says) [*Fragmente der griechischen Historiker*, 244 F68c; 2.1039] he was born during the fortieth Olympiad [620–617] and lived on until the times of Darius and Cyrus. (From the same source, Sextus Empiricus *Against the Professors* 1.257:) Xenophanes of Colophon was born around the fortieth Olympiad[14] [cf. fragment 8].

A9

Eusebius *Chronology*

(a) Fifty-sixth Olympiad [556–553] Xenophanes of Colophon became known.

---

13 The period of Hieron's reign was 478–467 BC.
14 Von Fritz (1945, 228n) comments: 'Clement ... and Sextus Empiricus ... cannot be correct when they say that Apollodorus placed the birth of Xenophanes in the fortieth Olympiad, i.e., 620 BC. This would also be at variance with the statement of Timaeus (also quoted by Clement) that Xenophanes came to the court of Hieron of Syracuse. The error in Sextus and Clement is probably due to a confusion of the figures M and N [i.e., reading M – the fortieth Olympiad – rather than N – the fiftieth].' See also the discussion of Apollodorus by Woodbury.

(b) Fifty-ninth to Sixty-first Olympiads [corrected to the first year of the Sixtieth Olympiad = 540] Ibycus the lyric poet and Pherecydes the historian and Phocylides and Xenophanes the natural philosopher and Thespis the tragic poet. Cf. A1 and A6 above.

A10

Theologoumena Arithmeticae p. 40 Ast. [= 14 A8, 26ff.]. For nearly five hundred and fourteen years are recorded from the time of the Trojan wars until the time of Xenophanes the natural philosopher and the times of both Anacreon and Polycrates and of the siege and desolation of the Ionians by Harpagus the Mede, which the Phocaeans fled when they settled Massilia.

SAYINGS [Cf. A1]

A11

Plutarch *Sayings of Kings and Commanders* 175c. But addressing Xenophanes the Colophonian who was saying that he could hardly support two servants, he (D-K: Hieron) said: 'But Homer, whom you disparage, supports more than ten thousand even though he is dead.'

A12

Aristotle *Rhetoric* B 23, 1399b5. Another [D-K: sc. line of argument] is this: if the conclusion is the same then the antecedents are the same. For example, Xenophanes used to say that 'those who say that the gods are born are as impious as those who say that they die'; for it follows on both views that there is a time when the gods do not exist.

A13

Aristotle *Rhetoric* B 26, 1400b5. For example, the citizens of Elea asked Xenophanes if they should sacrifice to Leucothea and mourn for her, or not; he advised them not to mourn if they took her to be a goddess, and not to sacrifice to her if they took her to be human.

Plutarch *On Loving* 18.12.763d. Xenophanes urged the Egyptians, if they considered Osiris a mortal, not to honour him in so far as he was a mortal, but if they considered him a god, not to mourn for him.

Plutarch *On Isis and Osiris* 70.379b. Quite rightly Xenophanes the Colophonian insisted that the Egyptians not mourn if they considered them gods, and if they mourned, not to consider them gods [cf. 22 B127].

Plutarch *On Superstition* 13.171e. Xenophanes the natural philosopher, observing the Egyptians singing dirges and conducting mourning rituals, properly suggested: 'if these are gods,' he said, 'do not mourn for them; and if they are human, do not sacrifice to them.' [cf. Pseudo-Plutarch *Roman Sayings* 26.228e].

A14

Aristotle *Rhetoric* A 15, 1377a19. And it is a fitting saying of Xenophanes that the same challenge [D-K: to the oath] is not equal for an ungodly man in comparison with a godly man, but rather like a strong man challenging a weak man either to hit or be hit.[15]

A15

Aristotle *Metaphysics* Γ 5, 1010a4. ... wherefore they speak plausibly, but they do not say what is true. For it is fitting to put it thus rather than to speak as Epicharmus puts it against Xenophanes.[16]

15 We should understand Xenophanes' comment in light of the ancient practice of giving and taking oaths as a way of advancing one's side of a dispute in a court of law (cf. Aristotle *Rhetoric* 1377a7ff.). The ungodly man, since he has no reason to fear divine punishment for false swearing, will always be willing to take an oath or propose that both parties to the dispute take one. Hence an offer of an oath or a challenge to an oath from such a person should carry less weight in the adjudication of a dispute than the same offer by a godly man; as Aristotle explains, the ungodly man's offer is as gratuitous a gesture as a strong man offering a weak man the opportunity to take the first punch in an exchange of blows. (For a recent discussion of the legal practice, see the study by Mirhady, 25–26.)

16 Ross comments on this passage, 'Epicharmus may have said that Xenophanes' views were "neither plausible nor true," or that they were "true but not plausible."' The source of Epicharmus' remark might have been Xenophanes' fragment 35, ἐοικότα τοῖς ἐτύμοισι (cf. Aristotle: εἰκότως μὲν λέγουσι, οὐκ ἀληθῆ). Since Epicharmus seems to follow Xenophanes' teachings in some respects (e.g., Epicharmus, fragment 12, on νοῦς; fragment 36, on the gods as the source of goods; fragment 38, 44a, on pleasures; etc.), 'neither true nor plausible' would be unlikely. Hence what Epicharmus said against Xenophanes was probably that 'he spoke the truth although it did not appear plausible.'

A16

Plutarch *On Being Shamefaced* 5.530e. Don't be ashamed or afraid of being scoffed at, but (do) just as Xenophanes who, when Lasus of Hermione called him a coward for not wanting to play dice with him, confessed to being both very much afraid and cowardly about doing shameful things.

A17

Plutarch *Against the Stoics on Common Conceptions* 46.3.1084f. Indeed Xenophanes, when someone told of having seen eels living in hot water, said, 'Very well then, we will cook[17] them in cold.'

POETRY

A18

Diogenes Laertius 9.22. ... and he himself (D-K: Parmenides) philosophizes in verses just as did Hesiod, Xenophanes, and Empedocles. Cf. 11 B1 (1.80.8ff), 21 A5 (1.114.20).

A19

Diogenes Laertius 9.18 (1.113.18); 2.46 (cf. 1.103.10). [D-K: sc. Homer was criticized] after his death by Xenophanes of Colophon just as Hesiod was criticized during his lifetime by Cercops[18] and after his death by the Xenophanes just mentioned.

A20

Strabo 14.643. Xenophanes, the natural philosopher, the composer of the *Silloi* in verses ...

---

17 Lit. 'boil' ($\xi\psi\omega$). Even 'cooking in cold water' is a peculiar idea, but the point of Xenophanes' comment may have related to the conditions necessary for life: if eels can live in hot water, they will die in cold water; cf. Heraclitus, fragment 61 (on seawater as life-sustaining *and* deadly). For a discussion of the tradition of 'inter-species relativism,' see Kahn 1979, 185–89.

18 Cercops of Miletus, 6th(?)-century BC epic poet.

A21

Apuleius *Florida* 20. ... for Empedocles composed poems, Plato dialogues, Socrates hymns, Epicharmus comedies, Xenophon histories, Xenophanes [D-K: ?][19] satires.

A22

Proclus, on Hesiod *Works and Days* 284 (from Plutarch). It is said that Xenophanes produced his strange *Silloi* against all philosophers and poets because of a certain animus toward the philosophers and poets of his own era.

A23

Scholium ABT on *Iliad* 2.212. Homer and not Xenophanes was already the first to compose *silloi* in which he himself attacks Thersites and Thersites (attacks) the best (of the Achaeans).

A24

Arius Didymus in Stobaeus *Physical Selections* 2.1.18 (p. 6, 14 Wachsmuth). There was a respectable tradition among the Greeks concerning first Xenophanes that he rebuked in jest the audacity of others and demonstrated his own piety (in holding that) god therefore knows the truth, while 'opinion is allotted to all' (fragment 34.4). Cf. 21 A35.

A25

Cicero *Prior Academics* 2.23.74. Although in less good verses [D-K: i.e., than those of Empedocles], nevertheless in verses Parmenides and Xenophanes rebuke almost like angry men the arrogance of those who dare to say that they know when in fact nothing can be known.

A26

Philo *On Providence* 2.39. Nevertheless, neither Xenophanes nor Parmenides nor Empedocles nor any other theologians taken by the poetic muse are divinely inspired men [D-K: sc. they fashioned the gods

19 Perhaps instead 'Xenocrates' (mss, Helm) or 'Crates' (Rohde, Vallette).

as liars] but rather they are known as the best sort of men, having embraced the contemplation of nature and dedicating their entire lives to piety and honour for the gods. But as poets they were not successful: (and those were men) who ought to have received from the gods heavenly grace in meter, song, and rhythm so that they might leave behind true poems as a finished work and fine example for all.

Ibid. 42. . . . moreover, why did Empedocles, Parmenides, Xenophanes, and the crowd of their imitators not receive the inspiration of the Muses when they practised theology?

A27

Athenaeus *Scholars at Dinner* 14.632c–d. That the ancient poets were naturally accustomed to music is clear also from Homer, who because he wrote all of his poems to be sung, often without thinking composes lines which drop the first short syllable or replace a long syllable with a short one either within the line or at its ending. But Xenophanes, Solon, Theognis, Phocylides, and also Periander the Corinthian elegiac poet, and the others who do not add music to their poems execute their verses according to the number and arrangements of the meters and see to it that not one line is shortened at the outset or made to contain shortened syllables within the line or at its end.

TEACHING

A28

Pseudo-Aristotle *On Melissus, Xenophanes, Gorgias* 3, 4 (ed. Bekker). Ch. 3.977a14: (1) He[20] says that it is impossible, if something exists, for it to have come into being, saying this about god. For it is necessary that what comes into being come either from what is like or what is unlike. But neither is possible. For it is not fitting for what is like to have been begotten from what is like rather than to beget it (for all are the same, are related to one another in equal ways, and exist similarly) nor can what is unlike come into being from what is unlike. (2) For if the stronger could come into being from the weaker, or the greater from the less, or the better from the worse, or conversely, worse things from better ones, what-is would come into being from what-is-not, which is

20 Xenophanes or 'Xenophanes': see the introduction to part 3.

impossible.[21] For these reasons accordingly god is eternal.[22] (3) And if god is the strongest of all things, he says that it is fitting for god to be one. For if there were two or more, he would no longer be the strongest and best of all things. For since each of the plurality would be a god, each would be similar to such a being. For this is what god and god's nature is: to master and not to be mastered, and to be the strongest of all things. So that in so far as he were not the strongest, to this extent he would not be god. (4) If then there were many gods, in some ways stronger and in other ways weaker than one another, they would not be gods. For it is inherent in the nature of the divine not to be mastered. (5) And if there were equal gods, they would not possess the nature of a god, who must be the strongest; the equal is neither better nor worse than its equal. So if there is a god and he is of such a sort, that god can only be one. For neither would he be able to do all that he might wish, if there were many gods. He must therefore be only one. (6) But being one he must be alike in every way, seeing and hearing and having all the senses in every part. For if this were not so, the parts of god would rule and he ruled by one another, which is impossible.[23]

(7) Being alike in all parts, he is spherical, for he cannot be of such a nature in one part but not in another, but (must be of such a nature) in every part. (8) But being eternal and one and <alike and> spherical, he must be neither unlimited nor limited. <For> what-is-not is unlimited since this has neither a middle nor beginning nor end nor any other part, and the unlimited is of this sort. But what-is cannot be the same sort of thing as what-is-not. If being were many, then the many would limit one another, but the one is similar neither to what is not nor to the many, for <being one> it does not have anything in relation to which it will have a limit. (9) The one, being of this sort – which he says god to be – neither moves nor is motionless, for it is what-is-not that is motionless – since another thing cannot go to where it is, nor can it go

21 The proverbial 'Parmenidean horror': what-is-not issuing forth into what-is. Here the impossibility of creation ex nihilo is used to argue that various qualities (strength, greatness, goodness) cannot come into being from their contraries (weakness, smallness, inferiority) or vice versa; in both respects, 'what-is' would have to come from 'what-is-not.'

22 Presumably since god can come into being neither from what he is like nor from what he is unlike.

23 Perhaps because a being with such dissimilar parts would no longer qualify as truly 'alike' in its very nature, or perhaps because the very idea of a 'subordinate divine part' would be regarded as absurd, in light of sec. 4 above (to be mastered is not in keeping with having a divine nature).

to where another thing is.[24] Movement belongs to pluralities, since one thing must move to where another thing is, and nothing could move to where what-is-not is, (10) for what-is-not exists in no place; but if they could change places with one another, the one would have to be more than one. For these reasons then two things, or more than one thing, could move, but that which is nothing is at rest and motionless. (11) And the one is neither at rest nor moving, for it is similar neither to what-is-not nor to the many.[25] Since god exists in all these ways, he is eternal and one, alike <in all his parts> and spherical, neither unlimited nor limited, neither at rest nor moving. Ch. 4 (1) First[26] then he too understands, as does Melissus [30 A 5], that what comes into being comes from what exists. And yet what would prevent that which comes into being coming not from what is like <or what is unlike> but rather from what-is-not? Further, god would be no more ungenerated than all other things, if indeed we assume that all things come into being either from what is like or from what is unlike – which is impossible. So either there is nothing else besides god or else all the other things are eternal.[27] (2) Further, he understands that god is the strongest, meaning by this the most powerful and best. But this does not appear

24 Lit. 'for another cannot go to it nor it to another.' The argument rests on a distinctive conception of motion, seen elsewhere in the *MXG* (sec. 18 following), in fragment 26, and in Parmenides' account of his motionless one: 'movement' means 'change of location,' 'vacating one's spot and going to the location of another thing.' As Mourelatos observed (1970, 118–19), this is a conception of motion rich with the possibilities of paradox.

25 The argument of sections 9–11 appears to parallel the argument of section 8: 'it' (being god) must be neither moving nor motionless since in being motionless it would share in the nature of what-is-not (which is motionless) – and this is impossible – nor can it move (i.e., relocate itself to the location of something else) since only 'it' exists.

26 Chapter 4 represents a different authorial voice, reviewing in a critical vein the main lines of argument laid out in ch. 3, along with several assumptions on which those arguments rest. For a discussion of the author's philosophical orientation see the introduction to part 3.

27 Two separate objections are raised: the author asks why that which comes into being couldn't come from what-is-not (the naiveté of this comment is perhaps explained by a prior argument against Melissus at 975a7–17, citing *sophoi* who have held that something could come into being from nothing). There is no indication that the author is aware of Aristotle's response to the Eleatic objection to qualitative change (*Physics* 1.8), and of Aristotle's opinion (191b12) that, in a certain absolute respect, the Eleatic thesis is correct. He also points out that the arguments of 3.1–3.2 will serve equally well to prove that coming into being is impossible generally, hence either nothing other than god has come into existence, or (if anything has) then it has always existed. Although this is not said to be unacceptable,

to be the conventional view, which on the contrary is that the gods are in many respects superior to one another. He did not therefore acquire this idea of god in concurrence with what is commonly thought.[28] (3) That god is the strongest is not to be understood in the sense that his nature is of such a sort relative to something else, but rather relative to his own disposition – since, were it in fact relative to another, there would be nothing to prevent his excelling in strength and goodness except the weakness of the others. But no one would want to say that god was strongest in this way, but rather that he exists in the best possible way, and lacks nothing for existing well and in an excellent way, and these other (attributes) would also result for one who was his equal.[29] (4) For nothing would prevent (these gods) – even if there were more than one-from existing in this way, all of them in the best possible state, and superior to the others, though not to themselves. (5) But, as it appears (from what Xenophanes says), there *are* also other things, for he says that god is the strongest, and this is necessarily among (that is, in comparison with) some things.

And, being one, it does not befit it at all to see and hear in every part, for if it were not to see in some particular part, it wouldn't be seeing worse, it just wouldn't see at all.[30] But perhaps this means that it perceives in every part because in existing in this way it would be in the best condition, being alike in every part. (6) Further, being of such a sort, why should its being spherical rather than its being some other shape cause it to hear (and see) and master in every part? For when we

---

'things' do exist and they are not all eternal, hence the 'proof' against ungenerability should be rejected.

28 Xenophanes' view of god's unmatched strength is characterized as 'unconventional' (οὐ ... κατὰ τὸν νόμον). Mansfeld (1988) suggests that this argument is best construed as an example of Aenesidemus' fifth sceptical trope, a form of an argument *ex consensu omnium* or, conversely, from *diaphōnia*, thus revealing the Pyrrhonian orientation of the anonymous author. Yet pointing out that an opponent's premise is not drawn from common agreement would be a familiar feature of dialectical argument (cf. Aristotle *Topics* 110a33: ἐξ ὁμολογίας διαλέγεσθαι).

29 Reading ἅμα as in mss, primarily to provide some continuity to what is otherwise a jumbled train of thought. The author seems to be arguing against the idea that god's greatness in strength or power implies that there can only be one god (3.3–3.5), but gets sidetracked into a discussion of 'absolute' as opposed to merely 'relative' strength. His 'refutation' appears to rest on the conceptual possibility of several gods, all maximally strong, but none of this is clearly explained.

30 The point is apparently that divine perceptiveness in all parts is not required either by god's unity or perfection; not being perceptive in a particular part would not necessarily imply being perceptive in some bad or inferior way, just not being perceptive (in that part) at all.

say of white lead that it is white in every way we mean only that white-
ness colours it in all its parts. In just the same way what would prevent
'seeing and hearing and being master in every way' from meaning
there too that every part of it which one might take would be characterized in this way? (7) Further, how is it possible for it to be a body
and have magnitude and yet be neither unlimited nor limited? Since
that is unlimited in so far as it lacks a limit – while capable of having
one – and since a limit is inherent in magnitude and number and in
everything that possesses quantity, then if it had no limits, wouldn't it
– in so far as it was a magnitude – be unlimited? (8) Moreover, if it is
spherical then it necessarily has a limit, for it has extremities – if it has
a middle point from which they are furthest away. And being spherical, it has a middle point, for this is what a sphere is: that which has
its extremities equally distant from the centre. (9) It makes no difference whether the body has 'extremities' or limits *** (for in either case
it would be limited. But it is also possible that what-is is unlimited)
***[31] for even if what-is-not is unlimited, why wouldn't what-is also be
unlimited? For what prevents some of the same things being said of
what-is as well as of what-is-not? For there are existing things which no
one now perceives (as well as) non-existing things, since one may fail
to perceive even the existing thing one currently perceives.[32] Both can
be said and thought *** (Similarly there are non-white existing things
as well as) *** non-white non-existing things.[33] Either for this reason
all existing things would be white[34] – so that we wouldn't be speaking
in the same way about existing and non-existing things – or, as I think

31 Following Diels' notation of a lacuna in the text (as appears evident from the
   change in subject-matter). The material within parentheses is merely one of many
   possible ways to fill in the lacuna.
32 The lacunae in the text make an exact translation difficult here (and in lines 28ff.),
   but the main point is that it is legitimate to apply some predicates to both existing as well as non-existing things. Here, 'not perceived' is an attribute which can
   be applied to both sorts of things (and even existing things can be 'not perceived'
   from time to time). The objective of this argument is to show that (contrary to the
   earlier claim at 977b5–6) one *can* say that what-is can be unlimited even though
   what-is-not can also be said to be unlimited. The same issue arises in sections
   4.12 and 4.15–4.18.
33 Something like the material I have supplied in parentheses is necessary in order
   for the argument about 'non-white' to parallel the argument about 'not perceived';
   i.e., that these predicates can be ascribed to existing and non-existing things alike.
   The overall objective remains that of showing that what-is can be spoken of as
   unlimited (even though what-is-not may also be unlimited).
34 Everything would be white, that is, if we assumed both that what did not exist was non-white and that what-is and what-is-not could never share any of the
   same attributes.

is true, nothing prevents any one of the existing things from being non-white. Hence, if in accordance with what was said earlier something is unlimited from its not having <a limit>, it might even more readily accept the negative [the unlimited]. So what-is is either unlimited or has a limit.[35] (10) But it is perhaps strange to attribute being unlimited to a non-existent thing. For we do not say that everything which lacks a limit is unlimited, just as we would not say that 'not equal' is 'unequal.'[36] (11) <Further>, why, since god is one, wouldn't he have a limit, but not relative to god? And if god is only one, the parts of god would also be one. (12) Further, this is also strange: that since the many attributes limit one another the one would have no limit. For many of the same qualities belong to the many and to the one, since even existence is common to them (both). It would accordingly perhaps be strange to deny for this reason that there was a god in so far as there are many things – to prevent him from being like them in this way. (13) Further, what prevents god from being limited and having limits in so far as he is one thing? As Parmenides also says, it is one 'in every way similar to the bulk of a well-rounded sphere, equally balanced from the centre' [fragment 8.43]. For while the limit of a thing must exist, it needn't exist as a separate *thing*, nor is it necessary that that which has a limit have its limit in relation to another thing – as something is limited in an infinite series by being next to something else. But while being limited is having extremities, something having extremities need not have those (extremities) relative to something else. (14) It might be true in some cases that things were limited <and> in relation to something, but in other cases it might be possible for things to be limited and not be limited by something else relative (to them). (15) Again, concerning the motionlessness of what-is and of what-is-<not>, <it must be said that the assumption that what-is-not is motionless> because what-is moves, is perhaps as strange as the previous absurdities. And further, no one would assume that 'not moving' and 'unmoved' were the same thing, but the former is the denial of movement (just like 'not equal'), which can be truly said of what-is-not. But doesn't 'unmoved' already speak of something as existing in a certain way, just as 'unequal' (does), and in a state opposite to that of moving,

---

35 Rather than *neither* unlimited *nor* limited – as was maintained at ch. 3.8.

36 The general thesis is that, for any predicate 'x,' we may properly predicate 'x' or 'un-x' only of existing things; while 'not x' may also be predicated of what does not exist, even 'what-is-not' itself. Hence, we may say that what-is-not is 'not limited' or 'not moving,' etc., but we may not say that it is either limited or unlimited, moving or unmoving, etc. The discussion of this point is continued, even belaboured, in ch. 4.15, following.

(namely) being at rest, as negations by means of an 'un'-prefix[37] just mean their opposites? Accordingly 'not moving' can truly be predicated of what-is-not, but 'at rest' cannot belong to what-is-not. Similarly 'unmoved' does not mean the same.[38] But he uses it in the sense of 'at rest' and says that what-is-not is at rest because it cannot change. (16) As we have said above, it is perhaps strange to say that whatever we attribute to what-is-not cannot (also) be truly spoken of what-is, especially if what is said is a denial, as for example 'not moving' and 'not changing.' For, as has also been said, this would greatly reduce our ability to speak about existing things. For then it would not be true to say that the many were 'not one,' if indeed what is not were 'not one.' (17) Further, in some cases the opposites seem to follow from the same denials; for example, it is necessary for something to be either equal or unequal if it is any quantity or magnitude, or odd or even if it is a number, perhaps similarly with being either of necessity 'at rest' or 'moving' if it is a body. (18) Further, if god and the one do not move because the things that are many move by exchanging places with one another, what prevents god from moving into another (place)? For he nowhere says that only one thing exists, but rather that there is only one god,[39] (19) and if this is so, what prevents god from moving in a circle by having his parts move into one another's locations? For he will certainly not say, as Zeno does, that a one of this sort is a many. For he himself says that god is a body, whether this is 'the whole' or whether he calls it anything else; for how, lacking a body, could god be spherical? (20) And the only way in which he could neither be moving nor at rest would be if he existed in no way at all.[40] And since he is a body, what would prevent him from moving, as was said?

A29

Plato *Sophist* 242c–d.[D-K: the Eleatic Stranger is speaking] It seems to me that each narrates a certain story to us as though we were children.

---

37 In Greek, the alpha privative: ἀκίνητος, ἄνισος, etc.
38 That is, again, 'unmoved' (ἀκίνητος) does not mean the same as 'not moving' (τὸ μὴ κινεῖσθαι).
39 The author appears finally to drop the pretence that Xenophanes presented a general metaphysical account. Greater candour on this matter at the outset (e.g., at 977a1: 'saying this about god') might have made manifest the limited utility of the *MXG* as testimony on Xenophanes' teachings.
40 The sense seems to require moving the Greek semi-colon (as in Diels) to the end of the sentence.

One says that there are three realities, and on occasion some of them war with one another in some way, but then they also become friends and arrange for marriages and offspring and the raising of their children. But another one says there are two realities, the wet and the dry, or the hot and the cold, and he also gives them away in marriage and has them settle down together [cf. 60 A4?] But our Eleatic tribe, beginning from Xenophanes as well as even earlier [cf. 1 B6; *Philebus* 16c–d], relates its stories on the assumption that what are called 'all things' are really one.

Philoponus *Commentary on Aristotle's Physics* 125.27 (Vitelli). Porphyry says that Xenophanes held that the dry and the wet were first principles, I mean (by this) earth and water, and he cites a passage from him to make this clear: 'All things which come into being and grow are earth and water' [fragment 29]. It seems that Homer is also of this opinion when he says: 'But may you all become water and earth' [*Iliad* 7.99].

A30

Aristotle *Metaphysics* A 5, 986b18 For it seems that Parmenides conceived of it as one in definition, Melissus of it as one in matter; accordingly the former says it is limited while the latter says it is unlimited. But Xenophanes, the first partisan of the One, for Parmenides is said to have been his pupil, made nothing completely clear nor does he seem to have touched on the nature of either of these, but with regard to[41] the whole universe,[42] he says that the one is god.[43] [cf. fragment 23] Accordingly these men, as we said, must be set aside for the purposes of the present inquiry, two of them – Xenophanes and Melissus – entirely aside as being rather naïve.

41 εἰς ... ἀποβλέψας: 'with a view toward,' i.e., 'in regard to,' 'with reference to,' etc. (cf. *Metaphysics* 991a23; *On the Soul* 404b7; *Categories* 5b1; etc.; and note 1 of the concluding essay of chapter 2.

42 τὸν ὅλον οὐρανόν: 'the whole heaven,' 'the heavens,' 'the whole universe' (LSJ, I, 4). Since Aristotle has just alluded to the Pythagorean theory of τὸν ὅλον οὐρανόν (986a3) = τὴν ὅλην διακόσμησιν (986a5–6), it is clear that it is the nature or arrangement of the entire physical universe that is under discussion.

43 τὸ ἓν εἶναί φησι τὸν θεόν: 'he says that the One is god' (KRS); 'the one exists and it is God' or 'the one exists, namely the god' or 'the One exists, the god' (Guthrie); perhaps 'he says that (the) god is (the) one.' The meaning of Aristotle's comment has been much debated (see the introduction to part 3 and the commentary on fragment 23 in chapter 2 above).

A31

Simplicius *Commentary on Aristotle's Physics* 22.22ff. (1) It is necessary then for the first principle to be either one or not one, which is to say more than one; and if one, either moving or unmoving; and if unmoving, either unlimited as Melissus of Samos seems to say, or limited as Parmenides son of Pyres from Elea holds; they were speaking not in terms of the physical element, but concerning the real nature of being. (2) Theophrastus [*Opinions of the Inquirers into Nature*, fragment 5; Diels, 480] says that Xenophanes of Colophon, the teacher of Parmenides, supposes that the first principle is one, or that what exists and the whole universe[44] are one – and neither limited nor unlimited nor moving nor at rest – admitting that the citing of this man's opinion belongs more to another inquiry than to an inquiry concerning nature. (3) For this is what god is: one and the whole universe, and he proves that it is one on the basis of (god's) being the strongest of all things. For if there were more than one, he says, the strength would necessarily belong in like fashion to them all; but god is the strongest and best of all. (4) He showed that it is ungenerated from the fact that it is necessary that a generated thing must come either from the like or the unlike. But he says that the like cannot be affected by the like, for it is in no way fitting for the like either to produce or be produced from the like. But if it were to come from the unlike what is would be coming from what is not. And that is how he showed it was ungenerated and eternal. (5) It is neither limited nor unlimited since what is not is unlimited in so far as it has neither beginning nor middle nor end, and a plurality of things limit one another. (6) In much the same way he eliminates motion and rest, for what is not is unmoving, since another thing could not go to where it is, nor could it go to the place of another; and it is a plurality which moves, for they can exchange places with one another. (7) So also when he says that it remains in the same place and does not move, 'always ... different times' [fragment 26], he does not mean that it remains at rest as the state of being opposite to movement, but only that it is deprived of motion and rest. (8) In his *Concerning the Gods* Nicolaus Damascenus records him as saying that the first principle is unlimited and unmoving, but Alexander says that it is limited and spherical in form. (9) But it is clear from what has been said that he shows it is neither unlimited nor limited. And yet it is also

---

44 τὸ ὂν καὶ πᾶν: 'what is and the whole' or 'that which is and the all.' For πᾶν as 'whole,' cf. LSJ, s.v. πᾶς II, 1, and the use of ὅλον at *Metaphysics* 986a3 and 986b19.

limited and spherical since he says that it is 'alike in every way.' And he says that it thinks all things, saying 'but ... shakes' [fragment 25].

A32

Pseudo-Plutarch *Miscellanies* 4 [Eusebius *Preparation for the Gospel* 1.8.4; Diels, 580]. But Xenophanes of Colophon, having gone his own way and departing from all those spoken of earlier [D-K: Thales, Anaximander, Anaximenes], abandons the idea of coming-into-being and passing away but says that the whole is always alike. For if this were to come into being, he says, then necessarily before this there would have been not being. But what is not cannot come into being, nor can it produce anything, nor can anything come into being from what is not. And he declares that the senses are deceptive and generally rejects reason itself along with them. He declares also that as the land is gradually and continuously carried downward, in time it gives way to the sea. He says also that the sun is gathered together from many small fires. He declares also that there is no one of the gods in single command over them, for it would be impious for any of the gods to be mastered; and not one (of the gods) needs any of the other gods or anything else. But (god) hears and sees as a whole and not in a particular part. And he declares also that the earth is unlimited and is not surrounded in every part by the air; and all things come into being from the earth;[45] but he says that the sun and the stars come into being from the clouds.

A33

Hippolytus *Refutation of All Heresies* 1.14 (Diels, 565; Wendland, 17). (1) But Xenophanes, son of Orthomenes, of Colophon, lived on until the time of Cyrus. He was the first to speak of the incomprehensibility of all things, saying 'for even if ... is allotted to all' [fragment 34.3–4]. (2) He says also that nothing comes into being or perishes or moves, and that the whole is one and outside the process of change. He says also that god is eternal and one and alike in all parts and limited and spherical in form and perceptive in all his parts. (3) And he says that the sun comes into being each day, from the gathering together of small fires, and the earth is unlimited and surrounded neither by the air nor by the heavens. And there are unlimited numbers of suns and moons,

45 ἐκ γῆς; see the commentary on fragment 27 in chapter 3 above.

but that all things are from the earth.[46] (4) He said that the sea is salty because of the many mixtures flowing along in it. But Metrodorus [70 A19] says that it is on account of its filtering through the earth that it becomes salty. (5) Further, Xenophanes thinks that a mixture of the land with the sea comes about, but that in time (the land) becomes freed from the moisture, and he asserts that there are proofs for these ideas: that shells are found inland and in mountains, and he says that in quarries in Syracuse imprints of fish and seals were found; and in Paros[47] the imprint of coral[48] in the deep of the marble and on Malta slabs of rock[49] containing all sorts of sea creatures.[50] (6) He says that these things came about when long ago everything was covered with mud, and then the imprint dried in the clay. And he says that all men will perish when the land sinks into the sea and becomes mud, at which time generation begins again, and this change comes about in all worlds[51] [see fragment 33].

A34

Cicero *Prior Academics* 2.18 [see 1.114.18]. (Xenophanes said that) all things are one, that this is unchanging, and is god, that this never came into being and is eternal, and has a spherical shape.

Cicero *On the Nature of the Gods* 1.11.28. Next, Xenophanes, joining the universe with mind, maintained that it was god because it was infinite. His view about the mind is subject to refutation as are the others, but his view of the infinite even more so, for the infinite can neither perceive nor be conjoined with anything. Cf. Aristotle *Poetics* 25.1460b35.

A35

Pseudo-Galen *On Philosophical History* 7 (Diels, 604.17). Xenophanes however was in doubt about all things, firmly believing only that all

---

46 ἐκ γῆς; see the commentary on fragment 27 in chapter 3 above.
47 See Marcovich 1959, 121.
48 Reading δάφνης (mss, Kranz, KRS, Guthrie, and others) rather than ἀφυής (Diels, Gronov, Marcovich), but as 'coral' (LSJ, IV) rather than 'bayleaf' (Guthrie).
49 Or perhaps 'tail fins' (of crustacea), LSJ, s.v. πλάξ, 3.
50 For further discussion of Xenophanes' views on inquiry into nature, see the commentary on fragment 18 in part 2, chapter 4
51 Properly 'world arrangements' rather than 'in all possible worlds' (KRS, 178).

things were one and that this was god, limited, rational, and change-less.

Timon, fragment 59 [Sextus Empiricus *Outlines of Pyrrhonism* 1.223].
... for having praised him [Xenophanes] in many places, even ded-icating the *Silloi* to him, he [Timon] rendered him as lamenting and saying: '... that I also with a double view[52] ought to have gained a share of wisdom, but being elderly and not attending carefully I was beguiled by a deceptive path away from total doubt. For in whichever way I might direct my mind, it returned to one and the same thing; and all that ever existed ended up in a single, uniform, stationary na-ture.'

Timon, fragment 60 [Sextus Empiricus, 1, 224; Diogenes Laertius 9.18; 1.113.12]. Xenophanes (*Xeinophanēs*), partly free of conceit,[53] critic of Homeric deception. It was he who fashioned a god distant from men, equal in every way, <unshaken> and unscathed, either thought or very great in thought.

[D-K: Sextus explains:] and for that reason he speaks of him as 'partly free of conceit' and 'not completely free of deceit' in which he says 'Xenophanes ...' [D-K: as in Sextus above]. He spoke of him as 'partly free of conceit' since he was somewhat free of conceit; and as 'critic of Homeric deception' since he disparaged the deception there is in Homer. Contrary to the conceptions of other men, he firmly believed that the whole is one, and that god is bound up with all things, and is spherical, impassive, changeless, and rational.

Sextus Empiricus *Against the Professors* 7.14. ... Xenophanes of Colo-phon, however, among those who divided philosophy in its founda-tions, is said by some to have pursued the natural along with the logical.

---

52 ἀμφοτερόβλεπτος: Lit. 'viewing both,' perhaps a reference to the sceptical pursuit of suspension of opinion by mounting arguments on both sides of the question (cf. D.L. 9.78–79). Timon speaks of Xenophanes as a less than consistent sceptic (cf. fragment 60 following). See further, Diels (1897b), 530–31, and Long (1978), 68–91, esp. 74–78.

53 ὑπάτυφος: 'not entirely free of τῦφος'; for τῦφος LSJ offers 'delusion,' 'affectation,' 'vanity' (or less relevant here: 'fever'), and for ἄτυφος, 'not puffed up.' Long (74) comments: '*tuphos*, meaning "trumpery" and referring to self-importance and self-deception, was constantly attacked by the Cynics ... [they] preached the need to struggle against *truphē* [a luxurious lifestyle], the prime source, along with *poluteleia* [extravagance], of all civic discord according to Crates.'

A36

Theodoretus *Treatment of Greek Afflictions* 4.5; from Aëtius (Diels, 284n). Accordingly Xenophanes, the son of Orthomenes from Colophon, leader of the Eleatic School, said that the whole is one, spherical, and limited, not generated but eternally and totally motionless. And, forgetting these accounts, he has also said that all things grow from the earth, for this is his remark 'from the earth[54] ... finish' [fragment 27].

Stobaeus *Physical Selections* 1.10.12. Xenophanes (says that) the earth is the first principle of all existing things; for he writes in the *Concerning Nature* 'from ... finish.'

Olympiodorus *On the Sacred Art* 24 [M. Berthelot *Collection des anciens alchimistes grecs* 1.1], 82, 21. ... for no one held the earth to be a first principle except Xenophanes of Colophon.

Galen *Commentary on the Hippocratic Treatise on the Nature of Man* 15.25k. Some of the interpreters also treat Xenophanes badly, reporting falsely concerning him just as Sabinus has written in the following words: 'for I say that man is neither completely air as Anaximenes (says) nor water as Thales (says), nor earth as Xenophanes somewhere (says) [D-K: fragment 33?], for you will nowhere find Xenophanes making such a declaration ... and Theophrastus would have recorded this as a doctrine of Xenophanes in his summaries of the physical opinions, if he held such a view [cf. Aristotle *Metaphysics* A 8, 989a5].

A37

Aëtius 2.4.11 (Diels, 332). Xenophanes (says that) the world is ungenerated and eternal and imperishable [cf. 2.1.3; 1.86.16].

A38

Aëtius 2.13.14 (Diels, 343). Xenophanes (says that) [D-K: the stars come into being] from burning clouds; and they are extinguished each day but ignited again at night like coals; for their risings and settings are kindlings and extinguishings.

---

54 ἐκ γῆς; see the commentary on fragment 27 in chapter 3 above.

A39

Aëtius 2.18.1 (Diels, 347). Xenophanes (says that) the sort of fires that appear on ships – whom some also call the Dioscuri[55] – are tiny clouds glimmering in virtue of the sort of motion (they have).

A40

Aëtius 20.3 (Diels, 348). Xenophanes (says that) the sun consists of burning clouds. Theophrastus has written in the *Physics* [fragment 16; Diels, 492] (that) the sun is a mass of little fires, themselves constituted from the massing together of the moist exhalation.

A41

Aëtius 2.24.4 (Diels, 354). Xenophanes (says that) [D-K: the eclipse[56] – or more correctly – the setting of the sun comes about] by being extinguished, and that another (sun) rises again in the east. He mentioned incidentally that there was an eclipse of the sun lasting a whole month and also a total eclipse so that the day appeared to be night.

A41a

Aëtius 2.24.9 (Diels, 355). Xenophanes (said that) there were many suns and moons throughout the regions, sections, and zones of the earth, and at a certain time the disk falls down into some section of the earth not inhabited by us and so, like someone treading on emptiness[57]

55 Cf. the *Homeric Hymn to the Dioscuri* 6ff.: 'these are deliverers of men on earth and of swift-going ships when stormy gales rage over the ruthless sea'; later known as St Elmo's fire. Cf. also Alcaeus, fragment 34 = Diehl, fragment 78.

56 I adopt the usual translation 'eclipse' but ἔκλειψις (throughout) may be merely a 'cessation' or 'departure' (ἐκλείπειν) of the sun, e.g., its month-long absence at a northern latitude. Pace KRS (174–75), there is no reason to accuse either Xenophanes or Aëtius of either irony or fantasy. See also West 1971, 229n.

57 Convincingly explained by P.J. Bicknell, (1967b, 73–77): the sun ceases to burn because it enters a region of the world devoid of water, hence both uninhabitable and incapable of supplying the moist vapours essential to the sun's kindling. For 'treading on emptiness' Bicknell cites Plutarch *Flaminius* 10, κενεμβατοῦσι; i.e., 'The birds fly into a region devoid of air, and in so doing, "as it were κενεμβατοῦσι"' (76).

makes the eclipse appear. He (also says) that the sun goes onward indefinitely,[58] but appears to go in a circle because of the distance.[59]

A42

Aëtius 2.30.8 (Diels, 362). Xenophanes (said that) the sun was useful with respect to the world and for both the generation and sustenance of living things on it, but the moon is redundant.

A43

Aëtius 2.25.4 (Diels, 356). Xenophanes (says that) [D-K: sc. the moon] is compressed[60] cloud.

Ibid. 2.28.1 (Diels, 358). Anaximander, Xenophanes, and Berosus (say that) it (the moon) has its own light.

Ibid. 2.29.5 (Diels, 360). Xenophanes (says that) the monthly disappearance (of the moon) [D-K: comes about] because it is extinguished.

A44

Aëtius 3.2.11 (Diels, 367). Xenophanes (says that) all things of this sort [D-K: sc. comets, shooting stars, meteors] are either groups or movements of clouds.

58 Following Zeller (1920, 1, 669) and Guthrie (1, 38ln): 'not "to infinity"; it burns out in a short time.'
59 Usually explained as an optical effect: as bodies move across the sky and approach the horizon they may appear to curve downward in their paths, hence 'move in a circle.' Xenophanes may, however, have had in mind the quite different psychological phenomenon (later much discussed by the British empiricists) of believing that various appearances are the appearances of *a single substance*, e.g., believing that the sun that sets in the west is identical with the one that rises in the east the next morning. Since ἀπόστασις can mean 'departure,' as well as 'distance' (LSJ, s.v. ἀπόστασις, B, 4), Xenophanes' point might have been that men believe that the sun travels in a circle (under as well as over the earth) because it departs from our point of view (and reappears in the east). Cf. Hume *Treatise* 1, iv: 'When we have been accustom'd to observe a constancy in certain impressions [of the sun or ocean] ... we are apt not to regard these interrupted perceptions as different ... but on the contrary consider them as individually the same, upon account of their resemblance' (ed. Selby-Bigge, 199). Xenophanes' own view would be that the sun goes onward εἰs ἄπειρον, i.e., indefinitely (downward), because that is after all just what the earth itself does (according to fragment 28) until it is extinguished. Both interpretations are possible.
60 D. Runia has recently proposed πεπυρωμένον πεπιλημένον for Aëtius' text ('condensed ignited' cloud), which would accord with the report (at 2.29.5) that Xenophanes held that the moon was extinguished on a monthly basis.

A45

Aëtius 3.3.6 (Diels, 368). Xenophanes (says that) flashes of lightning come about through the shining of the clouds because of the movement.[61]

A46

Aëtius 3.4.4 (Diels, 371). Xenophanes (says that) things in the heavens occur through the heat of the sun as the initial cause; for when the moisture is drawn up from the sea, the sweet portion, separating because of its fineness and turning into mist, combines into clouds, trickles down in drops of rain due to compression, and vaporizes the winds.[62] For he expressly writes, '(sea is) the source of water' [fragment 30.1].

A47

Aristotle On the Heavens 2.13, 294a21. For some say for this reason that the (region) below the earth is infinite, saying that it is rooted in the infinite, as does Xenophanes the Colophonian [fragment 28], in order to avoid the business of searching for the reason, wherefore Empedocles also censures him, saying 'if ... seeing (little of the whole)' [31 B 39].

Cf. Simplicius Commentary on Aristotle's On the Heavens (Heiberg, p. 522, 7). Not finding Xenophanes' words concerning this subject, I do not know whether he is saying that the part of the earth that lies below is infinite – saying for this reason that it remains (at rest) – or whether the space and aether which lie below the earth are infinite, and because of this the earth extends to infinity and appears at rest.[63] For Aristotle does not make this clear, nor do Empedocles' words make this distinction clearly, as 'depths of the earth' might also mean 'that to which it reaches down.'

Aëtius 3.9.4 (Diels, 376). Xenophanes (says that) [D-K: sc. the earth] from its lower portion is rooted in an infinite portion and that it is compounded of air and fire.

---

61 The nature of the movement (κίνησις) here, in A39, and in A44 (κινήματα) is unclear. Mourelatos (1989) suggests 'agitation,' perhaps an internal disturbance in the clouds which results in a flashing of light. Elsewhere, however, fires are described as a result of the massing together of moist vapours (cf. A32, A33, A40).
62 See the commentary on fragment 30 in ch. 3 above.
63 Fragment 28 makes it virtually certain that the former (in some sense of ἄπειρος) was really Xenophanes' view. See the commentary on fragment 28 in ch. 3 above.

Aëtius 2.11.1.2 (Diels, 377). Those following Thales (say that) the earth (is) at the center; (according to) Xenophanes, (it is) first – for it is rooted in the infinite [cf. fragment 28].

Cicero *Prior Academics* 2.39.122. But can we in the same way dissect, open up, and separate the natures of things in order to see whether the earth is fixed deep down and is fastened as if by its roots [D-K: i.e., the view of Xenophanes] or whether it hangs suspended in the centre?

Ibid. 2.39.123. Xenophanes [D-K: or rather Anaxagoras] says that the moon is inhabited and is a land of many cities and mountains. Cf. Hippolytus 1.14.3 [1.133.34]. From Pseudo-Aristotle *MXG* 2.21; 976a32 [30 A5]. Diogenes of Oenoanda, fragment 21.10 (William, 26f.).

A48

Pseudo-Aristotle *On Marvellous Things Heard* 38; 833a15 [D-K: perhaps from Timaeus]. Xenophanes says that [D-K: sc. the fire] on Lipara[64] once ceased for sixteen years, but recurred in the seventeenth.[65]

A49

Aristocles *Concerning Philosophy* 8 [Eusebius 14.17.1]. ... since they think that sense perceptions and appearances must be rejected and trust only reason. For at an earlier time Xenophanes, Parmenides, Zeno, and Melissus said something of this sort, and later on those following Stilpo and the Megarics. These therefore held that being was one and other than not being, neither coming into being at all nor perishing nor moving at all.

Aëtius 4.9.1 (Diels, 369). Pythagoras, Empedocles, and Xenophanes (say that) sense perceptions are deceptive.

---

64 Largest of a group of volcanic islands off north-eastern Sicily, hence a reference to a resumption of volcanic activity.

65 Xenophanes' use here of ἐκλιπεῖν led K. Freeman to connect the reference to intermittent volcanic activity with his ideas about periodic rekindling in the heavens (i.e., to regard the comment as an argument to the effect that the fires above a volcano can 'suffer eclipse' too). But ἐκλείπω might have signified nothing more elaborate than 'cessation' or 'departure' (cf. LSJ, sv. ἐκλείπω II, 2, and the month-long ἐκλείψις mentioned in A41 above). Periodic volcanic activity might have been of interest to Xenophanes simply in connection with his idea (as reported by Aëtius in A47) that there were mixtures of air and fire located below ground.

A50

Macrobius *Commentary on Scipio's Dream* 1.14.19. Xenophanes (says that) [D-K: sc. the soul consists] of earth and water.

A51

Tertullian *On the Soul* 43 [on sleep]. Anaxagoras with Xenophanes (says that it is) weariness [D-K conjectures κόπον τῆς σωματικῆς ἐνεργείας for the original Greek in Tertullian's source].

A52

Cicero *On Divination* 1.3.5. Certain carefully worked out arguments of the philosophers for the reality of divination have been collected; among these, to speak of the earliest, Xenophanes of Colophon, one who said that gods existed, repudiated divination in its entirety. The remainder, except really only Epicurus who spoke rather obscurely about the nature of the gods, approved of divination.

Aëtius 5.1.1 (Diels, 415). Xenophanes and Epicurus did away entirely with divination.

IMITATIONS

C1

Euripides *Heracles* 1341 [cf. fragments 11 and 12, A32].
    But I do not think the gods desire to have illicit relations
    and I never believed nor will believe that chains are
    fastened on their hands,
    nor that one god is master over another.
5 For god, if indeed truly he is a god, lacks nothing.
    Such ideas are the sorry tales of singers.

See chapter 2, pp. 92–94.

C2

Athenaeus *Scholars at Dinner* 10.413c.
    ... on which account Euripides in the first edition of his *Autolycus*
    also says:

Of all the countless evils that exist in Greece
not one is worse than the tribe of athletes.
First they do not learn how one should live,
nor would they be able to do so. For how could one
5 who is a slave to his jaw and defeated by his own belly
acquire wealth beyond that which his father had achieved?
. . .
13 I also fault the practice of the Greeks,
who holding an assembly for the sake of such as these,
15 pay them the honour of the useless pleasures of a feast.
For what aid to his native city does someone give who wins a
crown
for having wrestled well or being a swift-footed man
or having thrown the discus or landed a good shot to the jaw?
Will they engage the enemy in battle
20 with the discus in their hands or without their shields
throw the enemy out of their homeland by striking with their fist?
No one up against the sword indulges in such follies.
But I think we ought to crown wise and good men with leafy
crowns;
25 him also who leads the city best by being wise and just,
someone who also through his words liberates the city from evil
deeds,
ridding it both of battles and of civic strife. For noble deeds like
these
are good for the whole city and for all Greeks.

See chapter 1, pp. 59–61.

Sources and Authorities
Select Bibliography

SOURCES AND AUTHORITIES

For discussions of the value of these ancient sources see Burnet *Early Greek Philosophy* (London and Edinburgh 1930) 31–38; KRS, 1–6; and the Introduction in Heath *Aristarchus of Samos* (Oxford 1913). The following notes are meant to serve only as brief identifying descriptions of the authorities cited and the standard editions of their works. For additional information on texts and editions see L. Berkowitz, K. Squitier, and W. Johnson *Thesaurus Linguae Graecae: Canon of Greek Authors and Works* 2nd ed. (New York and Oxford 1986). References to the Loeb editions are to the multi-volume series of editions with facing translations in English of the major works of Greek and Latin literature, known collectively as the Loeb Classical Library.

ACHILLES, third-century astronomer and mathematician, author of a commentary on the *Phaenomena* of Aratus. See the *Commentariorum in Aratum reliquiae* ed. E. Maass, 2nd ed. (Berlin, 1898; repr. 1958). Often called 'Achilles Tatius' through a confusion with the more famous Alexandrian novelist.

AËTIUS, first- and second-century Eclectic philosopher, author of a summary of Greek philosophical ideas on physical topics. Two later summaries of Aëtius' work, the Pseudo-Plutarch *Epitome of Physical Opinions* and the *Physical Extracts* of Stobaeus' *Anthology*, form the basis of Diels' reconstruction of Aëtius' *Placita* in his *Doxographi Graeci*.

ALEXANDER of Aphrodisias, second- and third-century Peripatetic philosopher and commentator on Aristotle. His opinion on Xenophanes' cosmology/ontology was mentioned by Simplicius (A31). Alexander's commentaries on various works by Aristotle are contained in the *Commentaria in Aristotelem Graeca* (Berlin, 1883–1901).

APOLLODORUS, second-century BC historian and theologian, author of the *Chronology*, an account of events, individuals, and philosophical schools from the fall of Troy to 144 BC. The fragments are contained in *Die Fragmente der griechischen Historiker* ed. F. Jacoby (Leiden 1926–58; repr. 1954–60).

APULEIUS, second-century poet and rhetorician, author of *The Golden Ass* or *Metamorphoses* and, among other works, the *Florida*, which makes brief mention of Xenophanes. The text of the *Florida* has been edited by R. Helm (1910) and translated by H.E. Butler (1909).

ARISTOCLES, second-century Peripatetic philosopher, teacher of Alexander of Aphrodisias. The fragments are contained in *Aristoclis Messenii reliquiae* ed. H. Heiland (Giessen 1925).

ARISTOTLE (384–22 BC), student of Plato, founder of the Peripatetic school of philosophy, critical historian of Presocratic thought, and creator of what is arguably the most comprehensive and influential philosophy in the history of human thought. The complete works are available in English in the Oxford translations (ed. J.A. Smith and W.D. Ross) and in *The Complete Works of Aristotle, The Revised Oxford Translation* ed. J. Barnes (Princeton 1984); the major works are contained in the twenty volumes in the Loeb Classical Series and in R. McKeon *Aristotle* (New York 1941).

ARIUS DIDYMUS, first-century BC doxographer, author of a study of Stoic and Peripatetic ethics (portions of which were preserved by Stobaeus). The fragments are contained in H. Diels *Doxographi Graeci* 447–72.

ATHENAEUS, second- and third-century author of the *Deipnosophistae* or *Scholars at Dinner*, a miscellany on ancient foods and table talk containing extensive quotations from earlier writers, available in the Loeb series, ed. C.B. Gulick (7 vols., 1933).

AULUS GELLIUS, second-century grammarian, author of *Attic Nights*, a miscellany of some twenty books, also valuable as a source for earlier writers; available in the Loeb series, trans. J.C. Rolfe (1927–28).

CENSORINUS, third-century grammarian whose *De die natali* contains an abstract of a work by Varro, a Roman scholar of the first century BC. See the edition of Otto Jahn (Berlin 1845; repr. Hildesheim 1965).

CICERO, first-century BC Roman statesman, orator, and philosophical enthusiast, whose *Academica* provide valuable information on the development of scepticism. The *De divinatione* (which mentions Xenophanes in passing) seeks to free religious belief of some of its more superstitious features. These works are contained in the Loeb series, translated by H. Rackham (1933) and W. Falconer (1923).

CLEMENT, second- and third-century Christian philosopher whose *Stromata*, or *Miscellanies*, and *Protrepticus* contain extensive quotations from earlier poets and philosophers. The texts are contained in the series *Die griechischen christlichen Schriftsteller der ersten drei Jahrhunderte* (Leipzig 1905–09), the *Stromateis* (2nd ed., L. Fruchtel) in vol. 52 (Berlin 1960).

CRATES of Mallus, second-century BC grammarian, first head of the library at Pergamum. The relevant fragments can be found in H.J. Mette *Sphairopoiia: Untersuchungen zur Kosmologie des Krates von Pergamon* (Munich 1936).

CYRIL of Jerusalem, fourth-century ecclesiastical writer. The texts of various works are contained in W.C. Reischl and J. Rupp *Cyrilli Hiersolymorum Archiepiscopi Opera quae supersunt omnia* (Munich 1848–1860; repr. Hildesheim 1967).

DEMETRIUS of Phalerum, fourth-century BC Athenian writer and statesman. The most recent edition is that of W.R. Roberts (Cambridge 1902).

DIOGENES LAERTIUS, second- and third-century biographer. His *Lives of the Philosophers* is a valuable source of information about the Presocratics in part because of his extensive quotation from their writings. The work is edited by H.S. Long in the Oxford Classical Text series (Oxford 1964) and in the Loeb series, trans. R.D. Hicks (in 2 vols., 1925).

DIONYSIUS 'PERIEGETES,' third-century author of a geographical poem. The text is contained in *Geographi Graeci minores* ed. K. Müller (Paris 1861; repr. Hildesheim 1965).

EMPEDOCLES (c. 493 to c. 433 BC), Sicilian-born philosopher, poet, miracle worker, and mystagogue; author of a comprehensive theory of nature in which Eleatic principles are modified to accommodate change and plurality. There is some evidence (A5) that Empedocles associated with Xenophanes and disagreed with some of his ideas (D-K 31 B39). The texts of the fragments (with German translation) are contained in D-K, vol. 1, 308–72.

EPICHARMUS, fifth-century BC Sicilian playwright; identified by D.L. (8.3) as a student of Pythagoras, he seems to have known of Xenophanes' teaching (A15) and to have parodied some of his ideas (e.g., D-K 23 B1). See D-K, vol. 1, 193–210.

EPIPHANIUS, fourth-century ecclesiastical writer. His *Adversus haereses* is contained in *Epiphanius* ed. K. Holl, in *Die griechischen christlichen Schriftsteller* (Leipzig 1915).

EROTIAN, first-century grammarian and physician, author of a glossary to Hippocrates. The text is contained in *Erotiani Vocum Hippocraticarum collectio cum fragmentis* ed. E. Nachmanson (Göteborg 1918).

ETYMOLOGICUM GENUINUM, an early Greek etymological lexicon completed under Photius (ninth century).

ETYMOLOGICUM MAGNUM, a Greek etymological lexicon of unknown authorship, based in part on the *Etym. Gen.* (above) and the *Etym. Gudianum*. See the edition of T. Gaisford (Oxford 1848).

EURIPIDES, c. 485–406 BC. One of the three great dramatists of the Athenian 'golden age.' He appears to have associated with philosophers, dealt with the philosophical issues of his day in many of his plays, and been influenced in several respects by Xenophanes (see part 3, above – Imitation C1). His plays are included in D. Grene and R. Lattimore *The Complete Greek Tragedies* (Chicago 1959–60).

EUSEBIUS, second and third centuries, bishop of Caesarea and author of the *Preparation for the Gospel* – a study of pagan thought as prelude to Christianity. The text has been edited by J. Sirinelli and E. des Places (Paris 1974).

FAVORINUS, first- and second-century Roman historian, orator, and philosopher. The fragments have been edited by A. Barigazzi (Florence 1966).

GALEN, second-century physician and author who challenged the attribution to Xenophanes of a theory of earth as *archē* (A36). The complete works of Galen are contained in the *Corpus medicorum Graecorum* (Leipzig 1908–; 2nd ed., Berlin 1947–).

HERACLITUS, first-century author of the *Allegoriae* (or *Quaestiones Homericae*). See *Héraclite. Allégories d'Homère* ed. F. Buffière (Paris 1962).

HERACLITUS of Ephesus, late sixth- and early fifth-century BC philosopher, author of a series of obscure, often paradoxical aphorisms through which he expressed a comprehensive theory of the natural world as obedient to a universal principle of harmony in opposition. On the basis of this theory he proceeded to castigate the leading poets and philosophers of Greece (see fragment 40 for his mention of Xenophanes), insult the entire citizenry of Ephesus, and (according to Plato *Theaetetus* 179–80) captivate a small army of obnoxious followers. Fragment 40 notwithstanding, Heraclitus and Xenophanes both epitomized Ionian 'inquiry' into nature, society, and the divine. See D-K, vol. 1, 150–82.

HERMIPPUS, third-century BC Peripatetic biographer quoted by D.L. and Plutarch. There is an edition of the *Fragmenta* by F. Wehrli, *Hermippos der Kallimacheer* (*Die Schule des Aristoteles*, Suppl. 1; Basel 1974).

HERODIAN, second-century grammarian, author of several studies of accentuation and morphology, many of which survive only in later citations. His *Peri dichronōn*, or *On Doubtful Syllables*, and *Peri monērous lexeōs*, or *On Peculiar Speech*, are contained in *Grammatici Graeci* ed. A. Lentz (Leipzig 1867; repr. Hildesheim 1965).

HESYCHIUS, fifth-century Alexandrian lexicographer. See the *Hesychii Alexandrini Lexicon* ed. K. Latte, vols. 1 and 2 (Copenhagen 1966) and M. Schmidt, vols. 3 and 4 (Halle 1861; repr. Amsterdam 1965).

HIPPOLYTUS, second- and third-century, bishop of Rome, author of *Refutation of All Heresies*. Hippolytus summarizes and quotes extensively from the Greek philosophers in connection with his attempt to prove that supposed new revelations of Christian doctrine are ideas already developed by pagan thinkers. See M. Marcovich *Hippolytus: Refutatio omnium haeresium* Patristische Texte und Studien, 25 (Berlin 1986).

IAMBLICHUS, third- and fourth-century Neoplatonist philosopher, author of a summary of Pythagorean views, a life of Pythagoras, and various theological works. The *De vita Pythagorica liber* is edited by L. Deubner and U. Klein (Stuttgart 1975).

MACROBIUS, fifth-century Neoplatonist poet, author of a *Commentary on Scipio's Dream* (a work containing references to various Greek philosophers) and the *Saturnalia*, a symposiac poem. See *Macrobius Opera* ed. F. Eyssenhardt (Leipzig 1893).

NICOLAUS of Damascus, first-century BC historian and Peripatetic philosopher. His view of Xenophanes' cosmology/ontology was mentioned by Simplicius (A31). The testimonia and fragments are contained in *Die Fragmente der griechischen Historiker* ed. F. Jacoby (Leiden 1926–58; repr. 1954–60), 90.

OLYMPIODORUS, sixth-century alchemist and philosopher, author of *On the Sacred Art*, perhaps the same Olympiodorus who wrote commentaries on works by Plato and Aristotle. See the *Collection des anciens alchemistes grecs* ed. M. Berthelot (Paris 1887; repr. London 1963).

PANAETIUS, second-century BC Stoic philosopher. Selections appear in A.A. Long and D.N. Sedley, eds *The Hellenistic Philosophers*, vol. 1 (Cambridge 1987).

PHILO JUDAEUS, first-century author of a dualistic philosophy which draws extensively on the ideas of Plato, Aristotle, and the Stoics. The fragments have been edited by H. Lloyd-Jones and P. Parsons, *Supplementum Hellenisticum* (Berlin 1983). His major works are contained in the edition of L. Cohn and P. Wendland (Berlin 1896–1915).

PHILOPONUS, sixth-century Christian commentator on Aristotle. See the *Commentaria in Aristotelem Graeca* (Berlin 1887–97).

PLATO (428–348 BC), student of Socrates, teacher of Aristotle, founder of the world's first research institute, author of more than two dozen philosophical masterpieces, and creator of a philosophical system which shaped much of medieval and early modern thought. The texts of Plato's works are contained in the five volumes of the Oxford Classical Texts as *Platonis Opera* ed. J. Burnet; in the eleven volumes of the Loeb series, with English translations; and the dialogues generally accepted as genuine appear in English translation in one volume as *The Collected Dialogues of Plato* ed. E. Hamilton and H. Cairns (Princeton 1961).

PLUTARCH, first- and second-century Platonist philosopher and prolific author. Plutarch's dialogues and diatribes on philosophical topics are written under various titles and identified collectively as the *Moralia*, available in sixteen volumes of the Loeb series, by various translations, along with *The Parallel Lives* trans. B. Perrin.

POLLUX, second-century rhetorician and grammarian. His *Onomasticon*, or *Vocabulary*, has been edited by E. Bethe (*Lexicographi Graeci*, vol. 9.1–9.2; Leipzig 1900, 1931; repr. Stuttgart 1967).

PORPHYRY, third-century polymath, student of Longinus, and author of various works on philosophical, religious, and literary topics containing numerous quotations from earlier thinkers. His view of Xenophanes' *archē* theory was quoted by Philoponus (q.v.).

PROCLUS, fifth-century Neoplatonist, author of commentaries on Plato's *Parmenides* and *Timaeus*. His scholia on Hesiod have been edited by A. Pertusi, *Scholia vetera in Hesiodi opera et dies* (Milan 1955).

PSEUDO-ARISTOTLE, the author or authors of several works under the name of Aristotle, including the treatise *On Melissus, Xenophanes, Gorgias*. The text in D-K is from Bekker *Aristotelis Opera* (Berlin 1831–70). The 'Xenophanes' section is included in the Loeb volume *Aristotle, Minor Works*, with an English translation by W.S. Hett, based on the Teubner text by Apelt.

PSEUDO-GALEN, post-second-century author or authors of various scientific treatises and of the *De historia philosophica*, contained in Diels *Doxographi Graeci* 597–648.

PSEUDO-LUCIAN, post-second-century author or authors of *Macrobii* or *Long Lives*, also attributed to Lucian, second-century writer of satirical dialogues. The text is contained in *Lucian* ed. A.M. Harmon (Cambridge, Mass., 1913; repr. 1961), vol. 1, 222–44.

PSEUDO-PLUTARCH, post-second-century author or authors of a history of philosophy preserved by Eusebius in the *Preparation for the Gospel* and referred to by him as the *Stromata* or *Miscellanies* of Plutarch. The text is contained in Diels *Doxographi Graeci* 579–83.

SEXTUS EMPIRICUS, second-century physician and sceptical philosopher, follower of Aenesidemus, and author of the *Outlines of Pyrrhonism*,

Against the Dogmatists, and *Against the Professors.* These works are contained in the four volumes of the Loeb series (trans. R. Bury, 1933–49). The *Outlines* has also been translated by J. Annas and J. Barnes (*The Modes of Scepticism;* Cambridge 1985) based on the Teubner text of Mutschmann and Mau (Leipzig 1912).

SIMPLICIUS, sixth-century commentator on Aristotle, student of Ammonius, and important source for the teachings of the Presocratic philosophers. His *Commentary on Aristotle's Physics* is contained in vols. 9 and 10 of the *Commentaria in Aristotelem Graeca* (Berlin 1882–95).

SOTION, second-century BC Peripatetic philosopher, author of a book on Timon's *Silloi* and a source for D.L. The fragments have been edited by F. Wehrli, *Sotion* (*Die Schule des Aristotelis* Suppl. 2; Basel 1978).

STOBAEUS, fifth-century author of the *Florilegium* or *Anthology,* containing numerous extracts from Greek philosophical works. See *Ioannis Stobaei Anthologium* ed. C. Wachsmuth and O. Hense, 5 vols. (Berlin 1884–1912; repr. 1958).

STRABO, first-century historian and geographer. His *Geographica* was edited by A. Meinecke (Leipzig 1877; repr. Graz 1969) and is available in the eight volumes of the Loeb series (trans. L. Jones, 1917–32).

TERTULLIAN, second- and third-century Christian apologist. His *De anima* is edited by J.H. Waszink (Amsterdam 1947).

THEODORETUS, fourth- and fifth-century, bishop of Cyrrhus, author of theological studies and doxographies. Diels identified Theodoretus' statement of Xenophanes' views as an excerpt from Aëtius (q.v.); *Doxographi Graeci* 284n.

THEOLOGOUMENA ARITHMETICAE, various studies of the mystical properties of numbers, now attributed not to Iamblichus but to Nicomachus, second-century mathematician. The text has been edited by V. de Falco (Leipzig 1922).

THEOPHRASTUS, fourth- and third-century BC Peripatetic philosopher, successor to Aristotle as head of his school, author of a large number of works, most of which were lost. His *Physikōn Doxai,* or *Opinions of the Inquirers into Nature,* provided the main source for the ancient doxographers. See Diels *Doxographi Graeci* 475–95.

TIMAEUS, third- and second-century BC historian of Sicily. See the *Fragmenta historicum Graecorum* 5 vols., ed. K. Müller (Paris 1841–70).

TIMON of Phlius, fourth- and third-century BC philosopher, follower of Pyrrho, and admirer of Xenophanes. The fragments were edited by Diels in *Poetarum philosophorum fragmenta* (Berlin 1901) 184–206.

TZETZES, twelfth-century Byzantine polymath, author of works on grammar, Greek literature, and mythology. Tzetzes' comment on Xenophanes was contained in his remarks on Dionysius 'Periegetes' (q.v.), quoted by Diels from the edition of Dionysius by G. Bernhardy (Leipzig 1828) 1010.

SELECT BIBLIOGRAPHY

This bibliography lists only titles of works utilized in earlier chapters. The body of secondary literature on Xenophanes, while not nearly so extensive as that for Pythagoras, Heraclitus, or Parmenides, is still far larger than indicated here. The accounts of Xenophanes given by Barnes, Guthrie, Heitsch, and Kirk, Raven, and Schofield offer alternative interpretations of Xenophanes on many points. An analytic bibliography on the Presocratics has recently been compiled by L. Paquet, M. Roussel, and Y. Lafrance: *Les Présocratiques: Bibliographie analytique (1879–1980)* (Montreal–Paris 1988–89); the Xenophanes material is contained in vol. 1 421–43. Two surveys of earlier work on Xenophanes appear in the *Anzeiger für die Altertumswissenschaft* (see the entries following for Schwabl and Wiesner), and partial summaries of recent work on the Presocratics are provided by G. Kerferd (*American Philosophical Quarterly* 2 [1965] 130–40) and E.L. Minar, Jr. (*Classical Weekly* 47 [1954] 161–70, 177–82; *Classical World* 60 [1966–67] 143–63). For annual listings of classical scholarship across a wide range of topics and authors, see the volumes of *L'Année philologique* (Paris 1924–90). For surveys of recent scholarship in related areas see von Bies, Dee, Gerber, Holoka, and Packard and Myers (below).

Adkins, A. *Merit and Responsibility* (Oxford 1960)
– *Poetic Craft in the Early Greek Elegists* (Chicago 1985)
Babut, D. 'L'idée de progrès et la relativité du savoir humain selon Xénophane (fragments 18 et 38 D-K)' *Revue de philologie* 51 (1977) 217–28
Barnes, J. *The Presocratic Philosophers* 2 vols. (London, Henley, and Boston 1979); 2nd ed. 1982. Except where noted, all references to Barnes are to the 2-volume first edition.
– Review of Osborne (below), *Phronesis* 33 (1988) 327–44

Bicknell, P. 'A Note on Xenophanes' Astrophysics' *Acta Classica* 10 (1967) 135–36; cited as 1967a

– 'Xenophanes' Account of Solar Eclipses' *Eranos* 65 (1967) 73–77; cited as 1967b

von Bies, W., and H. Jung. *Bibliographie zur Symbolik, Ikonographie, und Mythologie, Internationales Referatorgan* 22 (Baden-Baden 1987); see previous volumes for work in earlier years.

Bouché-Leclercq, A. *Histoire de la divination dans l'antiquité* 4 vols. (Paris 1879–82)

Boudouris, K., ed. *Ionian Philosophy* (Athens 1989)

Bowra, C. 'Xenophanes, Fragment 3' *Classical Quarterly* 35 (1941) 119–26

– *Problems in Greek Poetry* (Oxford 1953)

– *Early Greek Elegists* (Cambridge, Mass., 1960)

Burkert, W. *Weisheit und Wissenschaft: Studien zu Pythagoras, Philolaus und Platon* (Nurenburg 1962); trans. E.L. Minar, Jr., as *Lore and Science in Ancient Pythagoreanism* (Cambridge, Mass., 1972)

Burnet, J. *Early Greek Philosophy* (London and Edinburgh 1930)

Campbell, D. *Greek Lyric Poetry* (New York 1967)

– *The Golden Lyre* (London 1983)

Cerri, G. 'Elea, Senofane, e Leucothea' *Annali dell'Istituto universitario orientale di Napoli* 16 (1994) 137–55

Chantraine, P. *Dictionnaire étymologique de la langue grecque* (Paris 1968)

Cherniss, H. *Aristotle's Criticism of Presocratic Philosophy* (Baltimore 1935)

– 'The Characteristics and Effects of Presocratic Philosophy' *Journal of the History of Ideas* 12 (1951) 319–45; in Furley and Allen 1, 1–28

– 'The History of Ideas and Ancient Greek Philosophy' In *Estudios de historia de la filosofia en homenaje al R. Mondolfo* ed. J. Vázquez (Tucuman 1957) 93–114

Classen, C.J. 'Xenophanes and the Tradition of Epic Poetry' In *Ionian Philosophy* ed. Boudouris, 91–103

Cornford, F. *Principium Sapientiae* (Cambridge 1952)

Cunliffe, R. *A Lexicon of the Homeric Dialect* (London, 1924; new ed. University of Oklahoma Press, Norman 1963)

Darcus, S. 'The *Phren* of the *Noos* in Xenophanes' God' *Symbolae Osloenses* 53 (1978) 25–39

Dee, J. 'A Survey of Recent Bibliographies of Classical Literature' *Classical World* 73 (1980) 275–90 (includes references to bibliographies of recent work on Herodotus, Homer, Euripides, Thucydides, and Greek lyric poetry, among many other authors and subjects)

Defradas, J. 'Le Banquet de Xénophane' *Revue des études grecques* 75 (1962) 344–65; cited as 1962a

– *Les Élégiaques grecs* (Paris 1962); cited as 1962b

Deichgräber, K. 'Xenophanes ΠΕΡΙ ΦΥΣΕΩΣ,' *Rheinisches Museum* 87 (1938) 1–31

Denniston, J. *The Greek Particles* 2nd ed., rev. K.J. Dover (Oxford 1954)

Dicks, D. *Early Greek Astronomy* (London 1970)

Diehl, E. *Anthologia Lyrica Graeca* Rev. R. Beutler (Leipzig 1952)

Diels, H. *Doxographi Graeci* (Berlin 1879)

– *Parmenides: Lehrgedicht* (Berlin 1897); cited as 1897a

– 'Ueber Xenophanes,' *Archiv für Geschichte der Philosophie* 10 (1897) 530–35; cited as 1897b

– *Aristotelis qui fertur de Melisso Xenophane Gorgia libellus*, Philosophische und historische Abhandlungen der königchen Akademie der Wissenschaften zu Berlin (Berlin 1900)

– *Poetarum philosophorum fragmenta* (Berlin 1901)

Diels, H., and W. Kranz *Die Fragmente der Vorsokratiker* 6th ed., 3 vols. (Berlin 1951); cited as D-K

Disandro, C. 'Lyrica da pensamiento: Jenófanes y Parmenides' *Discurso y Realidad* 6 (1991) 63–76

Dodds, E. *The Greeks and the Irrational* (Berkeley, Los Angeles, and London 1951)

– *The Ancient Concept of Progress* (Oxford 1973)

Dover, K. *Greek Popular Morality* (Berkeley and Los Angeles 1974)

Edelstein, L. *The Idea of Progress in Classical Antiquity* (Baltimore 1967)

Edmonds, J. *Greek Elegy and Iambus* 2 vols. (Cambridge, Mass., and London 1931). The material relating to Xenophanes is contained in vol. 1, 182–215.

Edwards, M. 'Xenophanes Christianus' *Greek Roman and Byzantine Studies* 32 (1991) 219–28

Eisenstadt, M. 'The Philosophy of Xenophanes of Colophon' Ph.D. diss., University of Texas at Austin, 1970

– 'Xenophanes' Proposed Reform of Greek Religion' *Hermes* 102 (1974) 142–50

Eucken, C. 'Die Gottesfassung in Symposium des Xenophanes' *Würzburger Jahrbücher für die Altertumswissenschaft* 19 (1993) 5–12

Farnell, L. *The Cults of the Greek States* 5 vols. (Oxford 1896–1909)

Feyerabend, P. 'Reason, Xenophanes, and the Homeric Gods' *Kenyon Review* 9 (1987) 12–22

Finkelberg, A. 'Studies in Xenophanes' *Harvard Studies in Classical Philology* 93 (1990) 104–67

– 'Xenophanes' physics, Parmenides' *doxa* and Empedocles' theory of cosmogonical mixture' *Hermes* 125 (1997) 1–16

Fränkel, H. 'Xenophanesstudien' *Hermes* 60 (1925) 174–92; repr. in *Wege und Formen frühgriechischen Denkens* 3rd ed. (Munich 1968)
- *Early Greek Poetry and Philosophy* Trans. M. Hadas and J. Willis (New York and London 1973) from *Dichtung und Philosophie des frühen Griechentums* (Munich 1962). Except where noted, all references to Fränkel are to the 1973 English translation.
- 'Xenophanes' Empiricism and His Critique of Knowledge (B 34)' In Mourelatos (1974) 118–31; trans. M.R. Cosgrove from 'Xenophanesstudien' *Hermes* 60 (1925) 174–92
Freeman, K. *The Pre-Socratic Philosophers* (Oxford 1959)
Fritz, K. von. 'Xenophanes' In *Paulys Realencyclopädie der classischen Altertumswissenschaft* (1894–1963) 1542–62
- 'Νόος and Νοεῖν in the Homeric Poems' *Classical Philology* 38 (1943) 79–93
- 'Νοῦς, Νοεῖν and their Derivatives in Presocratic Philosophy (excluding Anaxagoras),' *Classical Philology* 40 (1945) 223–42 and (1946) 12–34; repr. in Mourelatos (1974) 23–85
Furley, D., and R. Allen. *Studies in Presocratic Philosophy*, 2 vols. (New York 1970; London 1975)
Gera, D. 'Two thought experiments in the *Dissoi Logoi*' *American Journal of Philology* 121 (2000) 21–45
Gerber, D. 'Studies in Greek Lyric Poetry, 1975–1985' *Classical World* 81 (1987–88)
Giangrande, G. 'On Hexameters Ascribed to Xenophanes' *Orpheus* 2 (1981) 371–73
Gigon, O. *Der Ursprung der griechischen Philosophie* (Basel 1945)
Gilbert, O. *Die meteorologischen Theorien des griechischen Altertums* (Leipzig 1907)
Gomperz, T. *The Great Thinkers* Trans. L. Magnus and G. Berry (London 1901–12)
Goodwin, W., and C. Gulick. *Greek Grammar* (repr. New Rochelle, NY, 1981)
Guthrie, W. *A History of Greek Philosophy*, 6 vols. (Cambridge 1962–78). The material relating to Xenophanes is contained in vol. 1, 360–402. Except where noted, all references to Guthrie are to vol. 1.
Harrison, E. 'Notes on Homeric Psychology' *Phoenix* 14 (1960) 63–80
Havelock, E. *The Liberal Temper in Greek Politics* (London 1957)
- 'The Linguistic Task of the Presocratics' In *Language and Thought in Early Greek Philosophy* ed. Robb, 7–82
Heath, T. *Aristarchus of Samos* (Oxford 1913)
Heidel, W. 'On Certain Fragments of the Pre-Socratics: Critical Notes and Elucidations,' *Proceedings of the American Academy of Arts and Sciences* 48, no. 19 (May 1913) 681–734

– 'Hecataeus and Xenophanes' *American Journal of Philology* 64 (1943) 257–77
Heitsch, E. 'Das Wissen des Xenophanes' *Rheinisches Museum* 109 (1966) 193–235
– *Xenophanes: Die Fragmente* (Munich and Zurich 1983). Except where noted, all references to Heitsch are to this work.
– 'Klassische Philologie und Philologen' *Gymnasium* 93 (1986) 430–34
– *Xenophanes und die Anfänge kritischen Denkens* (*Abhandlungen der Geistes- und Sozialwissenschaftlichen Klasse* 7 (Stuttgart 1994) 1–23
Hershbell, J. 'The Oral-Poetic Religion of Xenophanes' In *Language and Thought in Early Greek Philosophy* ed. Robb, 125–31
Herter, H. 'Das Symposium des Xenophanes' *Wiener Studien* 69 (1956) 33–48
Holoka, J. 'Homer Studies 1978–1983' *Classical World* 83 (1990), 393–461 (part 1); 84 (1991), 89–156 (part 2)
Hudson-Williams, T. *Early Greek Elegy* (London 1926)
Hussey, E. *The Presocratics* (London 1972)
Jaeger, W. *Paideia: The Ideals of Greek Culture* Trans. G. Highet, 3 vols. (Oxford 1939–45)
– *The Theology of the Early Greek Philosophers* (Oxford 1947)
Kahn, C. *Anaximander and the Origins of Greek Cosmology* (New York 1960)
– 'On Early Greek Astronomy' *Journal of Hellenic Studies* 90 (1970) 99–116
– 'Pythagorean Philosophy before Plato' In Mourelatos (1974) 161–85
– *The Art and Thought of Heraclitus* (Cambridge 1979)
Keyser, P. 'Xenophanes' Sun (frr. A 32, 33.3, 40DK6) on Trojan Ida (Lucr. 5.660–5, D.S. 17.7.5–7, Mela 1.94–5' *Mnemosyne* 45 (1992) 299–311
Kirk, G., J. Raven, and M. Schofield. *The Presocratic Philosophers* 2nd ed. (Cambridge 1983); cited as KRS
Kleingünther, A. ΠΡΩΤΟΣ ΕΥΡΕΤΗΣ (Leipzig 1933)
Klessidou, A. 'La temps et l'espace chez Xénophane' *Philosophia* 19–20 (1998–9) 531–7
Lebedev, A. 'A New Fragment of Xenophanes' *Studi di Filosofia Preplatonica* (1986) 13–15; English précis of an article which appeared in *Eirene: Atti della XV Conferenza internazionale di studi classici dei paesi socialisti* (Sofia 1978) 47–50 (in Russian)
– 'Thales and Xenophanes' In *Antičnaja filosofija v interpretacii buržuaznych filosofov* ed. V.M. Boguslavskij (Moscow 1981) 1–16 (in Russian)
– 'Xenophanes on the immutability of God: A neglected fragment in Philo Alexdrinus' *Hermes* 128 (2000) 385–91
Lefka, A. 'The Xenophanean religious thought, a field of various interpretations' *Kernos* 2 (1989) 89–96
Lesher, J. 'Genetic Explanations of Religious Belief' *Philosophical Studies* 27 (1975) 317–28

- 'Xenophanes' Scepticism' *Phronesis* 23 (1978) 1–21
- 'Heraclitus' Epistemological Vocabulary,' *Hermes* 111 (1983) 155–70
- 'Parmenides' Critique of Thinking: The *poludēris elenchos* of Fr. 7' *Oxford Studies in Ancient Philosophy* 2 (1984) 1–30
- 'Socrates' Disavowal of Knowledge' *Journal of the History of Philosophy* 25 (1987) 275–88
- 'Xenophanes on Inquiry and Discovery: An Alternative to the "Hymn to Progress" Reading of Fr. 18' *Ancient Philosophy* 11 (1991) 229–48
Liddell, H., and R. Scott. *A Greek-English Lexicon* Rev. H. Jones and R. McKenzie, with 1968 Suppl. 9th ed. (Oxford 1976); cited as LSJ
Loenen, J. 'In Defence of the Traditional Interpretation of Xenophanes' Fr. 18' *Mnemosyne* ser. 4, 9 (1956) 135–36
Long, A. 'The Principles of Parmenides' Cosmology' *Phronesis* 8 (1963) 90–107; repr. in Furley and Allen 2, 82–101
- 'Timon of Phlius: Pyrrhonist and Satirist' *Proceedings of the Cambridge Philological Society* 240, n.s. 24 (1978) 68–91
- 'Socrates in Hellenistic Philosophy,' *Classical Quarterly* 38 (1988) 150–71
Lumpe, A. *Die Philosophie des Xenophanes von Kolophon* (Munich 1952)
McCoy, M. 'Xenophanean Epistemology: Empiricism leading to Scepticism' In *Ionian Philosophy* ed. Boudouris (Athens, 1989) 235–40
MacIntyre, A. *After Virtue* (Notre Dame, Ind., 1981)
Mansfeld, J. 'Theophrastus and the Xenophanes Doxography' *Mnemosyne* ser. 4, 40 (1987) 286–312
- '*De Melisso Xenophane Gorgia*: Pyrrhonizing Aristotelianism' *Rheinisches Museum* 131 (1988) 239–76
Marcovich, M. 'Was Xenophanes in Paros (Greece), Paros (Dalmatia), or Pharos (Egypt)?' *Classical Philology* 54 (1959) 121
- 'Xenophanes on Drinking-Parties and the Olympic Games' *Illinois Classical Studies* 3 (1978) 1–26
Marinone, N. *Lessico di Senofane* (Rome 1967; repr. Hildesheim 1972)
Milne, J. 'Herodotus i. 94: NOMIΣMA' *Classical Review* 63 (1949) 85–7
Mirhady, D. 'Non-Technical *Pisteis* in Aristotle and Anaximenes' *American Journal of Philology* 112 (1991) 5–28
Moore, J. *Selections from the Greek Elegiac, Iambic, and Lyric Poets* (Cambridge, Mass., 1965)
Mosshammer, A. 'Thales' Eclipse' *Transactions of the American Philological Association* 111 (1981) 145–55
Mourelatos, A. 'The Real, Appearances and Human Error in Early Greek Philosophy' *The Review of Metaphysics* 19 (1965) 346–65
- *The Route of Parmenides* (New Haven and London 1970)

– *The Pre-Socratics* (Garden City, NY, 1974)
– Review of Osborne (below), *Ancient Philosophy* 9 (1989) 111–17
– ' "X Is Really Y": Ionian Origins of a Thought Pattern' In *Ionian Philosophy* ed. Boudouris, 280–90
Murray, G. *Greek Studies* (Oxford 1946)
Mussies, G. 'Identification and Self-Identification of Gods in Classical and Hellenistic Times' In *Knowledge of God in the Graeco-Roman World* ed. B. van den Roelof, T. Baarda, and J. Mansfeld (Leiden 1988)
Nahm, M. *Selections from Early Greek Philosophy* (New York 1947)
Neugebauer, O. *A History of Ancient Mathematical Astronomy* 3 vols. (New York, Heidelberg, and Berlin 1975)
Nilsson, M. *Greek Folk Religion* (New York 1940)
Nussbaum, M. 'ψύχη in Heraclitus, I & II' *Phronesis* 17 (1972) 1–16, 153–70
O'Brien, D. 'Derived Light and Eclipses in the Fifth Century' *Journal of Hellenic Studies* 88 (1968) 114–27
O'Brien, M. 'Xenophanes, Aeschylus, and the Doctrine of Primeval Brutishness' *Classical Quarterly* 35 (1985) 264–77
Onians, R. *The Origins of European Thought* (Cambridge 1951)
Osborne, C. *Rethinking Early Greek Philosophy: Hippolytus of Rome and the Presocratics* (Ithaca 1987)
Owen, G. 'Eleatic Questions' *Classical Quarterly* 10 (1960) 84–102; repr. in Furley and Allen 2, 48–81
Packard, D., and T. Meyers. *A Bibliography of Homeric Scholarship, 1930–1970* (Malibu, Calif., 1974)
Palmer, J. 'Xenophanes' ouranian god in the fourth century' *Oxford Studies in Ancient Philosophy* 16 (1998) 1–34
Panchenko, D. 'How old were you? The chronology of the Presocratics and the Persian invasion in Asia Minor' *Hyperboreas* 1 (1994–5) 34–45
Popper, K. *Conjectures and Refutations* (London 1963)
Reiche, H. 'Empirical Aspects of Xenophanes' Theology' In *Essays in Ancient Greek Philosophy* ed. J. Anton and G. Kustas (Albany, NY, 1971) 1, 88–110
Reinhardt, K. *Parmenides und die Geschichte der griechischen Philosophie* (Bonn 1916; repr. 1959)
Reinhold, M. *History of Purple as a Status Symbol in Antiquity* (Brussels 1970)
Rivier, A. 'Remarques sur les fragments 34 et 35 de Xénophane' *Revue de philologie* 30 (1956) 37–61
Robinson, T. *Heraclitus: Fragments* (Toronto, Buffalo, and London 1987)
Robb, K., ed. *Language and Thought in Early Greek Philosophy* (La Salle, Ill., 1983)
Roller, D. 'Some Thoughts on Thales' Eclipse' *Liverpool Classical Monthly* 89 (1983) 58–59

Ross, W. *Aristotle's Metaphysics* (Oxford 1924)

Roth, P. 'Διέπω bei Xenophanes' *Hermes* 118 (1990) 118–21

Runia, D. 'Xenophanes on the Moon: A Doxographicum in Aëtius' *Phronesis* 34 (1989) 245–69

Russell, B. *A History of Western Philosophy* (New York 1945)

Schäfer, C. *Xenophanes von Kolophon: ein Vorsokratiker zwischen Mythos und Philosophie* (Stuttgart, 1996)

Schwabl, H. 'Xenophanes, 1939–1956' (Die Forschungsberichte: Die Eleaten) *Anzeiger für die Altertumswissenschaft* 10 (1957) 195–214

Seng, H. 'Ta Dikaia in the Context of the Symposium' *Quaderni urbinati di cultura classica* 3 (1988) 123–31

Shorey, P. 'Note on Xenophanes Fr. 18 (Diels) and Isocrates *Panegyricus* 32' *Classical Philology* 6 (1911) 88–9

Snell, B. *Die Ausdrücke für den Begriff des Wissens in der vorplatonischen Philosophie* (Philologische Untersuchungen 29; Berlin 1924).

- *Die Entdeckung des Geistes* (Hamburg 1948) Trans., with chapter added on 'Human Knowledge and Divine Knowledge among the Early Greeks,' as *The Discovery of the Mind* trans. T.G. Rosenmeyer (Oxford 1953)

- *Lexikon des frühgriechischen Epos* (Gottingen 1955–)

- 'Wie die Griechen lernten, was geistige Tätigkeit ist' *Journal of Hellenic Studies* 93 (1973) 172–84; repr. in *Der Weg zum Denken und zur Wahrheit* (*Hypomnemata* 57; Göttingen 1978)

Soverini, L. 'Nota sulla σοφιή di Senofane' *Annali dell'Istituto Italiano per gli Studi Storici* 13 (1995–6) 21–30

Steinmetz, O. 'Xenophanesstudien' *Rheinisches Museum* 109 (1966) 13–73

Stokes, M. *One and Many in Presocratic Philosophy* (Cambridge, Mass., 1971)

Thesleff, H. *On Dating Xenophanes* (Societas Scientiarum Fennica: Commentationes Humanarum Litterarum 23; Helsingfors 1957)

Tulin, A. 'Xenophanes fr. 18 D.-K. and the origins of the idea of progress' *Hermes* 121 (1993) 129–38

Untersteiner, M. *Senofane: Testimonianze e frammenti* (Firenze 1956)

Verdenius, W. ΚΑΛΛΟΣ ΚΑΙ ΜΕΓΕΘΟΣ *Mnemosyne* ser. 4, 2 (1949) 294–8

- 'Xenophanes 34, 3,' *Mnemosyne* ser. 4, 6 (1953) 197

- 'Xenophanes Fr. 18,' *Mnemosyne* ser. 4, 8 (1955) 221

Vlastos, G. 'Equality and Justice in Early Greek Cosmologies' *Classical Philology* 42 (1947) 156–78; repr. in Furley and Allen 1, 56–91

- 'Theology and Philosophy in Early Greek Thought' *Philosophical Quarterly* 2 (1952) 97–123; repr. in Furley and Allen 1 (1970) 92–129

- Review of Cornford (above), *Gnomon* 27 (1955) 65–76; repr. in Furley and Allen 1, 42–55

- *Plato's Universe* (Seattle, Wash., 1975)

Waerden, B. van der. *Die Anfänge der Astronomie* (Groningen 1956)

West, M. *Early Greek Philosophy and the Orient* (Oxford 1971)

– *Iambi et Elegi Graeci* (Oxford 1972)

– *Studies in Greek Elegy and Iambus* (Berlin and New York 1974)

Wiesner, J. 'Xenophanes, 1957–1970' (Die Forschungsberichte: Die Eleaten) *Anzeiger für die Altertumswissenschaft* 25 (1972) 1–15

– *Ps.-Aristoteles MXG: Der historische Wert des Xenophanesreferats* (Amsterdam 1974)

– 'Theophrast und der Beginn des Archereferats von Simplikios' Physikkommentar' *Hermes* 117 (1989) 288–303

– 'Wissen und Skepsis bei Xenophanes' *Hermes* 125 (1997) 17–33

Wilamowitz-Moellendorff, U. von. *Sappho und Simonides* (Berlin 1913)

– 'Lesefrüchte' *Hermes* 61 (1926) 278–81

– *Kleine Schriften* 4 (Berlin 1962)

Wöhrle, G. 'Xenophanes als didaktischer Dichter' *Elenchos* 14 (1993) 5–18

– 'Xenophanes' parodistische Technik' In *Literaturparodie in Antike und Mittelalter* ed. Ax and Reinhold (Trier, 1993) 13–25

Woodbury, L. 'Apollodorus, Xenophanes, and the Foundation of Massilia' *Phoenix* 15 (1961) 134–55

– Review of Guthrie (above), *Phronesis* 24 (1970) 348–56

Wright, M. *The Presocratics* (Bristol 1985)

– 'Presocratic Minds' In *The Person and the Mind* ed. C. Gill (Oxford 1990) 207–25

Zeller, E. *Die Philosophie der Griechen in ihrer geschichtlichen Entwicklung* 6th ed., ed. W. Nestle (Leipzig 1920) vol. 1, pt. 1, 640–78

– *Outlines of the History of Greek Philosophy* 13th ed., rev. W. Nestle, trans. L. Palmer (London 1963)

Ziegler, K. 'Xenophanes von Kolophon, ein Revolutionär des Geistes' *Gymnasium* 72 (1965) 289–302

Zunio, M. 'La testimonianza di Senofane su Lipari (21 A48 Diels-Kranz) e una nuova interpretazione dell' "eremia" eoliana' *Quaderni di storia* (1977) 145–53

NAMES AND SUBJECTS

This index lists the various aspects of Xenophanes' life and teachings discussed in preceding sections, the ancient authors and thinkers whose views were alluded to in the course of discussion, and the modern scholars whose works were cited. Succeeding indexes list all passages cited from ancient authors and all Greek terms discussed.

PASSAGES FROM ANCIENT AUTHORS

GREEK WORDS DISCUSSED

PHOENIX SUPPLEMENTARY VOLUMES